THE MOST
DEMOCRATIC BRANCH

The Annenberg Foundation Trust at Sunnylands'
Institutions of American Democracy

Kathleen Hall Jamieson and Jaroslav Pelikan, *Directors*

Other books in the series

*Schooling America: How the Public Schools Meet
the Nation's Changing Needs* (2005)
Patricia Albjerg Graham

*The Broken Branch: How Congress Is Failing America
and How to Get It Back on Track* (2006)
Thomas E. Mann and Norman J. Ornstein

THE MOST DEMOCRATIC BRANCH

How the Courts Serve America

Jeffrey Rosen

The Annenberg Foundation Trust at Sunnylands'
Institutions of American Democracy

OXFORD
UNIVERSITY PRESS

2006

OXFORD
UNIVERSITY PRESS

Oxford University Press, Inc., publishes works that
further Oxford University's objective of excellence
in research, scholarship, and education.

Oxford New York
Auckland Cape Town Dar es Salaam Hong Kong Karachi
Kuala Lumpur Madrid Melbourne Mexico City Nairobi
New Delhi Shanghai Taipei Toronto

With offices in
Argentina Austria Brazil Chile Czech Republic France Greece
Guatemala Hungary Italy Japan Poland Portugal Singapore
South Korea Switzerland Thailand Turkey Ukraine Vietnam

Copyright © 2006 by Jeffrey Rosen

Published by Oxford University Press, Inc.
198 Madison Avenue, New York, NY 10016
www.oup.com

Oxford is a registered trademark of Oxford University Press

Library of Congress Cataloging-in-Publication Data
Rosen, Jeffrey, 1964–
The most democratic branch : how the courts
serve America / by Jeffrey Rosen.
p. cm.
ISBN-13: 978-0-19-517443-4 (cloth)
ISBN-10: 0-19-517443-7 (cloth)
1. Political questions and judicial power—United States.
2. Courts—United States.
3. United States. Supreme Court.
4. Judges—United States—History.
I. Title
KF5130.R67 2006
347.73'26—dc22
2005037786

1 3 5 7 9 8 6 4 2

Printed in the United States of America
on acid-free paper

For Akhil Amar and Bruce Ackerman,
who taught me to love constitutional law.

The Judicial Department comes home in its effects to every man's fireside: it passes on his property, his reputation, his life, his all. Is it not to the last degree important, that [a judge] should be rendered perfectly and completely independent, with nothing to influence or control him but God and his conscience?

—CHIEF JUSTICE JOHN MARSHALL

I would make all the Judges responsible, not to God and their own consciences only, but to a human tribunal.

—GOVERNOR WILLIAM GILES

VIRGINIA CONSTITUTIONAL CONVENTION, 1829

Contents

Acknowledgments

This book was written at the suggestion of Tim Bartlett, whose good judgment, wit, and critical intelligence make him the platonic ideal of an editor and friend. After decamping from Oxford University Press to Random House, he edited the book as a pro bono project—an act characteristic of his generosity and thoughtfulness. Dedi Felman at Oxford inherited the book and then improved it immeasurably with judicious cuts and insightful suggestions—among the best edits I've ever received. I'm extremely grateful to her, and to the Annenberg Foundation for including me in its series on the institutions of democracy. Versions of the argument were presented to faculty colloquia at the University of Texas at Austin, Harvard Law School, the Annenberg Institutions of Democracy Advisory Commission on the Judiciary, and the Institute for Constitutional Studies at George Washington University, where the challenges of participants improved it greatly. Dean Frederick Lawrence of The George Washington University Law

School offered thoughtful and valued comments as well as research support. I was especially fortunate in having an unusually generous group of readers. Michael Klarman and Mark Graber went far beyond the call of duty in their close readings of the manuscript, and their detailed comments and corrections, along with the influence of their pathbreaking scholarship, are reflected on nearly every page. I am greatly in their debt. Sanford Levinson provided warm encouragement at the beginning of the project and many improvements at the end. Bruce Ackerman, Akhil Amar, Barry Friedman, and Benjamin Wittes offered treasured friendship, intellectual inspiration, and invaluable suggestions. I'm very grateful to my editors at the *New York Times Magazine*, Gerry Marzorati, Alex Star, and James Ryerson, who pointed me toward the fascinating subject of constitutional futurology, and parts of the article that emerged were incorporated in the epilogue. Many of the arguments about judicial restraint evolved over the years at *The New Republic*, where Martin Peretz, Leon Wieseltier and Franklin Foer continue to provide a unique home for the exploration of ideas for their own sake. Thanks to Christopher Bowman for able and valued research assistance. The thesis of the book emerged, like all my ideas, in the course of daily conversations with my beloved wife, whose influence, as always, is definitive.

Preface

When Oxford University Press and the Annenberg Foundation asked me to write about the U.S. courts and American democracy as part of a series of books about the institutions of democracy, I was delighted but also daunted by the challenge. This is an unusually polarized moment in American judicial politics, and many people define themselves based on their views about whether cases like *Roe v. Wade* or *Bush v. Gore* were good or bad for the country. I'm often struck, however, by how few citizens have opportunities to think about the role of the courts in a larger context.

As a result, perhaps, public opinion about the role of the courts in American democracy seems to be uncertain and conflicted. In a series of polls commissioned in 2005 by Syracuse University, 73 percent of the respondents embraced a view that many of us learned in high school civics: namely, that the role of courts is to protect minorities from the tyranny of the majority and that judges, as a result, should be shielded from outside pressures. But in the same poll, 47 percent of the respondents complained that courts were out of step with the American people, reflecting the familiar criticism by interest groups that judges have become out-of-control activists thwarting the will of the people. And nearly the same percentage, 44 percent, said that courts were in step with public opinion—a view hard to reconcile with both of the other two positions.

In this book, I argue that the third view—that courts are broadly in step with public opinion—has tended, throughout American history, to be the most descriptively accurate. Far from protecting minorities against the tyranny of the majority or thwarting the will of the people, courts for most of American history have tended to reflect the constitutional views of majorities. (The cartoon character Mr. Dooley was correct when he declared at the turn of the last century that "th' supreme coort follows th' iliction returns.") Moreover, on the rare occasions when courts have acted unilaterally—trying to impose a constitutional vision that a majority of the country rejects—they have tended to provoke backlashes that often undermine the very causes the judges are attempting to advance.

Although hard to reconcile with the claims of interest groups or romantic idealists, the historical claim that courts have tended, over time, to reflect the will of the majority rather than thwarting it is hardly novel; on the contrary, it has become a kind of underground conventional wisdom among the political scientists and legal scholars on whose work I've drawn in this book. Even at the risk of upsetting conventional pieties, I hope it may be useful to set out in some detail, on the theory that citizens cannot make intelligent choices about the kinds of judges they think should be confirmed to the federal courts without a realistic understanding of how judges have tended, over time, to behave.

Perhaps more controversial than my observations about how judges have behaved in the past will be my argument about how courts can best maintain their legitimacy in the future, as they confront a range of vexing issues—from human cloning and other technologies of assisted reproduction to attempts to patent human life. Not only have judges tended to reflect the constitutional views of national majorities in the past, they should, broadly speaking, continue to do so in the future if they want their decisions to be accepted as being based in sound constitutional principles as opposed to transitory political judgments. Paradoxically, the courts, often derided as the least democratic branch of government, have maintained their legitimacy over time when they have been more rather than less democratic in their constitutional views. By contrast, throughout American history, the least effective decisions have been those in which courts unilaterally try to strike down laws in the name of a constitutional principle that is being actively and intensely contested by a majority of the American people. When judges vainly imagine they can save the country from democratic excesses that they alone can perceive, they often imperil their own legitimacy and effectiveness in the process. Therefore, far from threatening judicial independence, judicial sensitivity to the constitutional views of the president, Congress, and the American people has tended surprisingly to preserve it.

Throughout the book, I'd like to defend a tradition that used to command widespread support among mainstream liberals and conservatives but is increasingly out of fashion: namely, the tradition of bipartisan judicial restraint. This tradition, famously associated with judges like Oliver Wendell Holmes, Felix Frankfurter, and Learned Hand, holds that courts should play an extremely modest role in American democracy. They should hesitate to strike down laws unless the constitutional arguments for second-guessing the decisions of a political majority are so powerful that people of different political persuasions can readily accept them. "If my fellow citizens want to go to hell, I will help them," Holmes said. "It's my job."

When I was lucky enough to become legal affairs editor of *The New Republic* magazine at the beginning of the 1990s, I absorbed the tradition of bipartisan judicial restraint, which had been championed over the years by editors such as Frankfurter, Hand, and Alexander Bickel.

This tradition led *The New Republic* to criticize the judicial invalidation of laws the editors' supported as well as those they opposed, from minimum wage laws during the Progressive era to health and safety regulations during the New Deal to postwar laws restricting abortion and permitting affirmative action. In both *Roe v. Wade* and *Bush v. Gore*, the magazine insisted that the Supreme Court should have resisted the temptation to plunge recklessly into the political thicket.

The tradition of bipartisan restraint is based on a strong—but, at the moment, hotly contested—claim about the relationship between the law and politics in American democracy: namely, that the most controversial political issues in American history always have been resolved in the political arena rather than the courts. When the courts attempt to short-circuit an intensely contested political debate, those of us in the bipartisan restraint crowd argue, they are likely to imperil their own legitimacy without dramatically influencing the ultimate outcome of the political debate in question. In the long run, majorities in America will always have their way.

Despite its venerable history, the claim that political questions should be resolved in the legislatures rather than courtrooms has increasingly less appeal, on the left and the right, now that so many of our political questions are being legalized—from assisted suicide to presidential elections. When judges take it upon themselves to decide the most divisive questions of politics, technology, and culture, who can blame both liberals and conservatives for selectively embracing judicial activism when it suits their purposes? Now that constitutional politics has become a blood sport, many believe, bipartisanship of any kind has become an unaffordable luxury.

Although the Supreme Court has generally tended to reflect the constitutional views of majorities in the past, that may change in the future. During the postwar era, liberals and conservatives were united around the importance of judicial deference to democratic decisions. But in the 1980s and 1990s, partly in response to *Roe v. Wade*, influential movements developed on the left and the right urging judges to ignore the constitutional views of national majorities. On the right, some activists now embrace an especially aggressive form of conservative libertarianism, calling on judges to strike down economic and environmental regulations by resurrecting limits on federal and state power that have been dormant since the New Deal. On the left, other activists are rallying around an equally aggressive form of liberal egalitarianism, encouraging judges to strike down other practices that national majorities embrace—from the death penalty to restrictions on gay marriage—in the name of an ill-defined and amorphous international consensus. These movements have not yet persuaded very many federal judges or Supreme Court justices to embrace their adventurous axioms. But the historically shortsighted assumption that courts are supposed to be aggressively antidemocratic is in the air, and judicial interest groups are trumpeting their indifference to the views of national majorities as a sign of their devotion to principle.

The book that follows is offered as a series of cautionary tales about the chaos that may result if judges heed this reckless and shortsighted counsel. It is also an attempt to persuade readers from both ends of the political spectrum to consider the virtues of bipartisan judicial restraint. Those of us who subscribe to this venerable tradition are, at the moment, a small but devoted band. Please join us.

THE MOST
DEMOCRATIC BRANCH

Introduction

The Most Democratic Branch

In March 2005, for the first time in history, Congress ordered the federal courts to reexamine a case involving the right to die. The case involved Terri Schiavo, a young woman who collapsed from a heart attack in 1990 and whose brain suffered a severe oxygen loss that left her in a coma. In 1998, after winning a malpractice suit against the doctors who failed to diagnose Terri's eating disorder, her husband, Michael, argued in court that she would have wanted her feeding tube to be removed. Her parents responded that Terri would have wanted to stay alive, insisting that Michael, who had become engaged to another woman, was not a reliable representative of Terri's wishes. A state judge agreed with Michael Schiavo that Terri would have wanted to refuse treatment, based on her statements to her husband and relatives; and after two other state courts affirmed the decision, he ordered the tube to be removed in 2001. After further legal wrangling, the Florida legislature passed "Terri's law," which authorized the Florida governor to issue a "one time stay" of a court order in Terri's case; nearly a year later, the Florida Supreme Court unanimously struck down "Terri's law" as an unconstitutional attempt by the legislature to delegate judicial powers to the executive branch. Another year of legal fights ensued, and in February 2005, the state judge once again ordered Terri's feeding tube to be removed.

At this point, the U.S. Congress intervened. Terry Schiavo received a subpoena ordering her to appear before the U.S. House of Representatives, with her feeding tube intact. The Senate delayed its Easter recess and passed a private relief bill giving Terri Schiavo's parents the right to contest her constitutional rights in federal court. Early the next morning, having suspended its rules, the House passed the bill and the president returned from Easter vacation to sign it. Despite this extraordinary intervention, the federal courts authorized to review Schiavo's case wasted no time in upholding the state judge's original order. A federal district court judge refused to order the reinsertion of the tube, and over the next few days, a federal appellate court and the U.S. Supreme Court refused to intervene. On March 31, 2005, Terry Schiavo died.

How did the courts perform in this stressful and illuminating case? By and large, state and federal judges performed well by following existing law rather than embracing novel constitutional arguments. The performance of Congress was less impressive. In the midnight House debate over the private relief bill for Schiavo's parents, there were frequent references to Terri Schiavo's "constitutional right to life." But there were no serious efforts to define the contours of that right or to make arguments about why it was not adequately protected by the judicial procedures that the Florida state courts had followed.

To the degree that Congress was attempting to challenge the constitutional vision of the courts, moreover, its competing vision did not seem to be embraced by the American people. After Schiavo's death, an overwhelming 82 percent of Americans in a CBS news poll said they disapproved of the decision by Congress and the president to intervene in the case.[1]

The reaction to the Schiavo case reveals something odd and unexpected about American judicial politics in the early twenty-first century. Conservative critics of the Schiavo ruling charged that unelected activist judges were thwarting the will of the people. But in fact, the critics had it exactly backward. In our new, topsy-turvy world, it was the elected representatives who were thwarting the will of the people, which was being channeled instead by unelected judges.

The Schiavo case was not unique. On a range of issues during the 1980s and 1990s, the moderate majority on the Supreme Court represented the views of a majority of Americans more accurately than the polarized party leadership in Congress. Congressional Republicans and Democrats are increasingly pandering to their respective bases: these include conservative and liberal interest groups who care intensely about judicial nominations because they are upset about the current direction of the Supreme Court, which has rejected their extreme positions on a range of issues, from abortion to religion. By contrast, the country as a whole is relatively happy with the Supreme Court and has no interest in paralyzing the federal government over symbolic fights about judicial nominations that will do little to affect the Court's overall balance. In 2005, only 22 percent of respondents in a Gallup poll said they trusted Congress "quite a lot" or "a great deal," compared to more than 40 percent who had similar trust in the Supreme Court and the president.

As these polls suggest, the Supreme Court in recent years has become increasingly adept at representing the views of the center of American politics that Congress is ignoring. In the 1980s and 1990s, as conservatives won the economic war to pass tax cuts and to scale back the size of government, the Court modestly followed their lead, striking down laws on the margins of the post–New Deal regulatory state, such as largely symbolic federal laws regulating violence against women and guns in schools. And as the public sided with liberals rather than conservatives in the culture wars—endorsing gay rights (but not gay marriage),[2] limited forms of affirmative action,[3] and protections for early (but not late) term abortions,[4]—so did the Court.

Of course, the Court's relationship to public opinion is complicated: sometimes the Court identifies a strong national sentiment and imposes it on a few isolated state outliers (striking down an obsolete state ban on contraceptives, for example); and sometimes it endorses a position that roughly half the public supports and that comes to be more widely embraced (striking down school segregation).[5] This is hardly consistent with a vision of an antidemocratic court boldly resisting popular will. Whether the moderate justices on the Supreme Court are self-consciously reading the polls, neutrally interpreting the Constitution, or trying to compensate for other polarities in the system, their high-profile decisions, for much of the past two centuries, have been consistently popular with narrow majorities (or at least pluralities) of the American public.[6]

How did we get to this odd moment in American history where unelected Supreme Court justices sometimes express the views of popular majorities more faithfully than the people's elected representatives? One obvious culprit is partisan gerrymandering. In the 2000 elections, 98.5 percent of congressional incumbents won with over 75 percent of the vote, thanks to increasingly sophisticated computer technology that makes it possible to draw House districts where incumbents are guaranteed easy reelection simply by catering to the interest groups that represent their ideological base. As a result, Democrats and Republicans in Congress no longer have an incentive to court the moderate center in general elections, resulting in parties that are more polarized than at any other point in the past fifty years. And since half of the current senators previously served as representatives, it's hardly surprising that the polarized culture of the House is infecting the Senate.

It's also not surprising that interest groups have continued to attack judges as tyrannical activists despite the fact that, in many cases, judges actually reflect the constitutional views of national majorities more precisely than the interest groups do. Throughout American history, the people most fervently devoted to judicial activism have been political losers who are no longer able to enact their agenda in the political arena, from the conservative Federalists of the early 1800s to the Democrats of the Civil War era to the conservative Republicans during the New Deal.[7] Today, the groups most devoted to judicial activism are once again those whose beliefs have been repudiated by a majority of the country—from the social conservatives represented by groups like Focus on the Family, who want a chance to resurrect statewide bans on early-term abortions, to liberal egalitarians represented by NARAL Pro-Choice America, who oppose restrictions on late term abortions and want the courts to impose gay marriage by judicial fiat.

The idea that the federal courts might represent the views of national majorities more precisely than Congress is hard to reconcile with the familiar, if romantic, vision of courts that many of us were taught in high school civics: courts are heroically antidemocratic institutions whose central purpose is to protect vulnerable minorities against the tyranny of the majority. It is also hard to reconcile with familiar criticisms of judges as antidemocratic activists in black robes. Critics of judicial activism frequently charge that whenever a court strikes down a law, it effectively thwarts the will of the majority that passed the law. "The root difficulty is that judicial review"—that is, the authority of the court to review the constitutionality of actions taken by other branches of government—"is a counter-majoritarian force in our system," wrote the legal scholar Alexander Bickel in 1962. "[J]udicial review is a deviant institution in the American democracy," he continued, because whenever the Supreme Court strikes down a law, "it exercises control, not in behalf of the prevailing majority, but against it."[8]

There are familiar answers to what Bickel called "the counter-majoritarian difficulty," and the most familiar comes from the American founders. In the course of defending the power of judges to strike down laws clearly inconsistent with the Constitution, Alexander

Hamilton rejected the charge that this power supposed that judges would be superior to legislators. "It only supposes that the power of the people is superior to both; and that where the will of the legislature declared in its statutes, stands in opposition to that of the people declared in the constitution, the judges ought to be governed by the latter, rather than the former," he wrote in *The Federalist Papers*.[9]

More recently, majoritarian scholars have argued that there's no need to worry about judges thwarting the will of the people, because the vision of antidemocratic courts protecting vulnerable minorities against tyrannical majorities is, in some sense, a romantic myth. For all the invective that it initially generated, *Brown v. Board of Education*, which struck down school segregation, was supported by more than half the country when it was handed down in 1954,[10] as were many of the most controversial decisions by the Warren and Burger Courts.[11] Beginning with Robert Dahl in the 1950s, political scientists have argued that the Supreme Court throughout its history has tended to follow national opinion rather than challenging it. Instead of protecting minorities against the tyranny of majorities, Dahl argued in 1957, "the policy views dominant on the Court are never for long out of line with the policy views dominant among the lawmaking majorities of the United States."[12]

According to this majoritarian view, courts play an important role as policy makers in American government, but their role tends to be more subtle than partisans of the countermajoritarian myth like to believe. Interest groups are not the only people who use the courts for parochial purposes; elected politicians, attempting to steer clear of controversial topics, often do the same.[13] Moreover, during periods when legislatures themselves are failing to represent the wishes of the majority, the Court may be able to remove an obstacle to democracy in the political process: the most obvious examples are the Warren Court's reapportionment decisions in the 1960s, which declared "one man, one vote" to be a Constitutional principle, over the objection of House incumbents who preferred the malapportioned old system that allowed them to protect their seats.

What the courts cannot do is thwart the will of national majorities for long. The great political scientist Robert McCloskey recognized that courts, always sensitive to sustained political attacks by the president and Congress, are ultimately constrained by public opinion even as their decisions can subtly nudge the country in one direction or gently apply the brakes in another. "[P]ublic concurrence sets an outer boundary for judicial policy making," McCloskey wrote. "In truth the Supreme Court has seldom, if ever, flatly and for very long resisted a really unmistakable wave of public sentiment. It has worked with the premise that constitutional law, like politics itself, is a science of the possible."[14]

The majoritarians offer a useful description of how courts actually behave as institutions of democracy: throughout American history, judges have tended to reflect the wishes of national majorities and have tended to get slapped down on the rare occasions when they have tried to thwart majority will. But this description doesn't tell us how courts *should* behave as institutions of democracy. It doesn't tell us, in other words, how the courts can best maintain their effectiveness and legitimacy over the long term, reaching decisions that will be accepted by the country, over time, as being rooted in constitutional rather than political values. To gain democratic legitimacy over the long term, after all, a court's decisions must not merely be popular with 50 percent of the country in an opinion poll, since opinion polls fluctuate and the people are often caught up in temporary enthusiasms. Moreover, judges are not supposed to be so crude as to simply follow the polls; that would make them politicians. Instead, successful judicial decisions must be accepted by the country as being rooted in constitutional principles rather than political expediency. Only with this kind of democratic legitimacy will the decisions be accepted, enforced, and followed by the political branches and the American people as a whole.

How can the courts serve America in this sense? That is, how can they maintain their effectiveness and legitimacy as institutions of democracy? Scholars and citizens disagree fiercely, of course, about the source of the courts' democratic legitimacy. Some embrace a more or less political view, arguing that the legitimacy of the courts flows less from the correctness of their legal reasoning than from their ability to predict and reflect future currents of public opinion. Others take a more principled view, insisting that the Supreme Court's legitimacy stems from its ability to convince American citizens that its decisions are rooted in correct constitutional principles rather than the personal preferences of judges.[15] Disagreement about which constitutional principles are the correct ones, of course, has always been the source of our fiercest constitutional battles.

Regardless of what vision of democratic legitimacy you embrace—regardless, that is, of whether you are persuaded by the political or principled account, and regardless of which principled account you find most convincing—judges throughout American history have tended to maintain their democratic legitimacy in practice when they practiced what might be called democratic constitutionalism; in other words, when they have deferred to the constitutional views of the country as a whole. By contrast, throughout American history, the decisions most likely to be attacked and resisted over time have been those where the courts engage in judicial unilateralism. By judicial unilateralism, I mean a court's decision to strike down federal or state laws in the name of a constitutional principle that is being actively and intensely contested by a majority of the American people.

The most notorious constitutional decisions in American history—the ones that have been most strenuously attacked as being based on politics rather than law—have been unilateralist in the sense that I've described: from Dred Scott, which held that Congress had no power to ban slavery in the federal territories, to the decisions in the 1930s striking down the New Deal to *Roe v. Wade*, which struck down restrictions on late- as well as early-term abortions. By contrast, the most successful constitutional decisions in American history—the ones that have been accepted over time as based in law rather than politics—have avoided trying to impose constitutional principles in the face of active contesta-tion by Congress, from *Marbury v. Madison*, which recognized the prin-ciple of judicial review, to *New York Times v. Sullivan*, which recognized the right to criticize government.

What is the best evidence of the views of a national majority on con-tested questions of constitutional interpretation? Polls are hardly a reli-able indicator, since polls seldom ask people what they think about constitutional issues, as opposed to policy issues, and judges are not sup-posed to follow the polls. Moreover, the Founders did not anticipate a direct democracy but a representative republic, in which the constitu-tional views of the people were channeled and represented by other branches of government. Instead, for much of American history, the most reliable representative of the constitutional views of the American people was Congress. The great constitutional debates in American history—over the meaning of free speech, equality, and political participation—all took place in Congress, and the congressional consensus was codified in amendments to the Constitution. For example, it was Congress, during the nineteenth and early twentieth centuries, that embraced the modern vision of free speech, which holds that government should not be able to ban speech except to prevent imminent lawless action, and it was Con-gress that defined the fundamental rights of American citizenship and insisted that they could not be abridged on the basis of race. Therefore, courts in the past have run the risk of acting unilaterally when they have tried to impose their own constitutional visions over the active objec-tions of congressional majorities.

But Congress has not always been a reliable representative of the con-stitutional views of the American people. When Congress's own pre-rogatives are under constitutional assault (in cases involving legislative apportionment or free speech, for example), it may be less appropriate for judges to defer to Congress's self-interested interpretations of the scope of its own power. Similarly, when courts are protecting their own powers against legislative assaults—in cases involving criminal procedure and the power of courts to review unlawful detentions—courts have properly been reluctant to defer to the legislature or the executive. When defining and enforcing the Fourteenth Amendment's guarantees of liberty and equality, however, Congress for much of American history has played a more important role than the courts, just as the framers of the Fourteenth Amendment intended.

For the Court to defer to the constitutional views of Congress, Congress must debate issues in constitutional (rather than political) terms. There are plenty examples of constitutional debates in Congress throughout American history: In the early years of the Republic, virtually every question—from the appropriate form of address for the president to the question of vice presidential succession—was a constitutional question; and when the constitutionality of early laws reached the Supreme Court, the judges tended to rehearse arguments that had been previously made by the president and Congress.[16] Before the Civil War, similarly, Presidents Lincoln and Buchanan as well as the Senate debated the constitutionality of the South's effort to secede from the Union far more thoughtfully and extensively than the superficial Supreme Court opinion declaring secession to be unconstitutional in 1869.[17]

In the twentieth century, however, the courts became increasingly aggressive about asserting their own exclusive authority to interpret the Constitution, embracing a defiant form of judicial supremacism. In response, the other branches of government became, not surprisingly, more passive. James Thayer of Harvard Law School, the famous advocate of judicial abstinence in the Progressive Era, worried that "the tendency of a common and easy resort to this great function [of judicial review], now lamentably too common, is to dwarf the political capacity of the people, and to deaden its sense of moral responsibility."[18] During the second half of the twentieth century, Congress vindicated Thayer's fears, increasingly citing judicial opinions rather than defending its own constitutional views. During the same period, as presidents became more aggressive in their assertions of executive authority, they became less willing to seek congressional authorization for constitutionally questionable acts—involving, for example, the detention of enemy combatants in the war on terror.

Thayer also worried that once the people became addicted to judicial activism, they would blame the courts for failing to strike down ill-advised laws, rather than directing their anger where it belonged: namely, to the offending legislatures. And here, too, Thayer's fears have been vindicated. For example, when the Supreme Court in *Kelo v. City of New London* (2005) upheld the city of New London, Connecticut's decision to use its power of eminent domain to seize private homes and then sell the land to a private developer to promote economic development, the decision unexpectedly provoked a firestorm of protest.[19] Uncontroversial among constitutional scholars, the principle that the Court should uphold economic decisions by local legislatures unless they were patently irrational had been well established since the New Deal. Nevertheless, eight out of ten Connecticut voters said they disagreed with the decision; a plurality in a national poll said private property rights was the issue before the Supreme Court they cared most about;[20] and more than two dozen states and both houses of Congress promised to propose legislation that would protect property owners from government seizure for economic development.[21] Although the Court may not have anticipated the popular resistance to its decision, it was right not to try to do so. After all, had the Court guessed wrong and imposed a narrower vision of eminent domain than the country embraced, its error would have been impossible to correct: in the face of uncertainty, courts should err on the side of upholding laws rather than striking them down. What was surprising about the response to the decision was the fact that Congress and the people were clamoring for the Court to spare them the need to resolve the issue politically. "By adhering rigidly to its own duty, the court will help, as nothing else can, to fix the spot where responsibility lies, and to bring down on that precise locality the thunderbolt of popular condemnation," Thayer wrote.[22] But although the

Supreme Court's deference to elected representatives in the *Kelo* case did indeed force Congress and the people to make their constitutional views clear, elected representatives seemed to resent this unsought responsibility, rather than thanking the justices for the favor.

As the Senate and House become increasingly unwilling to stand up for themselves, it is no wonder that Congress today seems to be a less reliable mirror of the people's constitutional views than it was for much of American history. If Congress is no longer a consistently representative of the constitutional views of national majorities, where else should courts look for evidence of those views? State constitutions and laws, certainly, remain an objective measure of a national consensus. For example, in identifying "evolving standards of decency" when in interpreting the Eighth Amendment's prohibition on cruel and unusual punishments, the Supreme Court has suggested that it is appropriate to consult the "primary and most reliable evidence of national consensus—the pattern of federal and state laws."[23] By the same token, the Court can look to past and present state constitutions and laws, including popular initiatives, in trying to identify a consensus about what rights should be considered fundamental under similar provisions of the U.S. Constitution.[24]

Many of the major schools of constitutional interpretation are useful in identifying the constitutional views of the American people, although each of them assigns different weight to different forms of evidence. For example, constitutional "originalists," who believe that constitutional provisions should be interpreted in light of the original understanding of their framers and ratifiers, agree on the importance of looking to the views of the Congress that proposed the Fourteenth Amendment after the Civil War. Originalists are reluctant, however, to recognize a shift in constitutional values unless it is codified in a formal constitutional amendment. Constitutional traditionalists are more willing to recognize shifts in values that have not been codified in the text of the Constitution, but only those that are deeply rooted in the traditions of the American people. Traditionalists often find the views of

Congress and the state legislatures to be reliable evidence of shifting traditions, and they are willing to strike down outlier laws, embraced by just a handful of states, that are inconsistent with a national consensus. Pragmatists who believe the Court should approach cases with a practical awareness of the consequences of its decisions may approve of the emphasis on interbranch cooperation that is at the center of democratic constitutionalism: a law should not be struck down unless there is broad national agreement about its unconstitutionality, reflected by a partnership between the Court and the political branches. In short, originalists, traditionalists, and pragmatists all should be able to embrace versions of democratic constitutionalism, although they will come to different conclusions about the right answer in particular cases. But this is not a "How To Interpret the Constitution" book championing one theory of interpretation over another. My point is that judges should identify the constitutional views of the people by using whatever combination of the usual methodologies they find most reliable and then enforce those views as consistently as possible.

In some of the most controversial cases, in other words, the Court may be uncertain about whether the institutional representatives of the people, such as Congress and the president, can plausibly represent the people's constitutional views. In the face of uncertainty, history suggests that courts can best maintain their democratic legitimacy—in both the political and the principled sense—by practicing judicial restraint. In other words, they should uphold the challenged federal or state law unless they are confident that the constitutional arguments for striking the law down are not being actively contested by a majority of the American people. Judges should be free to strike down laws if they believe, in good conscience, that the Constitution requires it, but they should be wary about rejecting the competing constitutional views of Congress, the presidents, or a majority of the states unless the case for invalidation is very strong. In other words, democratic constitutionalism is an argument that judges should defer to the views of the political branches and the states about constitutional issues in the face of intense opposition or uncertainty; it is not an argument that constitutional values should be primarily enforced in the streets rather than the courts.[25]

Judicial restraint is a cautionary principle, one that reflects the unsurprising fact that unelected judges often have a tin ear when they try to discern or predict the constitutional views of the country at any moment in time. Judges, after all, are rarely unilateralist in a self-conscious way: they seldom imagine themselves imposing their views on an unwilling nation, in the way that presidents occasionally pursue unpopular policies. On the contrary, judges sometimes mistake the views of their intellectual and social class with those of the country as a whole and therefore are surprised when the country rises up to criticize a decision that the judges imagined would be constitutionally uncontroversial. (This misreading of public opinion appears to have been the source of the Court's overreaching in *Roe v. Wade*.) But it's precisely because judges are often inept at reading public opinion on constitutional issues that they may sometimes overreach, inadvertently embracing a unilateralist constitutional vision that a majority of the country rejects. The best way to avoid inspiring political backlashes that can thwart the effectiveness of judicial decisions is for courts to defer to Congress or the states in the face of uncertainty. And the best way for courts to hand down decisions that are accepted by the country as being rooted in principle rather than politics is also to avoid judicial unilateralism by practicing judicial restraint.

Throughout this book, I want to explore a paradox: Why is it that judicial sensitivity to the constitutional views of the president, Congress, and the people, instead of threatening judicial independence, has tended over the long run to preserve it? By enforcing only those values that national majorities are willing to recognize as fundamental, it turns out, the courts can best sustain the legitimacy that allows them to reach unpopular decisions in particular cases. (The First Amendment is an obvious example: although national majorities disapproved of the

Court's decisions striking down state and federal bans on flag burning in 1989 and 1990, Congress refused to propose a constitutional amendment overturning the decisions because the country could accept the importance, in the abstract, of protecting free speech.) At the same time, sensitivity to the views of national majorities is not a recipe for ignoring federalism, states rights, or local diversity of opinion. Although the Court, in a deferential mood, can plausibly strike down an occasional state law that is dramatically out of line with a clear national consensus—such as Connecticut's ban on the use of contraceptives, the only law of its kind still on the books in 1965—it should hesitate to strike down state laws unless it is confident that a clear national consensus, represented by a strong majority of states, has, in fact, materialized.

The most controversial part of my argument, I expect, will not be the historical claim that judges have tended to maintain their legitimacy and independence in the past by deferring to the constitutional views of the American people; instead, it will be the prescriptive claim that they should continue to do so in the future. For example, enthusiastic liberal or conservative devotees of natural rights will find little that is appealing in the injunction to defer to the constitutional views of majorities; they believe that the duty of courts is to enforce principles of fundamental justice regardless of what the people think. And now that natural law-based theories of constitutional interpretation are once again becoming fashionable on the left and the right—embodied in the turn toward internationalism and pre–New Deal libertarianism—there may be increasing divergences between the constitutional views of the people and the constitutional views of the courts.

One of my goals in framing the argument for democratic constitutionalism in historical terms, however, is to emphasize that the notion that the courts should defiantly ignore the constitutional views of the other branches of government is relatively new. In the years before and immediately after *Marbury v. Madison*, the case that recognized the power of judicial review in 1803, federal courts were aggressive about protecting their own powers and those of juries. They were also willing to strike down state laws that encroached on clearly established federal powers. But outside these categories, courts generally practiced judicial restraint, upholding questionable assertions of congressional power, for example as early as 1796.[26] Under Chief Justice John Marshall, the Supreme Court continued this pattern of deferring to Congress and closely scrutinizing only laws that threatened federal power or judicial prerogatives.

It was not until the post–World War II era that the Supreme Court, in its rhetoric if not in its actions, became increasingly aggressive in asserting its own exclusive power to interpret the Constitution without consulting or deferring to the competing interpretations of the president or Congress. In 1958, for fear of being defied by a southern governor who opposed school desegregation, the Court declared not only that its interpretations of the Constitution bound other branches of government, but also that it was "supreme in the exposition of the law of the Constitution."[27] And the Rehnquist Court routinely adopted an imperious tone—the Constitution is what we say it is, period—even when striking down largely symbolic laws whose constitutional infirmity was that Congress had presumed to interpret constitutional guarantees more expansively than the Court. Between 1995 and 2003, the Court struck down thirty-three federal laws. turning on its head the historical pattern in which judges were willing to give Congress the benefit of the doubt.

The pages that follow offer cautionary tales for those who are urging the Courts to impose visions of constitutional law that are, at the moment, intensely contested by a majority of the country. After examining the courts' initial encounters with constitutional unilateralism, from *Marbury v. Madison* to the beginning of the twentieth century, I focus on cases involving race, love and death, politics, and civil liberties during wartime. Each of these chapters tends to confirm the observation that when the courts act unilaterally, their efforts are likely to be ineffective, to provoke backlashes, and ultimately to threaten the legitimacy of the courts. The epilogue, "What Are Courts Good For?", tries to imagine some of the constitutional controversies of the future, which offer further support for the thesis that courts should avoid short-circuiting political debates. I also suggest ways that courts can serve America in a positive way, not merely avoiding unilateralism but also encouraging the other branches of government to engage in a dialogue about constitutional issues and to reach bilateral consensus. I attempt throughout to defend a vision of judicial humility for an age of rancor, anchored not in romantic abstractions about the wisdom of Congress and the president but in respect for their prerogative to represent the people's constitutional views in ways that may differ from the courts.

The turn toward unilateralism has a long and fraught history. To understand it, let's begin at the beginning.

1

Cautionary Tales

John Marshall, America's greatest chief justice, took office in 1801 at the most vulnerable moment in the Supreme Court's history. Jeffersonian Republicans were determined to attack the independence of the largely Federalist bench by making judges entirely subservient to popular will; high Federalists, by contrast, viewed the judiciary as a monarchical protection against mob rule. Marshall's genius as chief justice was to find a middle ground between the populist and aristocratic positions, establishing judicial independence by avoiding judicial unilateralism. In case after case, he reinforced the paradoxical lesson that courts can best serve democracy by enforcing only those limitations on governmental power that national majorities have already approved.

Marshall succeeded in molding the Court in his own image as a result of his temperament as much as his constitutional philosophy: a genial, outgoing, and convivial man, he insisted that the justices board together so they could discuss cases over glasses of his excellent Madeira. Using the chief justice's most important power—the ability to assign cases when he is in the majority or to select a justice who will best reflect his views— Marshall persuaded colleagues of different ideological inclinations to join him in a series of unanimous opinions. He established judicial independence by repudiating the claim of radical Jeffersonians—that constitutional values should be enforced exclusively by legislatures, who were ultimately accountable to public opinion. But although Marshall established the power of independent judges to ignore public opinion in theory, he declined to press this power very far in practice, always taking care to defer to Congress on questions that the nation cared intensely about, and confining his invalidation of laws to cases affecting basic principles— such as federal power and property rights—that the nation as a whole was willing to support. In this sense, Marshall cannily achieved the Federalist vision of judicial independence by adopting the Jeffersonian counsel of judicial deference to the constitutional views of the people.

Marbury v. Madison

Marbury v. Madison (1803) is a monument to the inherent weakness of courts when challenged by a determined Congress and a popular president. *Marbury* recognized the power of courts to strike down laws inconsistent with the Constitution. This power, known as judicial review, may have been uncertain at the founding, but it became broadly accepted over the next fifteen years and was relatively uncontroversial when the case was decided.[1]

After losing the election of 1800 in an electoral cliff-hanger, President John Adams immediately signed the Judiciary Act of 1801, passed by the lame-duck Federalist Congress on February 13. The act expanded the judiciary by creating sixteen new circuit judges, who the Federalists would appoint. And it reduced the size of the Supreme Court after the next vacancy, to deny Jefferson the right to fill the seat. Two weeks later, Congress created the new position of justices of the peace for the District, who would serve for five-year terms.[2]

On March 1, Adams sent the Senate his nominations for the new justices of the peace, including that of William Marbury. By the next day, the Senate had confirmed Adams's nominees, and Adams stayed up late signing commissions which were then brought to the State Department and notarized by the secretary of state, John Marshall. Some of the commissions were immediately delivered to their recipients by Marshall's brother James, but others, including Marbury's, were not. When Jefferson took office on March 4, 1801, he ordered Lincoln Levi, the acting secretary of state, not to deliver the remaining commissions, and he replaced some of Adams's appointees with loyal Republicans (but not all—in the bipartisan spirit of his inaugural address, Jefferson was trying to be moderate). He also campaigned against the Federalist judiciary, encouraging Congress to repeal the Judiciary Act of 1801, thereby abolishing the nationwide circuit courts the Federalists had established and tossing the newly appointed Federalist judges out of office.[3]

It was the constitutionality of this Repeal Act—not the constitutional questions at issue in *Marbury*—that was intensely contested in Congress as John Marshall, the new chief justice whom Adams had appointed weeks before Jefferson's inauguration, prepared to decide the case. *Marbury* involved the relatively narrow question of whether or not an Adams appointee was entitled to his commission; by contrast, Congress was focused on the broader question of whether courts should be ultimately accountable to elected representatives. The Federalists predicted that a Congress unconstrained by judicially enforced constitutional limits might run roughshod over the liberties of the states and the people, as state legislatures had done in their assaults on property rights during the 1780s under the Articles of Confederation. The most sober Republicans, while conceding the authority of courts to strike down acts of Congress, emphasized that since the founding, Americans had tended to settle their constitutional disputes through the political process rather than in courts. In the long run, they emphasized, engaged citizens and representatives would prove to be more effective guardians of constitutional liberties than would unelected judges.[4] Over the course of American history, both the Federalists and Republicans proved half right: independent courts tended to enforce constitutional limitations, but only those that the people were willing to accept.

By the time the Court met again in February 1803, the *Marbury* case put the Court in an especially awkward position. If Marshall ordered Madison to deliver Marbury's commission, the order would be ignored and the Court's weakness exposed. If, by contrast, Marshall refused to order the delivery of the commission to which Marbury was arguably entitled, the Court would appear to be capitulating in the face of political pressure.[5]

Faced with two dangerous alternatives, Marshall deftly avoided both. And he did so with the combination of personal cunning and judicial modesty that was the touchstone of his legacy. By modern standards, he should never have agreed to hear the case in the first place: he himself had been the official responsible for the strategic error that gave rise to the dispute—the failure to deliver the commissions—and his own conflict of interest was hard to ignore. But Marshall minimized the inherent awkwardness of his position with his extravagant deference to the prerogatives of Congress and the executive. By appearing to rule against Marbury, a Federalist office holder, and in favor of Madison, the Republican secretary of state, he confounded his political enemies. And by pulling out of his hat a constitutional objection that hadn't occurred to the parties to the case, he enhanced judicial power over the long run.

In recognizing the power of judges to refuse to enforce clearly unconstitutional laws, Chief Justice Marshall claimed to be stating the obvious. "The question, whether an act, repugnant to the constitution, can become the law of the land, is a question deeply interesting to the United States; but, happily, not of an intricacy proportioned to its interest," he wrote.[6] All the conventional tools of constitutional interpretation—text as well as original understanding and pragmatic considerations—supported this modest conception of judicial review.

As Marshall noted, for a judge to allow a law not made in pursuance of the Constitution to trump the Constitution would be to deny the Constitution's status as fundamental law, undermining the very purpose of a written Constitution, which is to maintain limits on enumerated powers of government.[7]

What made *Marbury* a perilous test for Marshall was not his relatively uncontroversial assertion of the power of judges to refuse to enforce unconstitutional laws that affected their own jurisdiction. It was, instead, the danger that the Court would issue an order to Jefferson to deliver Marbury's commission that the new president and his congressional supporters were determined to resist. In sidestepping a potential conflict between the Court and the political branches, Marshall displayed judicial statesmanship of the shrewdest kind.[8]

In Marshall's opinion, he took care to distinguish between the president's "political" or discretionary powers, for which he was "accountable only to his country in his political character,"[9] and his legal or nondiscretionary powers, for which he was answerable to judges. This formal distinction was another sign of Marshall's humility: he made clear that not all of the president's actions were reviewable in court, but only those "affecting the absolute rights of individuals."[10] And in a judicial arabesque   or perhaps an act of jujitsu—at the end of his opinion, he held that although Jefferson was illegally violating Marbury's rights by refusing to deliver his commission, the Supreme Court had no power to grant him the remedy he sought. Section 13 of the Judiciary Act of 1789, passed by the First Congress, appeared to give the Supreme Court the power to order Jefferson to deliver the commission. Although Marshall read the Judiciary Act to confer jurisdiction in this case, however, he emphasized that this case did not fall within the narrow categories of the Court's original jurisdiction set out in the Constitution. Therefore, he concluded, Section 13 of the Judiciary Act was unconstitutional.

Marshall's constitutional conclusion may have been open to question, but no one had a political incentive to question it. He had given the

Jeffersonians the result they hoped for on several levels (Republicans had questioned Section 13 when it was being debated, while Federalists defended it) and declined to issue an order that would have been defied. He avoided judicial unilateralism, since the constitutionality of Section 13 of the Judiciary Act of 1789 was not a question that engaged the passions of the current Congress, which was focused instead on defending its power to abolish the national circuit courts. As a result, neither Republicans nor Federalists in the House or Senate offered any criticism of *Marbury* after it was decided. And a week later, in a far more politically charged case than *Marbury*, the Marshall Court deferred to Congress on the constitutional question that Congress cared about intensely, unanimously upholding the constitutionality of the Repeal Act in *Stuart v. Laird*. The Court had retreated in the face of Republican opposition, but by avoiding a direct confrontation, it had enhanced its power in the long term. *Marbury* is the paradigmatic example of how the Court can strengthen itself by restraining itself. In the end, Marshall realized, a determined majority in Congress can and will enforce its constitutional vision, and the Court attempts to thwart Congress at its peril.

McCulloch v. Maryland

During the rest of Marshall's chief justiceship, he kept these lesson firmly in mind: judicial authority could best be enhanced by deference to the democratizing forces of national sovereignty; and (conversely) the cause of national democracy is best served by a strong but restrained judiciary. For this reason, Marshall's greatest judicial achievements consisted not of attempts to challenge Congress but instead of simply getting out of its way. He upheld congressional authority after a consensus about broad national powers had crystallized in Congress and only struck down state laws in the name of the broader constitutional consensus that Congress had endorsed.

The greatest of his nationalizing decisions, *McCulloch v. Maryland*, which upheld Congress's power to charter the Bank of the United States,

is our second cautionary tale about the importance of judicial deference to Congress in the face of constitutionality uncertainty. Marshall
could have found plenty of ammunition in the conventional tools of
constitutional interpretation for questioning the constitutionality of the
Bank. But guided by his overarching principle—defending the sovereignty of the people of the United States as a whole rather than the
sovereignty of the people in the individual states—Marshall chose instead a more generous construction of Congress's power and avoided
entangling the judiciary in a series of policy judgments that it was ill
equipped to resolve.[11] (The fact that Marshall was a strong supporter of
the bank on policy grounds must have made his decision easier.)

The debate over Congress's power to charter a bank dated back to
the founding era. Alexander Hamilton, the first secretary of the trea-
sury, insisted that the United States needed a national bank whose notes
could be used as a national currency that would increase the money
supply; with the help of the bank, he hoped to collect national taxes and
to refinance the debts from the Revolutionary War. Opponents of the
bank, led by James Madison and Thomas Jefferson, objected that the
bank would favor urban financiers over rural farmers, but they also
opposed the bank on constitutional grounds.[12] The core of Madison
and Jefferson's constitutional objection was based on a strict construction of Article I, Section 8 of the Constitution, which, after enumerat-
ing a series of specific congressional powers, concludes by saying: "The
Congress shall have Power . . . [t]o make all Laws which shall be necessary and proper for carrying into Execution the foregoing Powers, and
all other Powers vested by this Constitution in the Government of the
United States, or in any Department or Officer thereof."

Opponents of the bank conceded that the "sweeping clause," as they
called it, might justify the chartering of a bank during wartime, when
the financing of war debts was arguably a necessity. But to charter a
bank after the emergency of war had passed, they argued, was not "necessary" but instead merely convenient or useful. To allow Congress to

claim any power that was convenient rather than necessary, they insisted, would transform the federal government from one of limited to unlimited powers. President Washington found Hamilton's constitutional arguments more convincing than Madison and Jefferson's and signed the bill chartering a national bank in 1791.[13]

Five years after the charter of the First Bank of the United States expired in 1811, Congress succeeded in renewing the charter after two failed attempts. The constitutionality of the Second Bank was accepted by the national Republican party: even President Madison, who had voted against the bank on constitutional grounds in 1791 and had vetoed on policy grounds Congress's effort to recharter the bank in 1815, abandoned his former objections and signed the bill into law.[14] But the bank became controversial in light of spreading allegations of corruption after the downturn of 1818, when it was blamed for the financial chaos following the War of 1812. Several states passed laws imposing special taxes on the bank, and one of these laws—passed by Maryland—became the vehicle for testing the constitutionality of the bank. The law in question required the bank to pay a $15,000 annual fee to operate in the state and imposed a fine on the local cashier of the bank, James McCulloch, for circulating money without having paid the fee. After the Maryland Court of Appeals upheld the state tax, the case presented itself to the Supreme Court as *McCulloch v. Maryland*, decided in 1819.

Far more than *Marbury v. Madison*, the McCulloch case presented as starkly as possible the two central questions regarding the relationships between the courts and American democracy: first, who was sovereign, the people of each state or the people of the United States, and, second, who should be trusted to determine the precise boundaries of congressional power—the courts, the states, or Congress itself? To both of these questions, the supporters and opponents of the bank gave different answers. The opponents insisted that the Constitution had been ratified not by the people of the United States as a whole but instead represented "a compact between the states," adding that "all the powers which are not expressly relinquished by it are reserved to the states." In order to preserve the limited character of federal power, they insisted on a narrow reading of the sweeping clause, which they said judges should construe to allow only those congressional actions that were unquestionably necessary and which they defined as "indispensably requisite" to the execution of a specifically enumerated power. Because Congress could exercise its enumerated powers to regulate foreign and interstate commerce without claiming the unenumerated power to regulate banking, they insisted, the bank was unconstitutional.[15]

Supporters of the bank responded that the people of the United States as a whole, not the individual states, had indeed ratified the Constitution, and, since all three branches of national government had assumed for years that the bank was constitutional, the court should defer to the judgment of the political branches as a faithful representation of the judgment of the national people. Citing contemporary dictionaries, they insisted that the words *necessary* and *proper* should be interpreted broadly, because Congress needed the flexibility to govern a changing nation. The core of their argument concerned judicial restraint: judges, they argued, were not competent to evaluate the degree of necessity presented by a particular law: this was a "question of political expediency, which . . . is exclusively for legislative consideration." If courts presumed to make case by case judgments about whether or not a particular law was necessary, they would be usurping the responsibility of the political branches.[16]

In upholding the constitutionality of the bank and striking down the Maryland state tax, Marshall was able to combine his twin commitments to judicial restraint and national power. He noted that the federal government, because it derives its sovereign power from the people of the United States as a whole, is "supreme within its sphere of action."[17] In defining the appropriate sphere of action of the national government, Marshall emphasized that judges should defer to the long-standing consensus of the president and Congress that the bank was constitutional: the bill to charter the bank "did not steal upon an unsuspecting legislature and pass unobserved," Marshall wrote, but had been consistently endorsed by the Congress and the president. Although there were plausible arguments for a broad or narrow reading, Marshall insisted on deferring to the political branches in the face of interpretive uncertainty. A narrow interpretation, he insisted, would thwart "the execution of those great powers on which the welfare of a nation essentially depends," making it impossible for Congress to adapt the Constitution "to the various *crises of human affairs.*"[18] Instead, he insisted that the word necessary "frequently imports no more than that one thing is convenient or useful or essential to another."[19] Since the necessary and proper clause added to Congress's powers, Marshall refused to construe it as a limitation on the powers that had already been enumerated. "Let the end be legitimate, let it be within the scope of the constitution, and all means which are appropriate, which are plainly adapted to that end, which are not prohibited but consist with the letter and spirit of the constitution, are constitutional," he wrote.[20]

The practical consequences of Marshall's opinion cannot be overstated. If Marshall had endorsed a stricter construction of the necessary and proper clause, the federal courts would have been forced into the position of being a perpetual censor on the political necessity of every law passed by Congress.

Although Marshall did not admit to uncertainty, his broad construction of congressional power was hardly beyond dispute—there was a vigorous disagreement between supporters and opponents of congressional power at the Constitutional Convention in 1787. But by 1819, the Republican Congress accepted the constitutionality of the bank, and the Republican president, James Monroe, instructed his attorney general to defend it before the Supreme Court. For Marshall to have imposed the southern and western states' narrow view of congressional power in the face of united opposition by the president and Congress would have been a foolish act of judicial unilateralism. Instead, Marshall had the humility to choose judicial deference to Congress in the face of constitutional uncertainty. In the long term, what Robert McCloskey called his "deft blend of boldness and restraint" once again enhanced the Court's power by avoiding a conflict.[21]

In the short term, too, Marshall disarmed his critics and enhanced judicial power. A few opponents of the bank denounced Marshall for failing to strike it down and in the process tacitly conceded the power of the court to invalidate federal and state laws that exceeded constitutional limits. And Marshall took advantage of this concession in cases where the constitutional and political opportunities for judicial activism were more propitious than they had been in the showdown about the bank. He focused his judicial activism on cases where state legislatures had interfered with property rights and with national power, and in the process managed to enhance the protection of both. Cases such as *Fletcher v. Peck* (1810), for example, involved the sanctity of contracts: the Georgia legislature had sold millions of acres that eventually became Alabama and Mississippi to New England land speculators, but a subsequent state legislature passed a law revoking the grant. Marshall struck down the revoking law as a violation of the contracts clause of the constitution ("No State shall . . . pass any . . . Law impairing the Obligation of Contracts"), which he interpreted broadly to include not only private contracts but public charters and grants. *Fletcher v. Peck*, as Marshall's biographer puts it, "was one of those rare cases in which everyone profited" and was hailed as "a decision in nearly perfect harmony with the attitudes and values of most politically conscious Americans."[22]

In *Gibbons v. Ogden* (1824), New York granted a monopoly to a group of steamship operators, led by Ogden, who ran a ferry across the Hudson. The monopoly was challenged by Gibbons, who had received a federal license to operate a ferry along the same route. Marshall struck down the state monopoly grant, holding that Congress's decision to require steamship licenses trumped the state's concurrent regulatory authority. The national reaction to the decision was uniformly positive; even New York, which had wanted to eliminate the steamship monopoly but feared that it would be sued for impairing its contractual obligations, supported the monopoly's destruction.[23] These cases had large financial consequences for the winners and losers but contributed broadly to the protection of vested property rights and therefore won support even among Marshall's Jacksonian opponents. And in other cases, he practiced the same "twistifications," to use Jefferson's uncharitable phrase, that he had deployed in *Marbury v. Madison* to protect his most controversial decisions from political assaults, deciding constitutional issues against the Southern partisans of states rights, but in a way that they found difficult to criticize in light of their Pyrrhic victories on the facts of the case.[24]

This, then, is the achievement of John Marshall: he expanded judicial authority by declining to exercise it in a heavy-handed manner. He was generally deferential to assertions of broad national power, where judicial activism would have created a national backlash, and he reserved his judicial invalidations for surgical strikes against local laws that could plausibly be attacked as special privileges. By staking the enhancement of judicial power to the enhancement of congressional power, he gained a crucial ally in his efforts to establish the judicial branch as fully coequal to the president and Congress. His combination of legal precision and political sophistication is unmatched in American history, except, as we will see, in the hands of our most constitutionally precise president, Abraham Lincoln.

Dred Scott

If Marshall is the prototype for a successful judge in American democracy, then his successor Roger Taney ended his career as the antitype. Taney succeeded Marshall in 1836, at a time when the Court, bowing to the new political ascendancy of Jacksonianism and localism, had begun to be more deferential to state laws. And at the beginning of his tenure, Taney preserved Marshall's achievements by generally following in his footsteps. As Jackson's attorney general, in opposing the Bank of the United States,

Taney had made clear his own views about the narrow scope of congressional power. In most of his opinions, Taney avoided judicial unilateralism, showing more restraint than Marshall in his inclination to uphold states laws, but refusing to abandon the Court's prerogative to strike them down in exceptional cases. Certainly Taney, like Marshall, insisted on the ultimate authority of the Court to decide constitutional questions; and during the long period when he managed to keep the Court out of political controversies, he served it well. But on the eve of the Civil War, Taney made a fatal error that destroyed his reputation and squandered the Court's carefully constructed reserves of legitimacy. In the *Dred Scott* decision, Taney became the most extreme example of what happens when judges succumb to the temptation to save the country from intense and unresolved constitutional disputes.

In *Dred Scott*, Taney ruled that Congress lacked the power to ban slavery in the federal territories. The case was decided in 1857, a time when the Democratic president and Senate opposed Congress's power to ban slavery in the territories, and the House, composed of Whigs and Republicans, supported it. *Dred Scott* was a unilateralist decision in a way that *Marbury v. Madison* (and *Brown v. Board of Education*) were not, because a majority of Americans in 1857 almost certainly believed that either Congress or the sovereign people, represented by territorial legislatures, had the power to ban slavery if they wanted to. Moderate Republicans and even many Northern Democratic voters were closer to the views of the moderately pro-slavery Stephen Douglas, who insisted on the right of each territory to decide the slavery question on its own, than the radically pro-slavery John Calhoun, who insisted that Congress and the states had to protect the natural rights of slaveholders and therefore had no power to ban slavery. Without Marshall's carefully calibrated deference to the constitutional views of national majorities, Taney squandered much of the legitimacy that his predecessor had established.

The question of who should decide whether new states and territories would be slave or free—Congress or the territories themselves—had triggered the most dramatic sectional conflict in the history of the early Republic. In 1787, the Northwest Ordinance prohibited slavery in the territory northwest of the Ohio River. When organizing the Louisiana and Missouri Territories in the early nineteenth century, however, Congress made no mention of this prohibition, and slavery expanded into the lands covered by the Louisiana Purchase. A controversy over the status of slavery in 1819 ended in the Missouri compromise the following year, which (among other provisions) admitted Missouri as a slave state and Arkansas as a slave territory while banning slavery in federal territories to the north. The question that the Court reached out to decide in *Dred Scott*—did Congress have the power to decide the boundaries of slavery in the territories?—was only sporadically debated in Congress in 1820. Although some Southerners (including Jefferson and Madison) questioned Congress's power as a matter of constitutional principle, their arguments were rejected by the majority, and President James Monroe signed the Missouri Compromise after satisfying himself that it was indeed constitutional.[25] It is fair to conclude, therefore, that when the Missouri Compromise was passed in 1820, both Congress and the president shared a consensus about its constitutionality.

That consensus became contested as the nation moved toward war, and a battle that had once been conducted in political terms began to be conducted in constitutional ones. Initially, the pro- and anti-slavery forces disagreed about whether Congress should or should not prohibit slavery in the territories, with anti-slavery forces favoring prohibition and pro-slavery forces preferring nonintervention, leaving it up to individual territories to decide for themselves. After the Missouri controversy, the pro- and anti-slavery forces continued to disagree about whether Congress had the constitutional power to prohibit slavery. The Union almost fell apart between 1846 and 1850 over the fate of slavery in the territories acquired in the war with Mexico: Northern Democrats introduced the Wilmot Proviso, which would have banned slavery in those territories. Secession was averted only by the compromise of 1850, which admitted California with an anti-slavery constitution and organized the Utah and New Mexico territories with no restrictions on slavery.[26] In the Kansas-Nebraska Act of 1854, Congress repealed the anti-slavery restrictions that applied in Kansas and Nebraska and allowed residents of those territories to decide the status of slavery on their own. Sponsored by Senator Stephen Douglas of Illinois, the act provoked pro- and anti-slavery partisans to rush into "bleeding Kansas" and to fight for control.

The Kansas-Nebraska Act transformed the political landscape. Most of the Northern Democratic House members who voted for the act were defeated in the next election. The Republican Party was founded in 1854 primarily in opposition to the Kansas-Nebraska Act, and the Republican presidential platforms in 1856 and 1860 insisted that slavery in the territories was unconstitutional because it deprived slaves of liberty without due process of law.[27] By contrast, Southern Democrats countered that by requiring the exclusion of slavery in the territories, the Republican platform itself was unconstitutional because it violated the property rights of slaveholders.[28] (Northern Democrats, for their part, thought that Congress had no enumerated power to exclude slavery from territories but that territorial legislatures could do so, without violating property rights.) The Thirty-fourth Congress, elected in the wake of the struggle over the Kansas-Nebraska bill, was divided on the constitutional questions. The Democrats lost control of the House, which, after a struggle of several months, elected as Speaker Nathaniel P. Banks of Massachusetts, a nativist Republican whose majority supported the constitutionality of the Missouri Compromise banning slavery in the territories.[29] The Democratic Senate took the opposite view. As the debate became constitutionalized, the calls for a judicial rather than a political resolution, which began with the compromise of 1850, became even more fervent.

When the Court first heard oral arguments in the *Dred Scott* case in February, 1856, only nine days after the Republicans triumphed by electing Banks as Speaker, the ultimate constitutional status of slavery in the federal territories was hardly a question that justices were compelled to answer. On the contrary, the case itself was initially presented to judges as a dispute about a far narrower and more technical question: namely, had Dred Scott, a slave who grew up in Missouri, a slave state, become free when he accompanied his new master, a hypochondriacal army sergeant named John Emerson, on tours of duty in Illinois, a free state, and Fort Snelling, Minnesota, on free federal territory? Or had he reverted to his former slave status when he accompanied Emerson back to Missouri?

The justices could have answered this question narrowly in a number of ways. They could have written a modest opinion, for example, simply affirming the circuit court's holding that Scott was a slave because his status was determined by Missouri law. But some Democrats and moderate Whigs were calling on the Court to rule much more broadly, finding a way to resolve the question of whether Congress had the power to ban slavery in the territories, which the political parties had been unable to settle on their own. This broad constitutional question was potentially relevant to the Dred Scott dispute, because if the Missouri compromise, which banned slavery in the territories, was unconstitutional, then Dred Scott might never have been set free when he ventured onto what he thought was free soil.

The broader question of Congress's power to ban slavery in the territories was intensely contested in Congress, and the justices were initially inclined to avoid addressing it in *Dred Scott*. But in May, because the justices were divided about technicalities, they asked for new arguments the following term, after the presidential election. In June 1856, Republicans nominated John C. Fremont for president, and their platform insisted that Congress had the right and duty to prohibit slavery in the territories. The same month, the Democrats nominated James Buchanan, and the Democratic platform insisted that each territory could decide for itself whether to accept or reject slavery.[30] Because some Republicans insisted slavery in the territories was unconstitutional and some Democrats insisted that banning slavery in the territories was unconstitutional, there were increasing calls for the Supreme Court to resolve the question.

In the election of 1856, Buchanan won the presidency as well as substantial majorities in both houses of Congress. The Republicans established themselves as the strongest opposition party and retained control of the House until the end of the Thirty-fourth Congress on March 3, 1857. On December 1, the outgoing president, Franklin Pierce, sent a farewell message to the lame-duck Congress denouncing the Missouri Compromise and denying that Congress had the power to enact it. But Pierce's constitutional claim was contested by a majority of the House, which remained under the control of the opposition, and, in the Senate, the Republican minority invoked the nationalist decisions of John Marshall on behalf of their claim that Congress did have the power to ban slavery in the territories.[31]

This was the constitutional debate that was raging in Congress when reargument in the *Dred Scott* case began on December 15, 1856, recapitulating much of the constitutional ground that Congress itself was actively considering. After hearing arguments in December, the justices were initially inclined once again to avoid answering the broad constitutional question. A holding affirming the circuit court's narrow holding that Scott was a slave because his status was determined by state law would have been unfortunate for Scott but a blessing for the nation. Nevertheless, at the urging of Justice James M. Wayne, who had become an enthusiastic partisan for the Democratic point of view, and, with the secret support of the incoming Democratic president, James Buchanan, who wrote to one of the justices at the suggestion of another, encouraging him to join Taney's decision striking down the Missouri compromise, the Court decided to act unilaterally, imposing its own constitutional vision in the face of congressional disagreement.[32]

Champions of judicial restraint argue, convincingly in my view, that *Dred Scott* shows that courts are most likely to act foolishly when they wrongly believe that they alone can save the nation from a dispute that the political branches are unable to resolve. The fact that Congress shared this foolish belief and encouraged the Court's intervention doesn't mean the Court should have accepted the invitation. It's true that the incoming Democratic president and Congress strongly urged the Supreme Court to resolve the constitutional status of slavery and strongly supported *Dred Scott* after it came down.[33] But the House that was in session when the justices decided the case clearly opposed the Court's decision. The fact that a majority in the sitting Congress, rather than the incoming Congress, opposed the Court's effort to save the country should have persuaded the Court that sufficient constitutional division existed in the country to leave the ultimate resolution to political actors.

Moreover, Taney's decision to endorse the constitutional vision of John Calhoun and the Southern Democrats—who insisted that the rights of slaveholders had to be constitutionally protected—was almost certainly rejected by a majority of the American people: even many Buchanan voters in states like Pennsylvania, Indiana, and Illinois were closer to the position of Stephen Douglas—who insisted that the people of each territory had the right to decide whether or not to ban slavery. We know this because Douglas himself, in his "Freeport Doctrine," felt compelled to question Taney's claim that Congress could not allow the slavery question to be decided by the territories—a position at odds with his own vision of popular sovereignty—and this disagreement eventually (although not immediately) split the Northern and Southern Democrats and destroyed the party. There may have been no clear majority position on slavery in 1857, but it's relatively clear that a national majority, made up of Republicans and Northern Democrats, would have disagreed with the Court's attempt to impose the constitutional vision of Southern Democrats. That is what makes *Dred Scott* an example of judicial unilateralism.

Although *Dred Scott* galvanized the Republican party, it did not, in fact, cause the Civil War. The most immediate causes of the war were political, not judicial—namely, President James Buchanan's endorsement in 1857 of the pro-slavery LeCompton constitution for Kansas, and the demand by Southern Democrats in 1860 that the Democratic national convention endorse slave codes for the territories. The best evidence we have of why marginal voters shifted to the Republican Party in 1858 was their revulsion against the LeCompton Constitution, which declared that the natural right of property owners to hold slaves could not be violated and therefore rejected Douglas's position that each territory could decide for itself, through popular sovereignty, whether or not to protect slavery. This divided the Democrats and destroyed their ability to pose as the party of accommodation.[34] And the extravagant victory that Taney had handed to the South was soon overwhelmed by the backlash it precipitated among Republicans, who resolved to reverse it by any means necessary. Although the Court couldn't have predicted the course of political events, it could have resisted the siren songs of politicians who flattered the justices into believing that they could resolve the nation's most intensely contested political dispute. By foolishly heeding calls for judicial intervention, the Court produced nothing very lasting for the nation and discredited itself with a self-inflicted wound.

Ultimately, of course, Taney's hope that he could resolve America's bloodiest political debate by judicial fiat was soon revealed to be deluded. Lincoln insisted, during his first inaugural address in 1861, that although any Supreme Court decision should bind the parties to the suit, its broader constitutional claims need not bind Congress because the Court had refused to defer to the will of the majority in an area of great constitutional uncertainty. Congress accepted Lincoln's invitation to ignore the decision. Indeed, Congress ended slavery in the federal territories in 1862, with no reference to *Dred Scott*; the Thirteenth Amendment, ratified in 1865, ended slavery throughout the United States; and the Fourteenth Amendment, ratified in 1868, overturned Taney's notion that native-born African Americans could not be citizens of the United States.

Lochner v. N.Y.

During the early decades of the twentieth century, the scope of the power of Congress and the states to regulate the economy remained contested. Beginning in the 1890s, the Court began to strike down state economic regulations as a violation of the due process clause of the Fourteenth Amendment, which says that "No State shall . . . deprive any person of life, liberty, or property, without due process of law." Opponents of these decisions attacked the doctrine of "substantive due process" as an oxymoron: instead of protecting substantive liberties, such as freedom of contract, they insisted, the due process clause merely guaranteed that any restrictions on life, liberty, or property would follow proper procedures. But in its Progressive Era decisions involving economic liberties, the Court was not, in fact, acting unilaterally; it was struggling to apply old common law categories to new economic circumstances. The Congress that passed the Fourteenth Amendment shared the widespread nineteenth-century belief that regulation in the public interest was permissible, but that redistributive "class legislation," which favored one group of economic competitors over another, was inherently suspect. In the Progressive Era, the Supreme Court tried to do what courts had done throughout the nineteenth century, resorting to formal categories to decide whether legislation was in the public interest or not—upholding laws that were designed to protect health, safety, or morals, for example, while striking down laws that the judges suspected were passed with purely redistributive motives.[35] As those formal categories became increasingly contested, the Court's attempts to apply them looked increasingly unilateralist.

In the notorious *Lochner* case (1905), the Court struck down a New York law prohibiting bakery employees from working more than ten hours a day or sixty hours a week. Justice Peckham's opinion for the Court held that the law was only masquerading as a health measure designed to safeguard the well-being of bakers, since baking (unlike working in a mine, for example) wasn't an unusually dangerous or unhealthy profession. The real purpose of the law, Peckham said, was to favor employees over employers. In one of the most famous dissents in American legal history, Justice Oliver Wendell Holmes chastised the Court for enacting "an economic theory which a large part of the country does not entertain." "The Fourteenth Amendment," he memorably announced, "does not enact Mr. Herbert Spencer's social statistics."[36] But although Holmes, in effect, accused the majority of indulging in judicial unilateralism—substituting a contested constitutional judgment in the face of a contrary judgment by a majority of Congress and the states—his charges, perhaps, were premature. *Lochner* was arguably an example of the Court's attempt to stand up against progressivism before progressivism had swept the country, which it did not do until after 1910.

The problem with *Lochner* was not that it applied the wrong constitutional principle; instead, the problem was that the Court presumed to second-guess the legislature's judgment about what kind of laws were necessary to promote health. In this sense, the dissenting opinion by Justice Holmes was more convincing according to the legal consensus of the day: because reasonable people could disagree about whether or not maximum hour laws were likely to promote health, the Court should have deferred to the legislative judgment about the utility of those laws in the face of constitutional uncertainty.

By 1907, two-thirds of the states had enacted laws banning child labor in factories and mines, and, in 1916, Congress banned the interstate shipment of goods manufactured with child labor. Nearly two years later, the Supreme Court struck down the federal child labor statute in *Hammer v. Dagenhart*, invalidating in a sweep a central element of the Progressive platform of 1912 and the Democratic and Republican Platforms of 1916.[37] In response to these decisions, progressives and organized labor attempted to mobilize Congress to resist the Court's commitment to federalism. In 1923 and 1924, for example, Representative James Frear, Republican of Wisconsin, proposed a right of appeal from the Supreme Court to Congress in constitutional cases, and Senator William E. Borah,

Republican of Idaho, proposed that at least seven justices should agree before striking down an act of Congress. Senator Robert M. La Follette of Wisconsin, the Progressive candidate for president, included an anticourt plank in his national platform. But La Follette was defeated and both houses of Congress in 1924 remained under Republican control. Because opposition to the Court was not sufficiently intense in the 1920s, Congress declined to adopt the Progressive proposals,[38] although it did in 1924 propose an amendment to the Constitution, which would have given Congress the power to prohibit child labor. Supported by political actors who had the power to cast crucial vetoes, the Court could continue to cast itself as what the president of the American Bar Association then called "the only breakwater against the haste and passions of the people—against the tumultuous ocean of democracy."[39]

By the mid 1930s, however, both houses of Congress were Democratic, and congressional indifference to the Court's constitutional vision evolved into active congressional resistance. In 1935 and 1936, the Court struck down a series of laws at the centerpiece of Franklin D. Roosevelt's New Deal. In 1935, the Court invalidated parts of the National Industrial Recovery Act as an excessive delegation of legislative authority to the president; it also held that the Railroad Retirement Act's mandatory pension plan was insufficiently related to interstate commerce. And in the *Schechter Poultry* case, the same year, the Court found an insufficient connection between a chicken slaughterer and the interstate poultry business, and held that Congress could not delegate to the federal government decisions about regulating the wages and hours of employees at a slaughterhouse that sold only to local retailers. The next year, in the *Carter Coal* case (1936), the Court struck down the Coal Conservation Act of 1935, which imposed collective bargaining agreements about wages, hours, and working conditions on miners who had not participated in the bargaining.

In these New Deal cases, the Court was trying to preserve an old constitutional consensus at a time when Congress had explicitly rejected it, while in *Dred Scott*, the Court was attempting to predict the constitutional vision of a future Congress at a time when the sitting Congress was actively contesting it. In retrospect, it is easier to sympathize with the Court when it was attempting to preserve rather than to transform a consensus, since in the absence of a constitutional amendment, the Court may have difficulty discerning when the old consensus has been displaced by the new. But in the 1930s, there was little doubt that Congress would assert its will if the Court refused to retreat.

In response to the judicial assault on the New Deal, Franklin D. Roosevelt in February 1937 proposed a Court packing plan that would have given him the power to appoint one additional judge to any court on which an incumbent refused to retire after the age of seventy. But on March 29, in the "switch in time that saved nine," Justice Owen Roberts joined a 5–4 majority in upholding a state minimum wage law applying to women and minors, even though he had voted to invalidate a similar law less than a year before. In *West Coast Hotel v. Parrish* (1937), the Court overruled an earlier decision from the Progressive Era as a "departure" from "true" constitutional principles. The most notable aspect of the Court's acquiescence to the constitutional vision of the president and Congress in the *West Coast Hotel* case was its self-conscious repudiation of its former unilateralism: recognizing that Congress no longer agreed which economic regulations should be considered "affected with the public interest," the Court deferred to a state legislature in the face of contestability. The legislature was "entitled to consider," said Hughes, that women were a vulnerable class with weak bargaining power; and the fact that many states had adopted similar regulations was evidence of a new national consensus about the necessity of such laws. Moreover, the economic reality of the Depression had dislodged the old assumptions that minimum wage laws should be considered special interest laws rather than laws affecting the well-being of all citizens; during a depression, what vulnerable workers lose in wages "the taxpayers are called upon to pay."[40]

The Court's retreat, whether strategic or not, helped to diffuse any political support for the Court packing plan, which the Senate Judiciary Committee rejected in June 1937. But the continued threat that Congress might pass bills restraining the Court may have contributed to the Court's complete capitulation. In the *Carolene Products* case (1938), the Court outlined the terms of its surrender. The case was the Court's most self-conscious disavowal of unilateralism: it would defer to the constitutional judgments of the legislatures in ordinary economic cases, where a national consensus about the scope of Congress's power was clear. And the Court would evaluate laws more skeptically only in cases where the legislative judgment might itself be distorted by prejudice or self-interest, or might clash with rights explicitly enumerated in the Constitution and its amendments.

The Court's disavowal of unilateralism in economic cases in the 1930s didn't prevent it from confronting the president in cases where Congress was sure to support the constitutional grounds for the confrontation. But in the 1950s, the Court became increasingly addicted to a rhetoric of judicial supremacy, based on the idea that courts alone can interpret the Constitution. This rhetoric was introduced most explicitly in *Cooper v. Aaron* in 1958, when the Warren Court ordered an Arkansas district court not to cave in the face of pressure from a local school board that wanted to delay desegregation. Governor Orville Faubus's earlier defiance of the district court had led President Eisenhower to send in federal troops in the fall of 1957. For fear of being defied, the Court lectured Faubus and the state legislature about their duties to obey the Supreme Court's interpretations of the Constitution, equating the Court's decisions with the text of the Constitution itself.[41]

A typical assertion of the Court's new supremacist temper is a good place to conclude our cautionary tales: *United States v. Nixon* (1974), which was, in many ways, the mirror image of *Marbury v. Madison*. During the Watergate scandal, the special prosecutor, Leon Jaworski, issued a subpoena ordering President Richard M. Nixon to turn over tapes of his conversations with aides who were being charged with obstruction of justice. Nixon invoked executive privilege, but the Supreme Court ordered the president to comply with the subpoena, holding that the needs of the judicial process outweighed the president's needs for confidentiality.

The Court was hardly engaging in judicial heroics: Congress had already expressed its own view about the constitutional propriety of subpoenaing tapes of the president's private conversations, and it coincided with that of the Court. Indeed, the House Judiciary Committee, preparing for an impeachment inquiry, had subpoenaed forty-two tapes on April 11, 1974, a week before the subpoena of the special prosecutor, and Nixon had already announced that he would comply with the Judiciary Committee's subpoena while resisting the one issued by Jaworski. Given the political confrontation between Congress and the president, the Court knew that there was no way that Nixon would resist a judicial order to turn over the tapes in the way that Jefferson would undoubtedly have resisted John Marshall. Moreover, if Nixon did resist, the Democratic Congress would back the Court, unlike the Republican Congress in Marshall's day, which would have backed Jefferson. In this sense, *Marbury* and *Nixon* are virtually the same case; only the political positions of the president are reversed. And in both cases, the Court was right to take its cues about how to interpret the Constitution in the face of uncertainty by consulting the constitutional views of Congress.

But if the Nixon Court reached a plausible result, the opinion was marred by grandiose and unnecessary language about the federal courts' duty (not just their right) "on occasion [to] interpret the Constitution in a manner at variance with the construction given the document by another branch."[42] Proclaiming its responsibility "as ultimate interpreter of the Constitution," the Court heavy-handedly cited *Marbury v. Madison* to establish its own "province and duty . . . 'to say what the law is.'"[43] But *Marbury* did not proclaim the Court to be the ultimate interpreter of the Constitution; it merely asserted the Court's power to be a coequal interpreter. The Nixon Court was reciting Marshall's mantra without his sense of humility.

This is the peculiar situation in which the modern Court finds itself: defiantly asserting its own supremacy in theory while (in most cases) sensibly declining to press it in practice. One could perhaps forgive all this as the posturing of a paper tiger; but there are costs to the rhetoric of judicial supremacy, even if it is only rhetoric. A Court that insists repeatedly that it alone is the ultimate and exclusive interpreter of the Constitution may discourage the other branches of government from engaging in constitutional interpretation of their own. Indeed, Congress in the post-Watergate period became less self-conscious about debating issues in constitutional terms, confident that the courts would save it from its excesses. This not only resulted in ill-advised legislation but also got Congress out of the habit of debating constitutional principles to which the Courts could plausibly defer. The result is a vicious cycle of judicial self-assertion and congressional acquiescence that is transforming the way American constitutional principles themselves emerge. Since those principles throughout most of American history were formulated by Congress as well as the courts, as we will see in the next chapters, this development is a cause for concern.

2

Race

After the Civil War, the Reconstruction Congress proposed the Fourteenth Amendment, promising all United States citizens equal civil (but not political) rights; in practice, however, these rights were denied or abridged by state laws and practice for nearly a hundred years and didn't begin to become meaningfully available to African Americans until after the civil rights movement of the 1960s. The framers and ratifiers of the Fourteenth Amendment expected that civil rights would be defined and enforced primarily by Congress, not the courts; but the courts high-handedly insisted on their own supremacy, denying Congress the right to interpret civil rights more expansively.

How effective a role did federal courts play in extending equal civil rights to African Americans? Accustomed as we are to celebrating the moral and constitutional heroism of *Brown v. Board of Education*, the case that struck down school segregation in 1954, many Americans tend to assume that racial progress in the United States is primarily the result of leadership by courageous and racially enlightened judges. This assumption, however, is mistaken. On the contrary, it's hard to avoid the conclusion that judges were most successful in enforcing civil rights when they followed a constitutional consensus about equality that was triggered by Congress or the White House, or both.

When the Civil War ended, it was Congress, not the courts, that attempted to extend equal civil rights to all Americans regardless of race. Even after the abolition of slavery, Southern states passed the notorious "Black Codes" restricting the rights of freedmen to own property and to make contracts, creating special criminal offenses for blacks only, and imposing discriminatory punishments for crimes committed by blacks. In 1866, the Reconstruction Congress passed the Civil Rights Act designed to repudiate the Black Codes. The Civil Rights Act extended to citizens "of every race and color" the same rights to make and enforce contracts, to sue and be sued, to inherit, buy, lease, and sell property and to the full and equal benefits of all laws and proceedings for the security of persons and property.[1] Because of doubts about whether Congress had the constitutional authority to pass the Civil Rights Act, Reconstruction Republicans in the Thirty-ninth Congress proposed the Fourteenth Amendment to the Constitution, which was ratified in 1868. The first section reads:

> All persons born or naturalized in the United States and subject to the jurisdiction thereof, are citizens of the United States and of the State wherein they reside. No State shall make or enforce any law which shall abridge the privileges or immunities of citizens of the United States; nor shall any State deprive any person of life, liberty, or property, without due process of law; nor deny to any person within its jurisdiction the equal protection of the laws.

At the very least, the privileges or immunities clause of the Fourteenth Amendment was designed to give constitutional protection to the rights protected in the Civil Rights Act of 1866—the right to make contracts, to sue and be sued, and so forth—and to prohibit the states from denying or abridging these rights. The courts and Congress, not the states, would have the final say when these rights were abridged—and therefore would protect fundamental rights throughout the nation. In addition to rights of contract and access to the courts, the question of what other rights the Fourteenth Amendment protected from state abridgment inspired vigorous disagreement. The principal drafter of the Fourteenth Amendment, John Bingham, believed that the "privileges and immunities of citizens of the United States" included most of the basic rights enumerated in the Federal Bill of Rights, including the First Amendment right to free speech, the Fourth Amendment's right against unreasonable searches and seizures, and the Fifth Amendment right against compelled self-incrimination. Under the original Constitution, Congress, but not the states, was forbidden to abridge these rights. It's not clear that all the states that ratified the Fourteenth Amendment—some of them under duress, as a condition for rejoining the Union—agreed with Bingham's expansive view. The precise scope of the Fourteenth Amendment was, therefore, an open question when the Supreme Court first attempted to define it in 1873. The Court's first encounter, in the *Slaughter-House* cases, was not auspicious. Afraid that a broad reading of privileges or immunities would make the Court into a perpetual censor on state laws, the justices unilaterally construed much of the amendment into irrelevance.

The *Slaughter-House* cases involved the constitutionality of a law passed by the New Orleans legislature in 1869 "to protect the health of the City of New Orleans." As refrigerated railroad cars made it possible to ship meat across the country, the slaughterhouses of New Orleans had a growing national market in the East. After the existing slaughterhouses in the city moved upstream, their offal and waste floated down the river and menaced the health of the citizens, contributing to yellow fever epidemics each summer in which thousands died. After the Civil

War, the New Orleans legislature responded by requiring slaughterhouses to operate below the city, but these required improvements on the riverfront. To fund the improvements, the legislature chartered the Crescent City Live-Stock Landing and Slaughter House Company, authorized it to build a "grand slaughter-house" south of the city, and allowed all butchers to use the grand slaughterhouse—including small businesses run by freedmen—by paying the necessary fees. At the same time, the law forbade competitors to set up any other slaughterhouses in and around the city.[2]

From the Jacksonian era onward, there was a powerful strand of thought in Congress and the courts that monopoly grants, designed to help some business interests at the expense of others, were an unconstitutional form of economic favoritism. The Reconstruction Republicans, following nineteenth-century state constitutions and judicial opinions, distinguished between laws enacted for the public good—that is, laws that protected all people equally—and what they called "class legislation"— that is, special interest laws that took property or vested rights away from some people for the purpose of giving them to others. Senator Jacob M. Howard of Michigan invoked the same idea in his speech introducing the Fourteenth Amendment to the Thirty-ninth Congress. After quoting the equal protection and due process language, Howard said, "This abolishes all class legislation in the States and does away with the injustice of subjecting one caste of persons to a code not applicable to another."[3]

Although the courts and Congress agreed that the Fourteenth Amendment prohibited the states from engaging in economic favoritism, there was a dispute in the *Slaughter-House* cases about whether or not the monopoly grant to the Crescent City Company should be considered an illegitimate form of "class legislation" or as a legitimate effort to protect public health. On the one hand, the New Orleans press and other defenders of the economic interests of the Old South claimed that the members of the Crescent City Company had bribed the governor's assistant to ensure his approval. On the other hand, revisionist historians have called the Crescent City Slaughter-House monopoly "a work of great genius."[4] The slaughterhouse was required to make its facilities available to any small proprietor who paid the fee and in this sense might be seen as a way of helping former slaves who were trying to establish themselves in business and would have suffered discrimination in trying to raise capital.

Unfortunately, after acknowledging this debate about whether the grand Slaughterhouse was a monopoly, a majority of the Supreme Court decided to save the country from the practical consequences of enforcing the Fourteenth Amendment according to the intentions of its framers. In a 5–4 decision by Justice Miller, the Court began by concluding, plausibly enough, that the Louisiana monopoly didn't deprive any butchers of the right to pursue their calling, since the slaughterhouse was open to anyone who paid the required fee. But after reaching this defensible conclusion, Justice Miller went on to ask whether the law abridged any other rights protected by the federal Constitution. For the first time, the Court was asked to construe the meaning of the first section of the newly ratified Fourteenth Amendment, which says, among other things, "No State shall make or enforce any law which shall abridge the privileges or immunities of citizens of the United States."

Faced with the possibility that the Fourteenth Amendment had transformed the relationship between the states and the federal government by giving Congress the power to enforce the protection of fundamental rights, the Supreme Court balked. More to the point, it proceeded, for purely pragmatic reasons, to read the privileges or immunities clause out of existence. Since requiring the states to respect the privileges or immunities of citizenship would "fetter and degrade the State governments by subjecting them to the control of Congress," the Court held, the Court would refuse to do so "in the absence of language which expresses such a purpose too clearly to admit of doubt."[5] This meant that if Congress wanted to force the states to respect the Bill of Rights, it would have to say so clearly and unequivocally.

In fact, the language of the privileges or immunities clause arguably did contain clear and unequivocal language that expressed Congress's purpose too clearly to admit much doubt. In a speech explaining why he used the words he did, John Bingham said explicitly that he chose the words of the privileges or immunities clause, beginning with "No State shall," for the specific purpose of making clear his intention that the Bill of Rights should bind the states.[6] But Justice Miller, determined to avoid the politically disruptive consequences of applying the Bill of Rights against the states, simply ignored the text and original understanding of the privileges or immunities clause. He read the first sentence of the Fourteenth Amendment to imply two different sorts of citizenship—federal and state—and then announced that the privileges or immunities clause only protects the privileges of federal citizenship. Miller embraced an implausible distinction between the privileges or immunities of United States citizenship—which he said included only a narrow category of federally protected right, such as the right to demand federal protection on the high seas or abroad—and the privileges or immunities of state citizenship, which, according to Miller, included the broader category of fundamental rights at issue in the *Slaughter-House* case, such as the right to make contracts and inherit property. As Justice Field noted in his dissent, if the Fourteenth Amendment protected only those rights already specifically designated in the Constitution, or implicit in the concept of federal citizenship, "it was a vain and idle enactment, which accomplished nothing, and most unnecessarily excited Congress and the people on its passage."[7]

Like *Dred Scott*, the *Slaughter-House* case is a cautionary tale about the dangers of judicial unilateralism. Although there may have been plausible disagreement in Congress between 1868 and 1873 about whether the Fourteenth Amendment incorporated all of the restrictions of the Bill of Rights against the states, there was little disagreement that it prohibited the states from passing either "class legislation" or caste-affirming legislation that disadvantaged one group at the expense of another. This was the central purpose of the amendment, after all. Moreover, the *Slaugh-ter-House* cases were decided in April 1873, just after the end of the Forty-second Congress, which had a strong Republican majority. Republicans in the Forty-third Congress would go on to pass the Civil Rights Act of 1875, which prohibited discrimination in places of public accommodations based on the constitutional understanding of majorities in the House and Senate that the Fourteenth Amendment required no less. For the Supreme Court to substitute its own cramped vision of federally protected rights for the far more generous vision of Congress was unilateralist in the extreme. (Although the Court should not attempt to predict the future, the Republican position on congressional power and civil rights was consistent and well known.) Instead of deferring to the congressional consensus, the Court presumed to save the country in the name of pragmatic expedience and in the process subverted the Fourteenth Amendment's promise of equality.

The Civil Rights Act of 1875 was passed by a lame-duck Republican Congress, which had just lost control of the House because of its liberal views on race. After the compromise of 1877 put an end to Reconstruction, and with it the hopes of congressional support for the rights of African Americans, the courts mirrored the increasingly intolerant public views about race, rather than challenging them in systematic ways. When the legal arguments in favor of an African American plaintiff were too clear and convincing to be ignored, judges occasionally applied the law and struck down especially egregious forms of discrimination. But when the legal materials were ambiguous—as they were in most cases—judges proved all too willing to tolerate dramatic violations of equality.[8]

Rather than indulging in judicial heroics, the courts might have attempted to do no harm, simply getting out of Congress's way and enforcing the few Reconstruction-era laws passed to guarantee equal civil rights for African Americans. Instead, they struck those laws down. In this sense, the Court's decision, in the *Civil Rights* cases (1883) to strike down the Civil Rights Act of 1875, was especially unfortunate. The Civil

Rights Act was the high-water mark of liberal reconstruction, and its guarantee of "full and equal access" to public accommodations such as inns, trains, ferryboats, and theaters was an important effort to make the promises of the Fourteenth Amendment a reality. Unfortunately, the political climate that made possible the passage of the Civil Rights Act was brief. The Republican majority in Congress had already been voted out of office when it passed the Civil Rights Act; and in the contested election of 1876 (which prefigured, in many ways, the contested election of 2000), Southern Democrats agreed to abandon their support for the Democratic candidate, Samuel J. Tilden, and throw their support behind his Republican opponent, Rutherford B. Hayes. In exchange, Democrats demanded the end of Reconstruction.[9]

Any hope for vigorous federal enforcement of the Civil Rights Act of 1875 was fanciful almost immediately after the act was passed, and it became even more fanciful after the electoral compromise of 1877, which ended Reconstruction and put Hayes in the White House. Indeed, the act was more or less moribund in practice by the time the Supreme Court considered its constitutionality. Some lower courts had already interpreted Congress's promise of "full and equal enjoyment" of places of public accommodations to guarantee separate but equal facilities, not integrated ones. Nevertheless, the Supreme Court's decision to strike down the Civil Rights Act, on the grounds that the Fourteenth Amendment doesn't give Congress the authority to forbid discrimination by private parties, was arguably an act of judicial unilateralism. When the *Civil Rights* cases were decided on October 15, 1883, there were still Republican majorities in both houses of the Forty-seventh Congress and no overt repudiation of the constitutional principle that Congress has the power, if it chooses, to forbid racial discrimination in places of public accommodation. The Republicans may have given up on Reconstruction as a policy matter, but they had not repudiated the broad constitutional vision of congressional power to enforce civil rights embodied in the Fourteenth Amendment.

As Justice Harlan wrote in his dissent, Republicans since Reconstruction had considered "exemption from race discrimination in respect of any civil right" as the preeminent privilege or immunity of U.S. citizenship that the Fourteenth Amendment meant to protect against state infringement. And it was plausible to consider railroad owners and keepers of inns and restaurants as agents of the state, because they are charged with public duties and amenable to government regulation. For this reason, Harlan concluded equal access to these "quasi-public" facilities should be considered a basic civil right, on par with the right to make and enforce contracts. Moreover, as Harlan noted, the Court was construing the boundaries of Congress's power in a far less generous spirit than it had done during the Taney era in 1842, when it upheld the fugitive slave law of 1793.[10] Was it really possible, Harlan asked, that Congress had more power to protect the rights of slave owners than those of the newly freed slaves? Because of the Court's decision to substitute its own vision of federal power for Congress's vision, advocates of equal rights had to wait nearly a hundred years, until the civil rights era of the 1960s, until they could again persuade Congress to prohibit discrimination in public accommodations.

After the Court struck down the Civil Rights Act, opponents of Jim Crow had no alternative but to rely directly on the Constitution. But constitutional arguments against segregation had even less success in the political climate that followed the end of Reconstruction than the arguments relying on the Civil Rights Act itself. Since before the Civil War, courts had upheld the creation of separate but equal facilities, holding that the inherent differences between the races made separation reasonable. More important, in some ways, the political support for segregation increased as the memories of Reconstruction faded. From 1887 to 1892, nine southern states passed laws requiring segregated accommodations on railroads and public conveyances.[11] The Louisiana law, passed in 1890, was fairly typical in purporting to require separate but equal accommodations for blacks and whites while containing an exception for black nurses, who were allowed to accompany their white charges only because of their status as subordinates rather than equals. The Louisiana Supreme Court refused to apply the segregation law to interstate travel, holding that such a regulation would have interfered with Congress's exclusive power to regulate interstate commerce[12]: this legalism—embraced by the U.S. Supreme Court in 1910[13]—suggests that courts actually were willing to side with racial minorities even in the face of popular support for segregation when the legal arguments were clear and convincing. But the same state Supreme Court held in 1893 that the law was a valid restriction on travel within Louisiana itself, noting that many other courts had concluded that "equality, and not identity or community, of accommodations is the extreme test of conformity to the requirements of the [Fourteenth Amendment]."[14]

Three years later, as public support for segregation continued to grow, the U.S. Supreme Court agreed. Upholding the Louisiana law in *Plessy v. Ferguson* (1896), the Supreme Court rejected the claim that the Fourteenth Amendment prohibited states from requiring segregated railroad cars. The Supreme Court conceded that "every exercise of the police power must be reasonable, and extend only to such laws as are enacted in good faith for the promotion for the public good, and not for the annoyance or oppression of a particular class."[15] In deciding whether a law was reasonable, the Court continued, "there must necessarily be a large discretion on the part of the legislature . . . to act with reference to the established usages, customs and traditions of the people." Plessy's lawyers had argued that mandatory segregation "stamps the colored race with a badge of inferiority." But "if this be so," the Court concluded, "it is not by reason of anything found in the act, but solely because the colored race chooses to put that construction upon it."[16]

Judged by the standards of the 1890s, *Plessy* was an uncontroversial demonstration of judicial restraint in the face of constitutional ambiguity. Lower courts and commentators had reached the same conclusion about the reasonableness of segregation on railroads, and dominant public opinion supported it; as a result, the opinion was barely noted in the inside pages of the major newspapers.[17] By contrast, judged in light of the text and original understanding of the Fourteenth Amendment, *Plessy* was arguably wrong on the day it was decided. As Justice Harlan noted in his prescient dissent, although the law formally applied equally to blacks and whites, "everyone knows that" its real purpose was to exclude blacks from white cars because of the belief that they were too inferior and degraded to ride with whites on equal terms. As a result, the law unconstitutionally interfered with the personal liberty of blacks and whites to travel—a freedom guaranteed by the Fourteenth Amendment— in a way that offended the constitutional guarantee that "there is in this country no superior, dominant, ruling class of citizens. There is no caste here." Harlan was not claiming that government had to be color-blind in all of its actions, as some modern conservatives claim, but only that "in respect to civil rights,"—as opposed to political or social rights— "all citizens are equal before the law,"[18] and the liberty to travel was widely acknowledged to be a fundamental civil right. Although the government was free to regulate civil rights to advance legitimate public purposes, Harlan continued, judges should refuse to credit the justifications offered by the legislature if they were nothing more than a "thin disguise" for an impermissible purpose: namely, the maintenance of a racial caste system. The law, therefore, had to fall not because it used a racial classification, but because its white supremacist purpose was too obvious to ignore.[19]

The original understanding of the Fourteenth Amendment about railroad segregation is hard to discern with clarity. The same Congress that passed the Fourteenth Amendment also passed a local railroad charter that the Court in 1873 interpreted to forbid segregation.[20] And the Congress that passed the Civil Rights Act of 1875 seemed to believe that segregated railroad cars violated the constitutional requirements of equal protection. Nevertheless, Congressional sentiment in 1875 may have been more liberal than it was a few years earlier when the Fourteenth

Amendment was passed, and Congress may also have believed that it had broader power to define constitutional rights of equality than judges did.

By 1896, there was no clear congressional consensus about the unconstitutionality of railroad segregation, but the question was not intensely contested. Two years earlier, Democrats found themselves in control of Congress and the White House for the first time since the 1850s, and they took advantage of this control to repeal most of the voting rights legislation of the 1870s. When Republicans once again controlled both houses of Congress and the presidency between 1897 and 1910, they did not attempt to resurrect these laws.[21] Nevertheless, Congress in the 1890s had not formally repudiated the Civil Rights legislation, since the Supreme Court had already struck it down.

If the Court had struck down railroad segregation laws in *Plessy* in 1896 rather than supporting them, would it have acted unilaterally? Arguably not, since the status of railroad segregation was not intensely contested in Congress or in national politics, and only nine southern states had required it. In fact, the Court might have claimed that it was merely bringing state outliers into a national consensus, embodied in the federal railroad law banning segregation and in the Fourteenth Amendment itself. Justice Harlan's constitutional argument for striking down segregation was sufficiently persuasive, after all, that in a posthumous tribute to Harlan in 1912, Justice Homer Brown, the author of the majority opinion in *Plessy*, expressed reservations about his own decision to uphold Jim Crow. Although "twenty-eight years have elapsed since *Plessy v. Ferguson* was rendered," Brown wrote, "there is still a lingering doubt whether the spirit of the amendments was not sacrificed to the letter, and whether the Constitution was not intended to secure the equality of the two races in all places affected with a public interest."[22]

On the other hand, there may have been less national support for striking down railroad segregation in 1896 than there was for the *Dred Scott* decision in 1857; and even if the Court had ruled the other way in *Plessy*, it seems unlikely that the spread of railroad segregation would have been meaningfully contained. Although Republicans won a land-slide victory in Congress in 1894 and took the presidency in 1896, there is no evidence that either Congress or the president would vigorously have enforced a Supreme Court ruling striking down segregation in the event that they had confronted it. If *Plessy* had come out the other way, southern whites would have refused to comply with a judicial ban on railroad segregation without federal coercion, and by the 1890s, it seems implausible that any president would have supported the courts by providing the coercion necessary.[23] Unless the president had been willing to send federal troops to enforce a hypothetical ruling striking down segregation, his other enforcement powers were limited: Democrats controlled nearly every southern legislature, and state judges, jurors, and prosecutors would have refused to cooperate. Even in the unimaginable event that the president had sent troops, segregation would have continued through informal practice: southern steamboat travel, courtrooms, theaters, and hotels were increasingly segregated in practice, although no laws commanded the segregation of courtrooms. And despite the Supreme Court ruling forbidding states from mandating segregation in interstate travel, southern railroads chose to mandate segregation on their own.[24] All this is to say that the Court's approval of railroad segregation laws reflected the determination of the public to enforce segregation rather than causing it; and without the support of the president and Congress, the courts had a limited ability to check this determination even if they had wanted to.

For the next sixty years, between *Plessy* and *Brown v. Board of Education*, the courts avoided unilateralism in cases concerning race discrimination. Courts were willing to strike down segregation in a few cases where the legal case for doing so was too strong to ignore. For example, even in the Progressive Era, at the height of Jim Crow, the Supreme Court questioned the constitutionality of an Oklahoma law that allowed railroads to provide unequal first class accommodations[25] (this was a clear violation of the principle of separate but equal) as well as striking down a Kentucky law that entrenched residential segregation by pro-hibiting black people from buying houses on primarily white streets.[26] (Although the law imposed similar restrictions on whites, the Court said it violated the right to own and dispose of property that the Four-teenth Amendment clearly was intended to protect.) As residential hous-ing patterns became increasingly segregated, however, this decision had little direct effect. Of more practical importance were decisions invali-dating white-only primaries in the South, which paved the way for American servicemen to demand voting rights when they returned from World War II. But by and large, the courts from the *Plessy* era until the 1950s followed the nation rather than leading it in confronting manda-tory legal segregation.

Meaningful political support for dismantling segregation increased after World War II, when Cold War politics made it embarrassing for America to practice segregation at home at a time when it was trying to win political support for democracy abroad.[27] The integration of the army and major league baseball in the late 1940s was a harbinger of increased sympathy for integration in the country as a whole. Prodded by the litigation of an increasingly energized National Association for the Advancement of Colored People, courts began to look beyond the formal pretense of separate but equal schools and to demand a measure of genuine equality. In challenging the Texas State University for Ne-groes, hastily established by Texas as a purportedly separate but equal alternative to the all-white University of Texas, the NAACP persuaded the Court that equal facilities were not all that blacks deserved. "More important" than the budget and curriculum, the Court agreed in *Sweatt v. Painter* (1950), were "those qualities which are incapable of objective measurement but which make for greatness in a law school."[28] Judged by this standard, the all-black law school was transparently unequal, and the Court ordered the University of Texas to integrate.

In border states between the North and South, where resistance to the integration of higher education was on the wane, *Sweatt* had a positive effect: six months after the decision, about a thousand African Americans were attending colleges that had been previously closed to them in Arkansas, Missouri, Oklahoma, and Kentucky.[29] But in the Deep South, massive resistance to *Sweatt* was itself fanned by the reaction to *Brown v. Board of Education*: as a result, ten years after the decision, not a single black student attended an all-white university, except in Louisiana.

The *Brown* case, a challenge to segregated public schools in Topeka, Kansas, might seem to challenge the thesis that the Supreme Court rarely acts to thwart the wishes of national majorities. But in fact, national opinion about public school segregation was evenly divided in 1954; and beginning that summer, a series of surveys about reactions to the school desegregation decisions, conducted by Gallup's American Institute of Public Opinion, found approval by over half the country.[30] In the face of constitutional ambiguity, therefore, the Court had the political support necessary to bring the twenty-one states that still endorsed segregation into line with a growing national consensus about the unconstitutionality of American apartheid.[31] Unlike the constitutionality of the Missouri compromise in the 1850s, the constitutionality of school segregation was not being actively contested in Congress in the 1950s: Republicans won control of the House and Senate in 1953 after a long period of Democratic rule, but southern Democrats continued to control the rules committee in the House and were able to threaten filibusters in the Senate. Therefore, the Court at the time of *Brown* was arguably in a better position to represent the constitutional views of a majority of the country than Congress itself.

Brown didn't merely reflect a constitutional consensus but also helped one to crystallize. The moral clarity of the decision helped to galvanize the civil rights movement, which in turn helped to provoke a southern backlash that ultimately turned Congress and the country strongly and unequivocally against segregation in the 1960s. *Brown*, then, is an example of how the Court, on rare occasions in American history, can play an educative role in encouraging Congress and the president to engage in a constitutional dialogue and ultimately encourage them to embrace a principle that the Court itself was the first to recognize. But the Court had the leeway to play this role only because a majority of the public was willing to recognize the constitutional principle of racial equality as fundamental.

The driving force behind the end of school segregation was not the Court or Congress but the White House—or perhaps more precisely, the Justice Department. Franklin D. Roosevelt, at the beginning of his second term, resolved to purge southern conservatives from the Democratic Party who had resisted his Court-packing plan as well as his constitutional vision of a strong executive branch with the power and flexibility to respond to national needs.[32] This didn't necessarily lead to more progressive views about race: even those southern senators who strongly supported the New Deal were fiercely committed to white supremacy. Still, Roosevelt appointed to the Court those justices who shared his constitutional vision of protecting individual rights and deferring to executive power, and his Justice Department encouraged groups like the NAACP to turn to the courts for civil rights victories (against antilynching laws and the poll tax, for example) that were being stymied by southern conservatives in Congress. Roosevelt instructed his Justice Department to enforce civil rights and individual liberties as a way of consolidating his power, mobilizing African American voters, and strengthening the national Democratic Party over state party organizations.

Although Roosevelt's interest in civil rights was politically opportunistic, he committed the Justice Department to moderately progressive views on race that continued in subsequent administrations. The Truman Justice Department first called for *Plessy v. Ferguson* to be overturned in 1950, a position that it reaffirmed in the brief it filed in *Brown*. And Eisenhower was persuaded by a liberal attorney general that quietly supporting the overturning of *Plessy* would maintain the GOP's traditional liberal base in the North while helping to erode Democratic support in the South. "In the eyes of the justices, two consecutive administrations—one Democratic, one Republican—had now told them that nothing prevented them from uprooting *Plessy*."[33]

The justices accepted the invitation in *Brown*, which involved five challenges to school segregation, including one in Kansas. At the initial conference in *Brown*, the Court seemed inclined to uphold segregation by a 5–4 vote. As Justice Robert Jackson noted in a concurring opinion that he drafted but never issued, there is nothing in the text of the Fourteenth Amendment that says clearly that segregation is unconstitutional. And nothing in the original understanding of the Fourteenth Amendment clearly condemns segregation either: the same Congress that proposed the Fourteenth Amendment presided over segregated public schools in the District of Columbia. Furthermore, Congress said nothing about ending segregation when it required Southern states to ratify the amendment as a condition of readmission to the Union. (Eleven of the Northern and border states that ratified the Fourteenth Amendment also had segregated schools.) The Supreme Court's own precedents had repeatedly said that segregation was consistent with the Fourteenth Amendment. In the early 1950s, moreover, it was hard to argue that changed circumstances had created an entirely new understanding of equality: twenty-one states and the District of Columbia required or allowed public school segregation. Finally, pragmatic considerations arguably counseled against invalidating segregation: the South was determined to resist by any means necessary, and Justice Jackson was concerned that the Court might weaken itself by issuing unenforceable orders in the face of public opposition.[34]

Despite Jackson's plausible arguments for judicial restraint, there were also powerful constitutional arguments for striking down school segregation. After the Court embraced them, they eventually became too compelling for even skeptics to resist. The central purpose of the Fourteenth Amendment, after all, was to eliminate a racial caste system in America. In a provocative effort to challenge the received wisdom that school segregation is consistent with the original meaning of the Fourteenth Amendment, Michael McConnell, the scrupulous conservative judge and legal scholar, has noted that between 1870 and 1874, majorities in the House and Senate repeatedly voted in favor of school desegregation. Although Congress had abandoned its focus on public schools when it passed the Civil Rights Act of 1875, majorities of those who voted for that act may have believed that the Fourteenth Amendment entitled all citizens to the same civil rights and access to public education was indeed a civil right.[35] Moreover, even if the precise legal status of education was unclear in the 1860s and '70s, when few state-sponsored public schools existed, the situation looked very different in the 1950s, when all states had committed themselves to requiring attendance at state-sponsored public schools. Although the argument for invalidating school segregation couldn't be strictly based on text or original understanding, therefore, it was at least deeply rooted in constitutional history and could be summarized along the following lines: The Fourteenth Amendment prohibits caste-based distinctions in the distribution of basic civil rights; access to school was a basic civil right in 1954, regardless of its status in 1868; and everyone knew, as Justice Harlan recognized in *Plessy v. Ferguson*, that the purpose and effect of segregation was to maintain a racial caste system. Therefore school segregation had to fall.

That, in any event, is more or less what the Court held. The fortuitous death of the mediocre Chief Justice Vinson (which led Justice Felix Frankfurter to remark "This is the first indication that I have ever had that there is a God") and his replacement by California governor Earl Warren changed the tentative vote at the justices' conference to at least 5–4 in favor of striking down school segregation. The Court recognized what appears in retrospect to be transcendently obvious—that segregation was based on the premise that black people are inferior. In the face of legal uncertainty, the undecided justices were able to embrace the principle that segregation was unconstitutional because Congress was not intensely committed to the opposite principle, public opinion was divided, and the support of the White House gave them room to do so. With some skillful lobbying from Warren, who urged the holdout justice, Stanley Reed, to resist the urge to dissent in order to protect the legitimacy of the Court, the decision became unanimous.

Although the point is arguable, *Brown* does not appear to be an example of judicial unilateralism. The Truman and (more grudgingly) Eisenhower administrations nominally supported the Court's claim that the Constitution required school desegregation, and majorities in the House and Senate at least were not actively insisting on the opposite principle, namely that segregation was consistent with the Constitution. Although Congress refused to pass resolutions supporting *Brown* after it came down, the Court was free to act without fear of a congressional backlash. Congress's attitude is best described as ambivalence, since the constitutional status of segregation was not intensely contested in 1954: McCarthyism, not school segregation, was the question of the day. Moreover, Congress was inhibited from reflecting national opinion about segregation because of a seniority system that gave disproportionate power to white southerners. Indeed, at the *Brown* oral argument, Justice Robert Jackson noted that "realistically the reason this case is here is that action couldn't be obtained from Congress."[36]

If the Court followed the White House's lead in declaring segregation to be unconstitutional, it was similarly deferential to the White House in devising a legal remedy for segregation. A month after Eisenhower won the 1952 election, the Truman administration filed a brief in *Brown* urging the Court to adopt a "gradualist" approach, neither upholding separate but equal nor demanding immediate desegregation.[37] In *Brown II* (1955), its second encounter with the case, the Court set out to formulate a remedy for the constitutional violation it had identified the previous year. Gratefully embracing this principle of gradualism, the Court urged desegregation "as soon as practicable" and "with all deliberate speed." Gradualism, moreover, was consistent with the national mood: polls suggested that, by nearly four to one, the country preferred gradualism to immediate desegregation, in the interests of avoiding more of the violence that followed *Brown*.[38] The more notable skepticism about this pragmatic compromise was expressed by Hugo Black, a southerner and far more hard-headed politician, who understood that the South would massively resist *Brown* no matter what the Court said. In predicting the political response to the Court's anxiously issued olive branch, Black turned out to be more prescient than his colleagues.

Months after *Brown II*, most southern members of Congress signed the "Southern manifesto," which denounced *Brown* as an abuse of judicial power and declared the right of states to ignore it. And school districts throughout the South embraced an impressive variety of stratagems to avoid complying with the decision, from so called "freedom of choice" plans that assigned students to their old schools unless they asked to transfer, to "pupil placement" laws that gave local officials broad discretion to assign students to different schools, supposedly without taking race into account. A few southern judges tried to invalidate these evasions of *Brown*, but in the face of overpowering public resistance, many of the evasions were upheld. The only moment during the 1950s when the Supreme Court itself intervened again in the desegregation battles was in *Cooper v. Aaron*, when Governor Orval Faubus ordered the Arkansas National Guard to thwart the efforts of nine black school children to enroll in the all-white Little Rock Central High School in 1957. In response to the governor's claim that he wasn't bound to respect *Brown*, the Court unanimously declared that "the interpretation of the Fourteenth Amendment enunciated by this Court in the *Brown* case is the supreme law of the land."[39] The Court's equation of its own decisions with the Constitution itself was far less convincing than John Marshall's more modest notion that the judiciary had a coordinate rather than exclusive authority to interpret the Constitution. In practical terms, however, neither the rhetorical excesses of the Supreme Court in *Cooper* nor the embattled efforts of a few southern judges made much difference: in 1964, ten years after *Brown*, scarcely more than 2 percent of the African American children in the South attended desegregated schools.[40]

By contrast, in the following decade, southern desegregation accelerated at an impressive pace: by 1966, that figure had climbed to 12.5 percent, and, by 1971, 44 percent of black students attended majority white schools in the South (compared to only 28 percent in the North and West.)[41] What can account for this transformation? Not the courts acting on their own but the support of the president and Congress, galvanized by the civil rights movement. The federal government's increased commitment to desegregation was represented most importantly by the passage of the Civil Rights Act of 1964. Title VI of that act prohibited the distribution of federal funds to any federal program that discriminated on the basis of race. Title VI proved to be a powerful financial carrot as well as a stick that could be yielded by federal judges against recalcitrant school districts. Around 1965, the Justice Department committed itself to suing southern school districts that had declined federal aid; and, in 1966, the Department of Health, Education, and Welfare issued new guidelines interpreting the Civil Rights Act to require effective desegregation. Lower courts, in turn, were able to use the new guidelines to announce elaborate desegregation plans that applied to every school in their districts. In short, it was not the *Brown* decision itself, but the political transformation that followed it, that made its commands a reality.

The precise relationship between *Brown* and the civil rights movement is hotly contested. The conventional view, favorable to the unilateralist myth, holds that there was a direct correlation between the decision and the freedom riders, and that white and black civil rights agitators took to the highways in the 1960s to make *Brown* a reality. Revisionist scholars offer a more complicated account. Michael Klarman, for example, argues that *Brown* was less directly responsible for the protests of the 1960s than it was for creating a southern backlash that ensured those protests were violently suppressed. It was the images of violence broadcast on national television that helped to transform public opinion about race in the North, creating a national constituency for civil rights legislation and leading to the Civil Rights Act of 1964.[42] Regardless of the precise relationship between *Brown* and the civil rights movement, it's obvious that courts weren't able to precipitate the desegregation of schools, transportation, or public accommodations on their own; at most the Court performed a collaborative role—putting the issue on the national agenda (with the support of the White House) at a time when public opinion was ready to support desegregation and inviting the political branches to follow. The only thing we can say with confidence is that the Court in *Brown* played an important educative role in helping to encourage a growing public consensus about the injustice of segregation, but that it was able to do so because a majority of the public was initially inclined to agree.

The period of harmony in the mid-1960s during which the courts, Congress, and the president were mutually committed to desegregation was brief. As the decade progressed, an ambiguity in the original *Brown* opinion became too pressing to ignore: as a remedy for intentional segregation, did the Constitution simply require an end to segregation or affirmative integration? Language in *Brown* could be read to support either vision, but the Court itself remained coy about what precisely it meant. In 1955, evaluating the effects of *Brown*, a southern appellate judge had announced "that Constitution, in other words, does not require integration. It merely forbids segregation."[43] But in the mid-1960s, Judge John Minor Wisdom on the U.S. Court of Appeals for the Fifth Circuit interpreted the new federal guidelines, and the Constitution itself, to require not merely desegregation but full integration in school districts that had been deliberately segregated in the past. This was a conclusion that the Supreme Court itself had been moving toward ever since *Cooper v. Aaron*, but the justices had been careful to use the word "desegregated" rather than "integrated" to avoid offending southern sensibilities.[44] Relying on the federal guidelines, Wisdom gave detailed instructions for the administration of the free choice periods, ordered that students had to be assigned by geographic proximity to the school, and included suggestions about where new schools should be built.[45] In the process, he put federal courts, rather than local officials, at the forefront of designing remedies for segregation.

In 1968, the Supreme Court endorsed Wisdom's approach and explicitly embraced integration as a constitutional requirement. In *Green v. County School Board of New Kent County*, the court struck down one of the "freedom of choice" plans that southern school districts were adopting in response to the threat of losing federal funds. Under the plan, no white students chose to attend the formerly all-black school, and only 15 percent of the black students chose to attend the formerly all-white school. In striking down the freedom of choice plan, the Supreme Court unanimously declared that any plan offered by the school board had to be judged by its effectiveness in achieving integration: the question was whether the plan promises "realistically to convert promptly to a system without a 'white' school and a 'Negro' school, but just schools."[46] The Court concluded that the freedom of choice plan wasn't working because 85 percent of the black students remained segregated. The invocation of statistics, the insistence on results, and the embrace of numerical goals ushered in a period of dramatic judicial activism in which the Supreme Court and lower courts began with mounting impatience to demand immediate integration in the form of court-ordered busing.

The Court's unilateral embrace of busing as a remedy for segregation produced a firestorm of resistance from the president and Congress that never abated. Busing had less popular support than desegregation, but it needed more support. Passive acceptance by the public wouldn't have been enough; officials had to take complex steps to make busing work. The more the courts require others to implement their decisions, the more support they need, and, in the case of busing, public opposition was clear. Richard Nixon was elected in 1968 on a "southern strategy" that included appeasing the South and denouncing the Supreme Court for judicial activism; he ordered his Departments of Justice and Health, Education, and Welfare to abandon the goal of threatening to cut off federal funds for districts that failed to integrate. The Nixon Administration sided with advocates of less integration in cases before the Supreme Court, and the White House promised to fire federal officials who advocated busing.[47] Congress was similarly quick to react. After the *Swann* decision in 1971, Congress passed the Education Amendments of 1972, which forbade the use of federal funds for transporting students to achieve racial balance. In 1974, Congress tried to ban any "court, department, or agency of the United States" from requiring "transportation of any student to a school other than the school closest or next closest to his place of residence." Constitutional amendments were also introduced in Congress, as well as legislation that would have deprived courts of jurisdiction to hear busing cases. And both the president and the Congress were faithfully reflecting the polls: A Gallup poll in 1973 found that a clear majority of the country supported integration, but only 5 percent supported busing. In the North, 63 percent of white parents objected to sending their children to mostly black schools.[48]

Initially, courts tried to ignore the opposition of the president and Congress. In 1973, the Supreme Court approved the first busing order in a northern city that had never formally required segregation, citing evidence that the Denver school board in the 1960s had subtly used gerrymandered attendance zones to maintain segregated schools. Soon, lawsuits and busing orders spread across the border states and the North, in cities like Baltimore, Detroit, Indianapolis, Kansas City, and throughout Ohio. In Boston, a Massachusetts law requiring school districts to desegregate any school more than 50 percent black led to riots after a federal district judge ordered the busing of black students from the inner city to the suburbs. In addition to riots, the white public expressed its opposition to busing plans by white flight, leaving the city for the suburbs, especially where white suburban schools were available as an alternative to urban schools with high percentages of blacks.

Court-ordered busing was judicial unilateralism of the most aggressive kind. It failed because it was intensely unpopular, even among its intended beneficiaries, and also because Congress and the president never came to agree with the courts that the Constitution required mandatory desegregation in the same way that it prohibited segregation. There were plausible arguments for and against busing as a legal and policy matter, but the connection between the wrongs of segregation and the remedy of busing was often attenuated and opaque: in many cases, the lack of integration resulted more from segregated housing patterns than from deliberate discrimination on the part of school districts, and yet the courts were unwilling to try to uproot segregated housing patterns root and branch. Busing would have been resisted even if its constitutional foundation had been more widely accepted, but the fact that the constitutional arguments were nationally contested (it's hardly obvious that the Constitution requires equality of results rather than equality of opportunity) gave opponents yet another excuse for resistance. In the face of congressional and presidential opposition, judges proved unable and ultimately unwilling to impose an unpopular and destabilizing social reform on their own. The failure of busing revealed the limits of the equitable powers of the courts, which are never able to enforce their decrees unilaterally, but which always rely on the cooperation of the political branches to transform the constitutional landscape over the long term.

With surprising responsiveness to the public backlash against busing, the Supreme Court, transformed by four Nixon nominees, soon changed direction. In *Milliken v. Bradley* (1974), the Court struck down an integration plan imposed by a federal court that would have enlisted mostly white suburban school districts to provide a remedy for deliberate segregation in the mostly black city of Detroit. The Supreme Court's deference to suburban autonomy marked the beginning of the end of the integrationist ideal. It became obvious in the 1980s and '90s that there was no way to achieve integration without coercion; diversity simply couldn't be reconciled with free choice, because given the option to choose, most white and many black parents increasingly preferred to have their children stay where they were. White suburban parents were generally happy with their local public schools and were determined to protect their geographic and financial exclusivity.

As a result, when inner-city school districts tried in the 1980s and '90s to introduce school choice in the form of vouchers and voluntary transfer plans, suburban parents fought them vigorously. Statewide voucher initiatives in California and elsewhere were defeated not primarily by teachers' unions but by Republican suburbanites. In Ohio, Wisconsin, and Florida—the three states in which publicly funded voucher plans were adopted—liberal African American legislators won white Republican support in part because they restricted their efforts to inner-city families in failing schools without threatening the physical or financial independence of suburban schools. More ambitious plans would have represented political suicide.[49]

But lack of enthusiasm for integration—whether forced or voluntary—wasn't limited to white suburbanites; it became increasingly widespread among African Americans as well. In Kansas City, Missouri, for example, after holding that the public schools were unconstitutionally segregated, a district judge ordered the city to spend nearly $200 million in 1987 to create a state of the art "magnet" school in the hope of attracting white students into the inner city. The white students failed to materialize, and the Supreme Court held that in 1990 the district judge had abused his discretion by ordering nearly a 100-percent increase in property taxes to pay for the school. When the district judge continued to order the district to spend more, the Supreme Court again held he had abused his discretion, because attracting white students from the suburbs wasn't an appropriate remedy for the inner city's segregation.

In a concurring opinion in *Missouri v. Jenkins* (1995), Justice Clarence Thomas declared that racial diversity is ultimately less important than ensuring a genuinely equal education for African American children.

"It never ceases to amaze me that the courts are so willing to assume that anything that is predominantly black must be inferior," Justice Thomas wrote.[50] As the leading conservative spokesman for black nationalism, Thomas was echoing the angry rejection of integration by his youthful hero, Malcolm X.[51] By the 1990s, many African American scholars on the left also had come to agree with Justice Thomas that "the assimilationism inherent in integration required African-Americans to embrace white norms."[52]

If courts were unsuccessful in unilaterally imposing a rule of compulsory integration during the 1970s, they were similarly unsuccessful in unilaterally imposing a rule of color blindness during the 1980s and '90s. After William Rehnquist became Chief Justice, a narrow and unsteady majority of conservative justices became increasingly committed to the proposition that the Constitution prohibits all racial classifications, even those ostensibly adopted as a remedy for the lingering effects of discrimination against African Americans. This proposition was hard to reconcile with the original understanding of the Fourteenth Amendment, which Justices Scalia and Thomas had repeatedly embraced as the touchstone of constitutionality fidelity. The framers of the Fourteenth Amendment, as we have seen, did not believe that government had to be color-blind in all circumstances; they believed that the Fourteenth Amendment prohibited racial classifications only with respect to fundamental civil rights, as opposed to political or social rights. It's hard to imagine that they would have considered access to all public benefits, such as the right to be hired by the government to build roads, as fundamental civil rights.[53]

Although hard to reconcile with the original understanding of the Fourteenth Amendment, the claim that the Constitution requires the government to be color-blind in all circumstances is not an implausible constitutional principle. It's an expansive attempt to translate the more limited color-blind aspirations of the nineteenth century into the modern era and in this sense is a powerful competitor to the similarly abstract claim of the more liberal justices that the Constitution prohibits only those racial classifications that are designed to maintain a caste system. But although they embraced the color-blind principle in good faith, the conservative justices were unable, in the end, unilaterally to impose it on American society in the late twentieth century. When push came to shove, neither Congress nor the American public was willing to accept its practical consequences, which would dramatically reduce minority representation in public contracts and public universities. Forced to choose between color blindness and public institutions that looked like America, politicians repeatedly preferred diversity.

The Court tried hardest to impose a rule of color blindness in a series of cases challenging the constitutionality of laws that gave public funds to state and local governments who were building public facilities. The laws often required that 10 percent of the funds had to be set aside for contracts with "minority business enterprises," originally defined by Congress in 1977 as businesses owned by "citizens of the United States who are Negroes, Spanish-speaking, Orientals, Indians, Eskimos, and Aleuts."

As a policy matter, the minority business set-asides were the largest and least defensible part of federal and state affirmative action programs: because they were so easy to manipulate by front operations, their intended beneficiaries did not always receive the intended benefits. When the Public Works Act was passed in 1977, it was the first federal law of general application containing an explicit racial classification. (Even the Freedman's Bureau Act of 1865, which set aside land and benefits for freed slaves, was amended to include loyal white refugees as well, because the Reconstruction Republicans were committed to the principle of "no distinction according to color" in the distribution of fundamental civil rights;[54] unlike modern welfare benefits, compensation for the deprivations of the war appears to have been viewed as a fundamental civil right.) Despite its rhetoric about correcting past discrimination in 1977, however, Congress never convincingly established a compensatory rationale for the contemporary set-aside program—there was little evidence of discrimination against recent Asian immigrants in the construction industry—and in the succeeding two decades, the program drifted even farther from its flimsy moorings. In response to heavy lobbying from interest groups, Congress expanded the number of groups presumed to be "socially disadvantaged," so that, by the 1990s, the list included: "Black Americans; Hispanic Americans; Native Americans (American Indians, Eskimos, Aleuts, or Native Hawaiians); Asian Pacific Americans (persons with origins from Japan, China, the Philippines, Vietnam, Korea, Samoa, Guam, U.S. Trust Territory of the Pacific Islands, Northern Mariana Islands, Laos, Cambodia, or Taiwan)." Women were added to the list in 1987. The Small Business Administration, on authority delegated by Congress, extended the preference to entrepreneurs from Burma, Singapore, Laos, Republic of the Marshall Islands, Federated States of Micronesia, Fiji, Kiribati, Sri Lanka, and Bhutan.

It was hard to justify the inclusion of most of the groups on this list by pointing to past discrimination they had suffered: few states have a large population of Aleutian road builders. In adding these groups to the list, Congress enshrined the presumption of disadvantage without considering evidence of discrimination, raising the suspicion that it was engaging in interest-group politics rather than a principled effort to compensate groups for the present effects of past discrimination. All this made the small business set-asides especially vulnerable to corruption and manipulation.

The congressional set-asides might be criticized on policy grounds, but they represented the outer limits of Congress's broad authority, under Section 5 of the Fourteenth Amendment, to enforce the equal protection of the laws. And when, during the 1980s and '90s, a competing constitutional principle arose in Congress, namely that the government must be color-blind across the board, it never commanded majority support. Repeated efforts to repeal the federal set-asides or to prohibit affirmative action by the federal government failed to pass the House or Senate.

Although the Supreme Court initially upheld the federal set-asides in 1980, newly appointed justices during the Reagan and first Bush administrations grew increasingly suspicious of racial preferences. Impatient with Congress's failure to repeal the set-asides, the Court attempted unilaterally to transform the existing constitutional consensus and thus narrow the circumstances under which racial preferences could be used. In *Adarand v. Pena* (1995), the Court held that "all racial classifications, imposed by whatever federal, state or local governmental actor, must be analyzed by a reviewing court under strict scrutiny."[55] Only close judicial scrutiny, the Court insisted, could "smoke out" the illegitimate use of race, distinguishing permissible attempts to remedy the effects of past discrimination from "illegitimate notions of racial inferiority or simple racial politics."[56]

Although the Supreme Court seemed to leave only a small window of opportunity for federal and state racial set-asides, the executive branch and Congress soon took advantage of the window for all that it was worth. In 1998, the Clinton administration ended the use of racial preferences in direct federal procurement of highway construction in forty-two states, including Colorado. At the same time, however, Congress considered and rejected proposals to end the use of racial and gender preferences in awarding federal funds to state and local governments for public works projects. Instead, Congress reaffirmed the minority set-asides for the original groups on the federal list, noting that prime contractors refused to hire minority subcontractors due to "old boy" networks." A national consensus about color blindness still failed to materialize. Two years later, a federal appeals court upheld the slightly revised federal set-asides, relying on Congress's finding that discrimination by prime contractors, unions, and lenders had impeded the formation of qualified minority business enterprises in the nationwide subcontracting market.[57] The second Bush administration supported the slightly revised federal set-asides, and the Supreme Court declined to review them.

All of this suggests that, more than twenty years after the Supreme Court first considered the constitutionality of federal set-asides for minority contractors, the set-asides have continued with only slight revisions, mostly because Congress and the president continued to support them. The persistence of contracting set-asides reflects the simple fact that it is politically awkward for the recipients of federal funds not to look like America. Although policy makers may be uncomfortable with racial preferences, they are even more uncomfortable with the consequences of eliminating them. As a result, Congress rejected the Supreme Court's invitation to end federal set-asides and chose to reaffirm them instead. Without the support of the president and Congress, the Court was unable unilaterally to enforce its vision of color blindness and, for the moment at least, has chosen to retreat.

The Supreme Court's retreat from color blindness was even more dramatic in the controversial area of affirmative action in higher education. In the mid-1990s, a series of lower court decisions and state popular initiatives began to prohibit racial preferences in higher education and state contracting. But instead of accepting the new mandates to be color-blind, state legislatures and public universities rebelled, bowing to political constituencies who insisted that racial diversity was more important. In both California, where affirmative action was banned by referendum in 1996, and Texas, where it was banned by a federal appellate court the same year, the political pressures to achieve racial diversity proved so overwhelming that when state universities were forbidden to take race into account in the admissions process, they simply refused to accept the decline in black and Hispanic enrollment that inevitably followed. Instead, universities responded to the widespread political demand for diversity by devising plans that, in effect, lowered academic standards across the board. This response had some success in keeping up minority enrollments but at the cost of an even more serious compromise of academic standards than the relatively modest concession represented by affirmative action itself.

The political salience of diversity was predicted by three University of Texas law professors in a brief filed in the Supreme Court in 1997. In the brief, they described with eerie accuracy the political pressures that would lead public universities to lower academic standards if the courts prohibited racial preferences. "If affirmative action is ended, inevitable political, economic and legal forces will pressure the great public universities to lower admission standards as far as necessary to avoid resegregation," wrote Douglas Laycock, Samuel Issacharoff, and Charles Alan Wright. "The complete end of affirmative action would be a formula for the destruction of the great public universities."[58]

As it happened, the pressures to lower admissions standards in Texas and California played out precisely as the professors predicted. After the U.S. Court of Appeals for the Fifth Circuit banned affirmative action in 1996, the Texas Legislature adopted a series of laws that required the University of Texas to lower its admissions standards in various ways. First, the Legislature adopted a "10-percent plan," which guaranteed that any students who graduated in the top 10 percent of their high school classes would be admitted to any public university in Texas, regardless of their test scores, the classes that they took, or their ability to contribute to intellectual diversity.

Before the 10-percent plan, the University of Texas admitted 93 percent of all applicants at the top 10 percent of their high school classes. After, it had to admit the remaining 7 percent of white and black students who would have been rejected under the old system. These were students with serious weaknesses elsewhere in their files, such as low test scores, poor recommendations, or questionable writing samples. In other words, by taking a single attribute—class rank—and requiring the university to throw out all the other more nuanced measures of intellectual diversity and academic ability, from test scores to musical skills to success in overcoming adversity, the 10-percent plans guaranteed the admission of white and black students who were both less academically prepared and also less likely to contribute to the diversity of the university as a whole than the white and black students they displaced. The effect on academic standards was tangible: the percentage of students admitted from the top 10 percent of their classes with SAT scores below 1000 tripled after the 10-percent plans were introduced. To keep the new admits from dropping out, the university had to offer remedial classes.

The experience of the states that attempted to ban affirmative action demonstrated that selective universities cannot achieve color blindness, diversity, and high admission standards at the same time. They can achieve only two out of the three goals. For the most part, schools would prefer to choose standards and diversity, using racial preferences to create a diverse class while keeping standards relatively high. But as soon as lower courts and popular initiatives demanded color blindness, America's finest public and private universities didn't hesitate for a moment to choose diversity as the second goal, allowing rigorous admissions standards to go out the window. This was a prospect, in the end, that both the president and Congress seemed unwilling to resist; and the Supreme Court bowed to this political reality by declining, in the end, unilaterally to impose the color-blindness rule on public universities across America.

Of course, there has never been an impassioned political constituency for academic meritocracy—standards that exclude most of the population aren't likely to have many defenders. But today, objective predictors of academic performance have as many detractors on the right as on the left. The most important revelation in the Supreme Court litigation challenging affirmative action at the University of Michigan Law School in 2003, for example, was the brief for the second Bush administration, which praised the so-called X-percent plans adopted in California, Texas, and Florida, and urged public universities to adopt "admissions policies that seek to promote experiential, geographical, political, or economic diversity" as a way of keeping up the number of racial minorities. The Bush administration's position disappointed principled conservatives who believe that students should be admitted on the basis of academic criteria alone, but it was a reflection of the great political pressure trained on the president and Congress to make sure that public universities look like America.

Faced with the opposition by the president, Congress, and even the military to the practical consequences of a rule of color blindness in higher education, the Supreme Court refused to impose one. In *Grutter v. Bollinger* (2003), Justice Sandra Day O'Connor candidly acknowledged the complexity of the political and legal challenges universities face as they struggle to balance the competing values of color blindness, diversity, and academic excellence. Rather than forcing universities to choose between selectivity and diversity, O'Connor said they had a constitutionally compelling interest in achieving both. Writing for a majority of her colleagues, she upheld the University of Michigan Law School's affirmative action program (which seeks a "critical mass" of minority students to achieve the intellectual benefits of educational diversity) on the grounds that universities have a compelling interest in the educational benefits that flow from racial diversity. To preserve the educational autonomy that the First Amendment protects, O'Connor concluded, judges should defer to the judgment of educators about how best to fulfill their educational mission. At the same time, O'Connor emphasized that race couldn't be used to insulate minority candidates from competitive consideration with other applicants. Along with Justice Stephen Breyer, O'Connor joined their four conservative colleagues in *Gratz v. Bollinger* (2003), rejecting the University of Michigan's undergraduate admissions policy on the grounds that it failed to treat applicants as individuals. The twenty-point automatic boost that all minority applicants receive, these justices held, precludes the university from assessing the particular contribution to educational diversity that each individual applicant brings to the table.

Dissenting in the Michigan law school case, Justice Thomas objected that Michigan's real interest isn't educational diversity for its own sake but a desire to maintain its high admissions standards as a selective university while, at the same time, achieving enough racial diversity to satisfy the political pressures for state universities to look like America. Contrasting what he called "the people's Constitution" with a "faddish slogan of the cognoscenti," Thomas insisted that "the Law School's decision to be an elite institution does little to advance the welfare of the people of Michigan," since most of its graduates don't practice in the state. "There is nothing ancient, honorable, or constitutionally protected about 'selective' admissions,"[59] he wrote, and he questioned the value of objective predictors of academic performance, such as standardized tests. Thomas and the color-blind conservatives, in other words, believe universities should have to choose between racial diversity and academic excellence; and they were willing to undermine the selectivity of the great public universities in order to vindicate the value of color blindness.

Although his argument was hard to reconcile with the original understanding of the framers of the Fourteenth Amendment,[60] Thomas insisted that there is no difference between laws designed to subjugate citizens on the basis of race and those designed to benefit citizens on the basis of race. Both, he claimed, unfairly stigmatize their victims (or beneficiaries) whether they are intended to hurt or to help. The question of whether racial preferences hurt their beneficiaries more than help them is a relevant constitutional question. The framers of the Fourteenth Amendment clearly intended to abolish racial classifications that created a racial caste system, such as the Black Codes, which, among other things, forbade African Americans from making contracts or inheriting property. And black conservatives such as Thomas argue powerfully that racial paternalism, and the low expectations it creates, can be just as caste affirming as racial segregation. But Congress has refused to endorse Thomas's presumption that all racial classifications are inherently stigmatizing. In the face of widespread disagreement among blacks and whites about whether preferences stigmatize their beneficiaries, combined with Congress's continued insistence that affirmative action in higher education was constitutionally permissible, the Court appropriately chose judicial restraint.

These, then, are the wages of judicial unilateralism in the struggle for racial equality. After Reconstruction, an attempt by judges to impose contested visions of constitutional equality in the face of contrary congressional understandings was responsible for thwarting Congress's efforts to force the states to respect the Bill of Rights and to guarantee equal access in public accommodations. The Court was able to end segregation in schools because the president and Congress were not intensely committed to a contrary understanding; but in the face of opposition from the national political branches, unilateralist judges were unsuccessful in imposing mandatory desegregation in the form of busing, as well as a highly controversial vision of color blindness whose practical consequences the country was unwilling to accept. In the end, vindication of the constitutional promise of equal rights for African Americans came not from the courts but from Congress and the president and ultimately the people, as the framers of the Fourteenth Amendment intended.

3

Love and Death

A t the beginning of the twenty-first century, the most hotly contested questions in American courts involve the right to privacy. Abortion, sodomy laws, and gay marriage: these are
the issues that roil judicial confirmation hearings and inflame interest
groups on both sides of the political spectrum. It is now impossible to
be confirmed to the Supreme Court unless you acknowledge that the
Constitution protects some right to privacy—when Robert Bork denied this during his confirmation hearings in 1987, his fate was sealed.
But although everyone from Chief Justice John Roberts to Justice Ruth
Bader Ginsburg acknowledges that the Constitution protects privacy in
some form, there is broad disagreement about what kind of privacy the
Constitution protects. When the Supreme Court, in *Roe v. Wade*, announced that the "liberty" guaranteed by the Fourteenth Amendment
includes a right to privacy broad enough to include the right to choose
abortion, it was widely criticized by both liberal and conservative scholars

for failing to offer convincing constitutional arguments to support its conclusion. I am among the pro-choice critics of *Roe*: although personally devoted to privacy, and convinced that restrictions on abortions represent serious restrictions on the autonomy and equality of women, I have always had difficulty understanding how the Court in *Roe* derived a broad right to privacy in the way that it did. Since more than two-thirds of the country has long opposed restrictions on early-term abortions, I also believe that the right to choose would be protected by Congress and the states even if *Roe v. Wade* were not on the books. In this chapter, I offer a challenge to liberals who believe that *Roe* is sacrosanct, arguing instead that it was a political and constitutional mistake when it was first decided, largely because of its aggressive unilateralism.

The truth is that sweeping abstractions about privacy tend to obscure the differences between a range of very different values that privacy protects, including dignity and personal autonomy, neither of which is protected explicitly in the Constitution. The Fourth Amendment prohibits unreasonable searches and seizures of "persons, houses, papers, and effects" and has traditionally guarded the privacy of the home by enforcing rights of private property. But abortions seldom take place in the home, and restrictions on abortion arguably violate a woman's autonomy and equality, rather than her sense of spatial privacy. The American legal tradition has always been more concerned about liberty and autonomy than personal dignity but has nevertheless struggled to find constitutional arguments for protecting these values in the absence of a national consensus about what they entail. Reaffirming *Roe v. Wade* in 1992, Justice Anthony Kennedy declared that the Constitution includes expansive protections for personal autonomy: "At the heart of liberty is the right to define one's own concept of existence, of meaning, of the universe, and of the mystery of human life," he wrote. "Beliefs about these matters could not define the attributes of personhood were they formed under compulsion of the State."[1] This paean to liberty, which Justice Scalia would later ridicule as the "sweet-mystery-of-life passage,"[2] had never been embraced by Congress or the president, and Justice Kennedy, by trying to impose it unilaterally, inflamed his critics rather than persuading them.

Throughout the twentieth century, judicial encounters with laws concerning sterilization, contraception, abortion, assisted suicide, and gay rights have confirmed the hazards of judicial unilateralism. In each of these controversial areas, courts have been powerless to challenge deeply felt currents of public opinion and have been most effective when they have followed a national consensus after it has crystallized, rather than trying to coax one into being ahead of schedule.

The fate of involuntary sterilization laws in America is the first illustration of the limited ability of courts to protect autonomy in the face of public enthusiasm for restrictions on reproduction. Today, it's hard to imagine anything more cruel and illiberal than involuntary sterilization: many people understandably believe that if the Constitution prohibits anything, it must prohibit such an appalling practice. But this is a relatively recent consensus: during the first half of the twentieth century, compulsory sterilization was extremely popular, encouraged by the American eugenics movement, which supported what it called the science of better breeding. Far from being imposed on an unwilling nation, eugenics was enthusiastically supported by progressive medical, political, and even religious leaders as a way of protecting the racial integrity of America from the perceived threats posed by immigration and urbanization. Theodore Roosevelt and Oliver Wendell Holmes were avid eugenicists, as were liberal Catholic, Protestant, and Jewish leaders who encouraged their churches to embrace modernity.[3] In response to this public enthusiasm (and lobbying from activist physicians), legislatures in sixteen states between 1907 and 1913 passed laws authorizing the sterilization of "defective" people, defined loosely as "idiots" and "imbeciles." The first of these laws, passed in Indiana, provided a model for the rest. Declaring that "heredity plays a most important part in the transmission of crime, idiocy, and imbecility," it authorized the sterilization of those "confirmed criminals, idiots, imbeciles, and rapists" who were confined in institutions, provided that a committee of expert physicians certified that their mental and physical condition was "unimproveable."[4]

During the next five years, seven of the state sterilization laws were challenged as unconstitutional by opponents of eugenics (many of them conservative Catholics who believed in a right to life), and, in the absence of a congressional consensus on the question, lower courts unilaterally struck all seven of them down.[5] The U.S. Constitution contains no explicit protection for personal autonomy, so the lawyers for the eugenics opponents presented a range of alternative arguments. A Nevada appellate court struck down a law authorizing the punitive sterilization of convicted child molesters, rapists, and habitual criminals as an "unusual punishment" prohibited by the state constitution. Courts in New Jersey, Michigan, and New York found that state laws violated the equal protection clause by allowing the sterilization of people who were confined in state institutions but not similarly affected people who were not institutionalized. By contrast, courts in Iowa, Indiana, and Oregon were more concerned about the due process of law, focusing on the lack of procedural safeguards to ensure that the sterilized individuals were correctly identified as habitually degenerate.[6]

These decisions appear to have had little practical impact on the debate over eugenic sterilization in America. In the face of continued public enthusiasm for eugenics, state legislatures simply passed new sterilization laws, with minor procedural protections added to inoculate them against future constitutional attack. The American Bar Association even had a committee on sterilization that designed a model sterilization bill to satisfy the requirements of equal protection and due process: state eugenicists had to survey the entire population, not simply inmates in state institutions, to identify "potential parents of socially inadequate offspring"; and after being identified by the state eugenicists, individuals were entitled to a hearing (followed by a jury trial and right of appeal) to ensure they had been correctly identified. Between 1923 and

1925, fourteen state legislatures passed sterilization laws, and, by the end of 1925, sterilization programs were operating in seventeen states.[7]

The Supreme Court had little difficulty dismissing the various constitutional attacks on these laws. In *Buck v. Bell* (1927), Justice Oliver Wendell Holmes wrote an 8–1 opinion for the Court vigorously rejecting constitutional challenges to a Virginia law that allowed the state to sterilize the feebleminded inmates of state institutions in order to prevent the birth of feebleminded children who might turn to indigency or crime. (The sole dissenting vote was cast by Justice Pierce Butler, the only Catholic justice, who reflected the general opposition to eugenics by conservative Catholics.) "Carrie Buck is a feeble-minded white woman. . . . The daughter of a feeble-minded mother in the same institution, and the mother of an illegitimate feeble-minded child," Holmes memorably began."[8] In fact, the state had offered no experts to testify on Carrie Buck's behalf, and the eugenics expert who certified her as a "low grade moron" had not examined her or her daughter, whom he noted, again without evidence, "was supposed to be a mental defective." (Neither Buck nor her daughter was mentally disabled by modern standards; the daughter was listed on her school's honor role before dying of measles in the second grade.)[9]

Carrie Buck hadn't been denied the due process of law, Holmes held, because the state had adopted "very careful" procedures to protect "the patient from possible abuse," including a petition by the superintendent of the hospital or colony to a special board of directors, notice to the inmate and guardian, an opportunity to attend hearings, written evidence, and a right of appeal. Nor had she been denied any substantive right or liberty of "bodily integrity," as her lawyer argued, because no such right could be located in history, tradition, or judicial precedent: the Court had recently sustained a compulsory vaccination law in the interest of public health and welfare, Holmes noted, and the same principle could justify "cutting the Fallopian tubes."[10] Holmes could not resist an editorial flourish that betrayed his own enthusiasm for eugenics.

"It is better for all the world, if instead of waiting to execute degenerate offspring for crime, or to let them starve for their imbecility, society can prevent those who are manifestly unfit from continuing their kind," he wrote. "Three generations of imbeciles are enough."[11]

As unthinkable as it seems today, *Buck v. Bell* was constitutionally uncontroversial by the standards of its time. Congress had no occasion to debate a national eugenics law, since family and domestic laws were viewed as the exclusive domain of the states. But congressional views about eugenics at the time of *Buck v. Bell* may be gleaned, at least in part, from the Immigration Act of 1924, passed in response to the growing numbers of immigrants arriving from southern and eastern Europe. Embraced by large majorities in the House and Senate, and signed by President Calvin Coolidge (another eugenics enthusiast), the law limited the immigrants from any European country to a small percentage of those that the 1890 census had recorded as being born abroad of the same national origin. (The quotas were renewed in 1927 and based on the 1920 census.) During hearings on the bill in 1923, the House Committee on Immigration and Naturalization heard a parade of witnesses who testified for the exclusion of most southern and eastern European "races" on the basis of their "biology." After the law passed, it was hailed by eugenicists for protecting the purity of American blood.[12] Clearly, there was little concern in Congress that eugenically motivated restrictions violated the Constitution. And in light of the (pseudo) scientific consensus that reproduction by the mentally ill imposed a burden on society, it was hard to resist the conclusion that sterilization, like compulsory vaccination, could be imposed to protect public health and welfare. (Once this scientific consensus collapsed in the 1980s, courts were able to see the power to reject sterilization as part of the well-established common law right to reject unwanted medical treatment.) The fact that the Constitution contains no explicit right of dignity or sexual autonomy forced opponents of the law to focus on concerns about equality and fair procedures, and, once these were addressed, courts in the 1920s and 1930s could think of no obvious constitutional arguments for striking the laws down.

The legal fate of sterilization laws helps to dramatize how imprecisely the Constitution protects a right to privacy: if the courts couldn't think of a clear constitutional basis for striking down a policy as harsh and jarring as mandatory sterilization, many citizens will ask today, what is the Constitution good for? It's hardly clear that the popular enthusiasm for sterilization laws would have been affected in any meaningful way even if the Court had asserted itself more aggressively. After *Buck v. Bell* removed any remaining constitutional doubts about sterilization laws, state legislatures continued to resurrect them with renewed vigor. During the next few years, thirteen more states adopted sterilization laws, bringing the total number to thirty, and the number of sterilizations performed on institutionalized patients rose dramatically, from 322 in 1925 to more than 2,000 in 1928, a rate that continued through the 1930s.[13] But although the Court was able to ratify popular enthusiasm for eugenics in the face of congressional enthusiasm, it lacked the same ability to discourage eugenics in the face of congressional indifference. Despite the Court's suggestion in *Skinner v. Oklahoma* (1942) that lower courts might use the equal protection clause to strike down habitual criminal laws, courts in only two out of thirty states accepted the invitation.[14] Antisterilization laws remained on the books in twenty-six states at the beginning of the 1960s; and as recently as 1985, the sterilization of the mentally retarded was allowed in at least nineteen states.[15] In the end, the American enthusiasm for sterilization was cooled not by the courts but by the Depression, World War II, and ultimately by the civil rights movement, whose insistence on the inherent equality of vulnerable groups made the sterilization laws seem like the brutal remnants of a distant era. Anyone who believes that the courts alone can protect vulnerable and unpopular minorities should remember the fate of sterilization laws as a cautionary tale.

The judicial response to laws restricting contraception followed a similar pattern. Passed by Congress and the states in the 1870s at the behest of the nineteenth-century moralist Anthony Comstock, the federal and state anticontraceptives laws were defeated not primarily by the courts but by the political agitation of activists such as Margaret Sanger. (Sanger, as it happens, was herself an enthusiastic eugenicist, who defined the purpose of birth control as "more children from the fit, less from the unfit." She hailed contraception as a way of "preventing the birth of defectives";[16] addressing an audience of fellow eugenicists, she enthused that birth control would create "a race of thoroughbreds.")[17] As in the case of sterilization laws, contraceptive bans were struck down by courts only after popular support for them had deteriorated. The 1873 federal Comstock law forbade interstate trading in obscene materials, including "any article whatever for the prevention of conception, or for causing unlawful abortion." During the following fifteen years, twenty-two states passed "little Comstock laws," modeled on the federal language, although some of the state laws went even farther.[18]

Sanger crusaded vigorously for the legislative repeal or judicial invalidation of contraceptive laws; but initially, she had limited success. She was imprisoned for distributing contraceptive literature in 1914 and jailed again two years later when she opened a birth control clinic in Brooklyn.[19] By the 1930s, however, popular opinion about contraceptives had changed dramatically: in a 1936 survey by the American Institute for Public Opinion, 70 percent of respondents said the distribution of information on birth control should be made legal; and, in a survey the following year, 71 percent of respondents said they favored the birth control movement.[20] At the same time, the American Medical Association reversed its long-standing position and found that birth control information was an integral part of medical advice. It was hardly an act of very aggressive judicial unilateralism, therefore, when the U.S. Court of Appeals in New York, in the *U.S. v. One Package* case (1936), largely struck down the 1873 federal Comstock law. (A dubious Judge Augustus Hand, noting that Congress had considered and rejected an exception for the medical use of contraceptives, observed that "a statute stands until public feeling gets enough momentum to change it, which may be long after a majority would repeal it, if a poll were taken.")[21]

The *One Package* decision permitted physicians to prescribe effective contraceptive methods to married couples but failed to make them available to low-income women. In the face of changing public opinion, the federal and state governments began to support publicly funded birth control, although not always for liberal reasons. In 1937, responding to racist fears of black population growth, North Carolina became the first state to support the use of tax dollars to provide contraceptives; six other southern states quickly followed; and the predecessor of Planned Parenthood proposed a special "Negro Project" because "the mass of Negroes . . . particularly in the South, still breed carelessly and disastrously."[22] During the baby boom of the 1950s, support for family planning became overwhelming: national fertility studies between 1955 and 1960 indicated that 81 percent of the wives surveyed had used some form of contraception. At the beginning of the 1960s, the National Council of Churches endorsed the practice of "mutually acceptable, non-injurious" birth control in marriage.[23] Between 1961 and 1964, twenty-three states adopted policies providing financial assistance for family planning.[24] By 1965, Connecticut was the only state that prohibited the use of contraceptives by married couples. (Massachusetts prohibited the distribution of contraceptives but not their use.)

The Supreme Court, therefore, was forcing a single state outlier to comply with an overwhelming national consensus when it struck down Connecticut's unique 1879 law in *Griswold v. Connecticut* (1965). Although Justice William O. Douglas's opinion locating a right to privacy in "penumbras, formed by emanations" from the Constitution was correctly criticized for its amorphousness and abstraction, the more modest and convincing rationale was provided by Justice John M. Harlan, who noted in a companion case that the "utter novelty" of the Connecticut law provided a good reason for striking it down as arbitrary and irrational. The positive reaction to the *Griswold* decision shows the degree to which the Court had ratified a popular consensus about the unconstitutionality of contraceptive restrictions that had crystallized in Congress as well.

In 1967, Congress required the provision of family planning services under two federal programs, and, by the end of that year, forty-seven states had endorsed family planning.[25] Far from having precipitated a social revolution, the Supreme Court was merely codifying it in conjunction with Congress, the president, and the states.

Roe v. Wade was a very different matter. The Court's decision in 1973 to strike down abortion laws in forty-six states and the District of Columbia represents one of the few times in the Court's history that it has unilaterally leaped ahead of a national consensus about liberty or equality to impose a complicated reform not yet accepted by a majority of the public. It's true that public opinion polls in the immediate wake of *Roe* superficially resemble those in the immediate wake of *Brown*: 52 percent of the respondents in a Harris poll in 1973 said they agreed with the part of *Roe* that made abortions up to three months of pregnancy legal,[26] just as a similarly narrow majority approved of the result in *Brown*. But in *Roe*, the agreement was only skin deep: supermajorities consistently said they favored many of the practices that the Court would later strike down in the name of *Roe*, including spousal notification laws, parental notification laws, and informed consent requirements.[27] And similarly large percentages said abortion should generally be illegal in the last two trimesters of pregnancy.[28] Moreover, while majorities in 1954 seemed to accept the constitutional principle that the Court had embraced—namely that the Fourteenth Amendment forbids racial segregation—there was no similar constitutional consensus in Congress or the states in 1973 that the right to liberty, protected by the Fourteenth Amendment, created an elaborate framework for the regulation of late-term abortions. Nor did subsequent legislation in the wake of *Roe* reflect a shift in public opinion in the Court's direction—the polls remained remarkably consistent in the thirty years after *Roe* was decided. This is why *Roe*, unlike *Brown*, provoked a political backlash in Congress and in the states, a backlash that transformed the dynamics of judicial confirmations and ultimately led in 1992 to something of a judicial retreat. Even today, *Roe* continues to distort and inflame our judicial confirmation process, giving social conservatives and liberal extremists an exaggerated sense of their own political power and sense of victimization in a debate where they have lost the hearts and minds of a majority of the country.

From the framing of the Constitution to the mid-nineteenth century, abortion was regulated by common law and was not considered a criminal offense if performed before fetal quickening, which occurs in the second trimester of pregnancy. In the years after the Civil War, however, states began with increasing frequency to restrict abortion by statute without reference to quickening. When the Fourteenth Amendment was ratified in 1868, thirty of the thirty-seven states in the Union had passed laws restricting abortion. All but three of these states—Arkansas, Minnesota, and Mississippi—banned abortion throughout pregnancy, with exceptions only for saving the life of the mother. These restrictive laws were enacted at the urging of the newly formed American Medical Association, which relied on recent discoveries about human development. (In addition to being concerned about protecting fetal life, the doctors were determined to protect their professional prerogatives against the challenges of midwives.)[29] By 1910, every state except Kentucky outlawed induced abortions at any stage of pregnancy, except for "therapeutic" abortions performed to save a mother's life.[30]

Restrictive laws remained on the books in most states for nearly a century, from the mid-nineteenth to the mid-twentieth century. In the late 1950s, however, as demand for abortions increased after the war, doctors found themselves unsure about what sort of "therapeutic" abortions they were allowed to perform. Accordingly, they began to lobby for reforms of state abortion laws that would define the statutory exceptions more precisely. In response to pressure from medical professionals, the American Law Institute in 1959 proposed a model Penal Code that would have codified some of the exceptions for abortion that doctors were informally embracing: rape, incest, fetal deformity, and the physical or mental health of the mother.[31]

In the 1960s, popular support for the reform of abortion laws grew in response to the women's movement, the sexual revolution aided by the contraceptive pill, and a few highly publicized abortion scandals, such as Sherri Finklebine's inability in 1962 to get an abortion in the United States after she discovered that her fetus had been deformed by the drug Thalidomide. The first successful efforts to reform American abortion laws took place in the spring of 1967, when legislatures in Colorado, North Carolina, and California adopted "reform" laws based on the American Law Institute model that allowed women with serious health problems to petition hospital committees for "therapeutic" abortions. By 1972, ten more states had passed reform statutes.[32] As it became clear that reform statutes gave few pregnant women access to abortions, activists shifted their goal from reform to repeal. In 1970, four states passed repeal statutes and legalized abortion entirely; but in 1972, when the Supreme Court heard re-arguments in *Roe*, a Michigan repeal referendum was soundly defeated.

This, then, was the state of public opinion about abortion in 1973, on the eve of *Roe v. Wade*. Nearly a third of the states had liberalized their abortion laws, but thirty states still had laws on the books forbidding abortion except to save the life of the mother. And nationwide public opinion when *Roe* was decided appeared to support reform but not complete repeal of abortion restrictions. According to a poll by the National Opinion Research Center in 1973, strong majorities thought pregnant women should be able to obtain legal abortions if the woman's health was seriously endangered (91 percent), if there was a serious chance of fetal defect (82 percent), or if the pregnancy was a result of rape (81 percent). By contrast, less than half thought abortion should be legal if a married woman doesn't want more children (46 percent) or if a single woman didn't want to marry the father of her child (47 percent).[33] Only 24 percent of respondents in a 1972 poll said that abortion "should never be forbidden."[34] In 1973, this public consensus about the desirability of reform but not repeal had not crystallized into anything like a constitutional consensus in Congress, and the efforts of reformers were focused on state legislatures. But the intense contestation about the status of abortion at the state level should have suggested to an attentive Court that Congress might react if the Court nationalized the issue.

In the years leading up to *Roe*, lower courts had acted with relative caution. In fourteen cases between 1969 and 1972, lower courts struck down convictions resulting from restrictive abortion laws as a violation of the constitutional right to privacy or as unconstitutionally vague.[35] But courts that invalidated the new reform statutes, like the California decision striking down the 1967 California law, left open the possibility that the legislature might adopt a more precise set of conditions under which abortion could be restricted.[36] And courts that invalidated the older, pre-reform laws, such as the Texas statute that allowed only abortions "for the purpose of saving the life of the mother," did not presume to specify the conditions under which legislatures could protect or prescribe abortion; instead, they said merely that any future legislative action had to respect the fundamental privacy rights of women and left it up to the legislature to fill in the blanks.[37] Even the Supreme Court, in its first encounter with abortion cases in 1971, modestly held that a District of Columbia abortion law forbidding abortion except when necessary to protect the mother's life or health was not unconstitutionally vague.[38]

Two years later, the Supreme Court in *Roe* acted far less modestly. With aggressive unilateralism in the face of intense contestation, it invalidated not only the extreme Texas law, which contained only an exception for the life of the mother, but also a Georgia reform law, passed in 1967, that allowed for abortions in the broader circumstances recommended by the American Law Institute. The opinion was criticized in its day by liberal constitutional scholars, such as John Hart Ely and Alexander Bickel, who found the Court's abstractions about the right to privacy unsupported by constitutional text, history, tradition, or precedent. It was hard to locate a fundamental right to abortion in the text or original understanding of the Fourteenth Amendment, as a majority of states in 1868 forbade abortion in nearly all circumstances. Nor could a shift in tradition be easily identified: although fourteen states (far less than a majority) had adopted reform laws in the five years before *Roe* was decided, only four states had repealed their abortion restrictions. Nor could a sweeping right to abortion be obviously located in the Court's precedents: while *Griswold v. Connecticut*, the contraceptives case, was most convincingly defended as a case about the privacy of the marital bedroom, the right at issue in *Roe*—involving the freedom to choose abortion in hospitals—had little to do with unreasonable searches of the home. In a case after *Griswold*, *Eisenstadt v. Baird*, the Court had included a sweeping dictum suggesting: "If the right of privacy means anything, it is the right of the individual, married or single, to be free from unwarranted governmental intrusion into matters so fundamentally affecting a person as the decision whether to bear or beget a child."[39] But the *Eisenstadt* Court supported its dictum with a citation to cases involving mental privacy and the right to refuse unwanted medical treatment. None of these cases easily supported a broad right of procreative autonomy. The right to privacy that the Court recognized in *Roe* was not completely implausible, but it required the Court to read its earlier cases at a high level of abstraction that opponents of the decision found unconvincing.

The most controversial part of the *Roe* opinion was not its derivation of a fundamental right to abortion but its almost legislative specifications about the boundaries of the new Right. In his opinion for the Court, Justice Blackmun said that the Constitution required an intricate set of guidelines for state regulations: abortions had to be available to women during the first trimester; could be restricted only to protect the mother's health in the second trimester; and could be restricted to protect the fetus's interests only in the third trimester. Instead of inviting state legislatures to balance the interests of the mother and the fetus, as the lower courts had done, the Court imposed a scheme of regulation by judicial fiat, and it did so without asking for guidance from the states or Congress. In a dramatic gesture, as David Garrow has

noted, *Roe* struck down the laws of forty-six states, unlike *Brown* which did not mandate any immediate school desegregation. "By extending constitutional protection for abortion all the way to the point of fetal viability," Garrow notes, the *Roe* court "handed abortion rights advocates a vastly more far-reaching victory than they ever could have attained through the legislative and political process."[40] In this sense, its unilateralism is clear.

How quickly abortion laws would have been liberalized if the Supreme Court had acted more modestly is impossible to say. Pro-choice critics of *Roe*, such as Justice Ruth Bader Ginsburg, have argued that national opinion about abortion in the early 1970s was becoming increasingly liberal; and, left to their own devices, the state legislatures would have continued to repeal the most restrictive laws such as the one in Texas, which banned abortion in nearly all circumstances.[41] By contrast, supporters of the decision, such as Laurence Tribe, emphasize that no states voted to repeal their criminal prohibitions on abortion between 1971 and 1973, and, in Michigan, a referendum that would have legalized abortion in the first twenty weeks of pregnancy was defeated by pro-life activists in 1972, despite the fact that a local poll showed 59 percent support for the measure.[42]

Although no one can be sure how quickly abortion laws would have been liberalized across the country, the fact that more than half the country since 1973 has consistently opposed restrictions on abortion during the first three months of pregnancy suggests that the reform movement could not have stalled for long without provoking a national reaction. Moreover, this national majority in favor of a right to choose abortion during the first trimester remained largely unchanged for nearly two decades after *Roe*: polls from 1975 to the present suggest that public opinion on abortion for the past three decades has consistently included extremes on both sides that favor either no restrictions or total bans—each of which command about 30 and 20 percent support, respectively—and a vast majority in the middle that opposes both early-term bans and late-term abortions. [43]

In the wake of *Roe*, as the University of Chicago scholar Gerald Rosenberg notes, there was no rapid or unusual increase in the number of legal abortions, but the legislative tide turned in the conservatives' favor: while states had been liberalizing their abortion laws before 1973, they increasingly limited access to abortion after *Roe* came down. State legislatures introduced 260 abortion-related bills by the end of 1973 alone, and enacted 39.[44] In Congress in particular, resistance to *Roe* was especially acute. In 1973, sixty-eight constitutional amendments were introduced in Congress by eight senators and sixty Representatives, although none of them garnered the necessary two-thirds support. Congress was more united on the question of banning federal Medicaid funding for abortion, except when medically necessary, which it first prohibited in 1976. The Supreme Court upheld restrictions on federal funding for abortion in 1980. But federal and state efforts to restrict abortion didn't end, showing more intense congressional and state opposition in the wake of *Roe* than there was in the wake of *Brown*. Between 1973 and 1982, Congress enacted thirty laws restricting abortion.[45] And in the states, there were more abortion restrictions passed in 1977 than in any year since 1973.[46]

When the Supreme Court struck some of these abortion restrictions down in the late 1970s and '80s, it finally energized abortion opponents who otherwise would have had to make their case in the political arena. The response to *Roe* created a series of conservative interest groups, from the Concerned Women for America to the Moral Majority, who shared common goals in the culture war, setting out not only to restrict abortion but also to oppose pornography, gay rights, and the ERA, and to resurrect school prayer. Above all, these groups sought the appointment of Supreme Court justices who would reverse *Roe*, their most galling judicial defeat.

In this ultimate goal, the conservatives were disappointed: in *Casey v. Planned Parenthood*, the Court voted 5–4 in 1992 to reaffirm the central holding of *Roe*. In 1992, strong majorities continued to support laws

requiring women seeking abortions to wait 24 hours (73 percent), laws requiring doctors to inform patients about alternatives to abortion (86 percent), laws requiring women under the age of eighteen to get parental consent for any abortion (70 percent), and laws requiring that husbands be notified if their wives seek abortions (73 percent). As if acknowledging this persistent public support, the Court upheld all of these restrictions in *Casey*, with the exception of spousal notification laws. At the same time, the Court reaffirmed the core of *Roe*—the holding that abortion may not be prohibited before fetal viability—a principle that, in the years since *Roe*, commanded even stronger national support. (In 1996, 64 percent of the respondents in a Gallup poll agreed with the Court that the right to choose abortions should be generally protected in the first three months of pregnancy, while 82 percent agreed that it should be generally illegal in the last three months of pregnancy.)[47] As an exercise in judicial representation, the Court in the *Casey* decision managed to reflect the complexity of public opinion about abortion even more precisely than Congress itself.

The Court in *Casey* cast its decision as an exercise in countermajoritarian judicial heroics, a principled refusal to overturn *Roe* "under fire" because to do so would subvert the Court's legitimacy. The joint opinion noted accurately that "the Court's power lies . . . in its legitimacy," and its legitimacy depends not only in "making legally principled decisions" but in ensuring that the decisions were perceived as such by the nation. The joint opinion then suggested erroneously that the compromise that it embraced was defying public opinion rather than codifying it. "Whether or not a new social consensus is developing on [the abortion issue], its divisiveness is no less today than in 1973, and pressure to overrule the decision, like pressure to retain it, has grown only more intense," the joint opinion concluded misleadingly. (In fact, the Gallup polls on abortion since 1973 had been essentially unchanged.) "A decision to overrule *Roe*'s essential holding under the existing circumstances would address error, if error there was, at the cost of both profound and unnecessary damage to the Court's legitimacy, and to the Nation's commitment to the rule of law."[48]

The suggestion that the Court should be especially reluctant to overrule decisions that inspired strong public opposition did not sit well with the dissenting justices. "The Judicial Branch derives its legitimacy, not from following public opinion, but from deciding by its best lights whether legislative enactments of the popular branches of Government comport with the Constitution," wrote Chief Justice Rehnquist."[49] Justice Scalia was even more scathing. "Whether it would 'subvert the Court's legitimacy' or not, the notion that we would decide a case differently from the way we otherwise would have in order to show that we can stand firm against public disapproval is frightening," he wrote. "We have no Cossacks, but at least we can stubbornly refuse to abandon an erroneous opinion that we might otherwise change—to show how little they intimidate us."[50]

In fact, both the majority and the dissenters in *Casey* seemed determined to ignore the fact that the decision had bowed to public opinion rather than defiantly resisting it, calibrating *Roe* so that it more precisely reflected the public's constitutional views. And since the Democratic House and Senate arguably supported the *Casey* compromise in 1992, the decision might have been defended as a codification of an emerging national consensus about abortion, rather than an exercise in judicial heroics. In the wake of *Casey*, moreover, even some conservative judges suggested that it should be viewed as a kind of "super-precedent" that subsequent courts should be especially reluctant to overturn, because *Roe* had been repeatedly reaffirmed by different courts, comprised of justices appointed by presidents and confirmed by Senates of both political parties.[51] Reasonable citizens can disagree, in fact, about the degree to which *Casey* has been embraced by the president and Congress; but if the Court had acknowledged that the constitutional views of the political branches deserve respect, it might have avoided the unilateralism that suffused the original *Roe* decision.

Although *Casey* may have been precisely calibrated to reflect the public's policy views, its failure to articulate a constitutional rationale that had been clearly embraced by a majority in Congress guaranteed that the decision would inspire further congressional opposition. The *Casey* plurality seemed to root the right to abortion not in the right to privacy, as understood in *Griswold*, but instead in the right to sexual autonomy, as Justice Kennedy suggested in that hyperbolic passage about the "sweet mystery of life." But as we saw in the courts' struggles over sterilization laws, the right to sexual autonomy does not have deep constitutional roots. In the years between *Roe* and *Casey*, many legal scholars had tried to argue that equality might be a more convincing basis for abortion rights than the right to privacy. And indeed, language in the *Casey* opinion suggested that the restrictions on abortion might violate women's right to equality by denying the right to participate in the workforce on equal terms with men and forcing them into an unwanted occupation—namely that of mother and caregiver. For many pro-life activists today, both women and men, views about abortion may be closely connected to traditional views of women's roles as caregivers rather than autonomous workers. And these views were very much present among the doctors who convinced states to restrict early-term abortions in the mid-nineteenth century.

But the equality argument was not developed at any length, and the Court failed to engage the obvious counterarguments. The Court has always demanded evidence of intentional discrimination before finding a violation of the equal protection clause. The historical evidence, however, is complicated, and it might be read to suggest that most of the states that banned first-trimester abortions in the mid-nineteenth century did so to protect human life, not because of stereotypical views about the proper roles of women. Although some of the doctors who lobbied for restrictions on abortions during the mid-nineteenth century clearly harbored what would be considered today stereotypical views of women—they talked about the importance of motherhood as a way of guaranteeing the survival of the race—the laws were designed on their face to protect fetal life. Moreover, many nineteenth-century feminists were pro-life rather than pro-choice, believing that men pressured women to have abortions. Today, those women and men (and a majority of pro-life supporters are women) who support restrictions on abortion often explicitly justify their arguments in terms of the protections of fetal life and disavow any interest in channeling women toward or away from particular careers. All of these objections might have been answered by an engaged Court, but the justices did not take the time to develop the equality argument with sufficient care to convince skeptics.

Of course, controversy over abortion would have continued even if the Court had ruled more narrowly. The minority of Americans who believe that abortion should be banned from the moment of conception will never be persuaded to change their minds by the majority of the country that has reached a different conclusion. But by ratifying the national consensus—that late-term abortions could be banned, while early-term abortions had to be protected—the Court created the mistaken impression among the pro-choice majority that abortion rights would be imperiled if *Roe* were overturned. Although the Court in *Casey* avoided the unilateralism that it had displayed in *Roe*, it kept abortion at the center of judicial politics long after the issue lost its salience at the center of national politics.

Thirty years after it was decided, therefore, *Roe* is far more important as a galvanizing symbol for interest groups in judicial nomination battles than it is a central issue in presidential or congressional elections. In the Reagan and both Bush administrations, lower court and Supreme Court nominees were selected largely because of their perceived opposition to *Roe*, which was seen as a sign of their judicial virtue. The result is a polarizing gap between the moderation of the country as a whole on abortion and the radical opposition it continues to inspire among conservative legal elites. Since the two sides in the culture wars are seeking symbolic as well as tangible victories, judicial nomination fights over *Roe* have become an angry proxy for the political battles that social conservatives and liberal pro-choice extremists increasingly despaired of winning in the legislatures.

Unfortunately, after implicitly reflecting the views of national majorities in *Casey*, the Court then reverted to inflammatory unilateralism in applying the decision. In response to *Casey*, Congress held hearings about so-called partial-birth abortions in 1995. And in the wake of the hearings, more than thirty states passed laws banning the rare and politically controversial procedure known as D&X, or Dilation and Extraction, which is used in the third trimester of pregnancy. In 2000, by a 5–4 vote, the Supreme Court struck a partial-birth abortion law from Nebraska, one of more than thirty partial-birth laws passed by the states. The definition of D&X was so vague, the Court held, that it might be construed to ban a more common procedure known as D&E, or Dilation and Evacuation, which is used earlier in pregnancy, thereby imposing an undue burden on the constitutional right recognized in *Casey*—namely, the right to chose abortion before fetal viability. The Court also objected that the Nebraska partial-birth law contained no exception for the preservation of the health of the mother, which *Casey*, again, had said was constitutionally required. Although some medical associations had concluded that partial-birth abortions are never necessary to preserve a woman's health, and Congress made findings to that effect, the Court unilaterally ignored those findings.

If the Court had been in a more modest mood, it might have followed Judge Frank Easterbrook on the U.S. Court of Appeals for the Seventh Circuit, who upheld partial-birth laws in Illinois and Wisconsin by construing them to prohibit only the D&X procedure and also interpreting their exception for the preservation of the woman's life to include a health exception as well. Certainly, there was no constitutional consensus in Congress about how broad the health exception had to be, nor had the Court explained clearly whether it had to cover only imminent threats to a woman's life or more marginal threats to her psychological health. By continuing to monopolize the constitutional regulation of late-term abortion, the Court discouraged legislatures from engaging in the quintessentially legislative judgment of spelling out what kind of threats to a woman's health could override a viable fetus's interest in life. Because the Court unilaterally struck down a ban on a symbolic, unpopular, but rarely used procedure, Congress had no incentive to engage in responsible constitutional debate on its own. Instead, in 2003, in an effort to goad the Court into further unilateralism, it passed a federal statute banning partial-birth abortions that again contained no exception for the woman's health.

There is a provocative argument, as I mentioned, that even if *Roe* was wrong when it was first decided, its acceptance by Congress and the president has turned it into a kind of "super-precedent" that should not be lightly overturned by the Supreme Court. But whether you find this argument convincing as a legal matter—it's not obvious that both Congress and the president have, in fact, accepted the *Casey* compromise— it's hard to avoid the conclusion that the best political gift that the Court could give to the pro-choice majority in the nation might be to over- turn *Roe*. If *Roe* were overturned, the relative political weakness of the extreme pro-life position would be exposed, and the Republican Party would be torn apart at the seams because many Republicans oppose early-term bans and would desert the party in droves. At the same time, if *Roe* were overturned, the expanded and moderate Democratic ma- jority would be free to distance itself from extremists in the pro-choice movement who persist in fighting restrictions on late-term abortions, which most Americans embrace.

Despite this national consensus, it's true that if *Roe* were overturned, some states would try to regulate early-term abortions. The precise num- ber is hard to estimate. After the Supreme Court gave the states greater leeway to restrict abortion in 1989, only two legislatures—Louisiana and Utah—passed laws to ban early-term abortions (except in cases of rape or incest or to save the woman's life), and both were quickly struck down.

Even legislators in the most conservative states (such as Louisiana, Mississippi, Missouri, and Utah) would feel pressure from the public to allow abortion not only in cases of rape or incest but also when a woman's physical or even psychological health is threatened, a broad category that would allow women and their doctors flexibility. And, in the handful of states that are most likely to restrict abortion except in cases of rape or incest or to save the mother's life, political scientists suggest that popular opinion tends to be more liberal than the pro-life base and that a sweeping ban might provoke a political backlash. In all these states, pro-choice voters were willing to vote for pro-life candidates because they knew *Roe* would prevent their positions from being enacted; if *Roe* were overturned, they would have to think again. Pro-life legislators, as a result, would themselves think long and hard before pulling the trigger to overturn *Roe*.

Even if a handful of state legislatures did pass new restrictions on first-term abortions (or resurrect old ones), as South Dakota did in 2006, the political consequences may energize the pro-choice movement and hurt the Republican Party far more than it now benefits from pandering to the pro-life extremists. A sizeable number of Republican women and men who tilt toward the pro-choice side could ultimately desert the GOP, precipitating a realignment that could make a significant difference in a country that is more or less at political parity.

In the face of this kind of pressure, Congress might at last feel compelled to pass a federal abortion bill that mirrored popular sentiments on abortion, protecting early-term and restricting late-term abortions. Even a Republican Congress could ultimately pass a moderate bill along these lines, in an effort to staunch the hemorrhaging of its moderate supporters. Once Congress finally passed a federal bill that protected early-term abortions and allowed late-term ones to be banned, the Court could abandon its unilateralist turn on abortion. And judicial nominations could go back to normal at last.

As if chastened by the reaction to the abortion decision, the Court behaved more circumspectly in another important set of privacy cases, involving the right to die. In the *Cruzan* case in 1990, the Court recognized a limited and modest right to refuse unwanted medical treatment, such as feeding tubes and hydration. This right was well established on a number of levels: the Fourth Amendment prohibits unreasonable searches and seizures, and the common law long recognized a right not to be subject to unwanted medical treatment, battery, or unwanted touching. And as early as 1905, the Court balanced an individual's interest in declining an unwanted smallpox vaccine (which was traditionally protected by the common law) against the state's interest in preventing disease. Although the *Cruzan* Court recognized a right to decline unwanted medical treatment, it said that states were free to require clear and convincing evidence of an individual's wishes before allowing family members to act on his or her behalf. In addition, the Court left undisturbed laws against assisted suicide on the books in more than thirty states. A patient who wants to commit assisted suicide is not seeking to have a feeding tube withdrawn, but to have lethal medication applied; and the courts had long recognized a distinction between actively killing and passively allowing a patient to die.

After the *Casey* decision, with its expansive paean to individual autonomy, lower courts began to wonder whether Justice Kennedy's paean to the "sweet mystery of life" called assisted suicide laws into question as well. In a pair of decisions in 1996, appellate courts in California and New York attempted to strike down assisted suicide laws. The California court was especially expansive in declaring a constitutional right to "determine the time and manner of one's own death." Writing for eight members of the full circuit court, Judge Stephen Reinhardt struck down a State of Washington law prohibiting physician-assisted suicide. "A common thread running through these [abortion and contraception] cases is that they involve decisions that are highly personal and intimate, as well as of great importance to the individual," he wrote.[52] The most striking feature of Reinhardt's right-to-die opinion was its unabashed reliance on opinion polls. In a section of his opinion called "Current Societal

Attitudes," Judge Reinhardt cited a 1994 Harris poll indicating that 73 percent of the respondents favored legalizing physician-assisted suicide under certain conditions. In fact, "current societal attitudes" were considerably more complicated. In the early 1990s, three states had held referenda on proposals to allow physician-assisted suicide for the terminally ill. Voters in two states—Washington and California—rejected the proposal by margins of about 54 percent to 46 percent. Oregon voters were the only ones to endorse a decriminalization measure, by a narrow margin of 51 percent to 49 percent. Six state legislatures had recently rejected bills that would permit physician-assisted suicide, and no legislature had passed a decriminalization bill. There was clearly no congressional consensus on the constitutional scope of the autonomy principle nor on the kind of legislative safeguards that would be needed to implement it.

In a repudiation of the unilateralism of the California court, the Supreme Court in 1997 unanimously rejected the claim that there was a constitutional right to physician-assisted suicide. In his opinion for the Court in *Washington v. Glucksberg*, Chief Justice Rehnquist refused to expand the Court's broad rhetoric about autonomy to include a fundamental right to die. When the Court recognized new liberties not enumerated in the text of the Constitution, he said in an implicit rebuke to *Roe*, it should look to history and tradition, and, rather than resorting to sweeping abstractions, it should require a "careful description" of the asserted fundamental liberty. The California Court's descriptions of the asserted interest at stake—from a right to "determine the time and manner of one's death" to "the right to choose a humane, dignified death"—were too broad to be endorsed. "This asserted right has no place in our Nation's traditions, given the country's consistent, almost universal, and continuing rejection of the right, even for terminally ill, mentally competent adults," Rehnquist wrote. "To hold for respondents, the Court would have to reverse centuries of legal doctrine and practice, and strike down the considered policy choice of almost every State."[53] Because there was no fundamental right to assisted suicide, the Washington law need merely be rationally related to legitimate government interest, and Rehnquist held that it was. The states' legitimate interests in banning assisted suicide ranged from "preventing the serious public-health problem of suicide, especially among the young, the elderly, and those suffering from untreated pain or from depression or other mental disorders" and "avoiding a possible slide toward voluntary and perhaps even involuntary euthanasia."[54]

Although concurring in the result of the right-to-die cases, five justices insisted on preserving the possibility that the Court might, in the future, recognize a more limited right to die with dignity, in circumstances where patients were terminally ill and suffering great pain. "Irrespective of the exact words used," Justice Breyer suggested, at the core of the right "would lie personal control over the manner of death, professional medical assistance, and the avoidance of unnecessary and severe physical suffering—combined." If and when the Court ultimately decides that there is a constitutional right to assisted suicide for the terminally ill who are in great pain, it should wait until Congress has reached its own constitutional consensus on the issue.[55]

The right-to-die decisions were models of judicial humility. The concurring justices were eager to seek more empirical evidence from countries that had legalized assisted suicide, such as the Netherlands, to see whether they experienced a rise in voluntary or involuntary euthanasia. They rejected the broad abstractions of *Roe v. Wade* and invited the political branches to take the lead in an important social reform. As it happened, public opinion about the right to die did not change notably in the wake of the Court's decision. After the Supreme Court spoke, no state joined Oregon in repealing its bans on assisted suicide (although Oregon voters passed their own repeal law again by even higher margins). In this sense, the right-to-die cases were successful in their self-conscious effort to avoid the backlash that had been provoked by *Roe v. Wade*.

In confronting cases involving gay rights, the record of the courts was more mixed. In its first encounter with sodomy laws, in 1986, the

Supreme Court rejected the claim that the Constitution protected a fundamental liberty to make intimate sexual decisions in the privacy of the bedroom. *Bowers v. Hardwick* involved a challenge to a Georgia law that prohibited sodomy whether committed by same-sex or different-sex couples. But in his opinion for the Court, Justice Byron White called the claim that the Constitution protects a fundamental right to sodomy "at best, facetious." Using the historical methodology that the Court would reaffirm in the right-to-die cases, he noted that "in 1868, when the Fourteenth Amendment was ratified, all but 5 of the 37 States of the Union had criminal sodomy laws. In fact, until 1961, all 50 States outlawed sodomy, and today, 24 States and the District of Columbia continue to provide criminal penalties for sodomy performed in private and between consenting adults."[56] White, a dissenter in *Roe v. Wade*, was unwilling to "take a more expansive view" of the Court's authority to discover new fundamental rights and said that the Court was most vulnerable when it "deals with judge-made constitutional law having little or no cognizable roots in the language or design of the Constitution."[57]

Although characteristically restrained, White's opinion was vulnerable to an obvious objection: the Georgia sodomy law, like most American sodomy laws in 1986, did not apply only to gays and lesbians, but proscribed oral and anal sex regardless of the gender of those who performed it. And yet Georgia had a policy of enforcing the law only against gays and lesbians. Since the state had failed to provide any reason— aside from dislike of homosexuals—to single them out in a discriminatory way, the law arguably violated the constitutional guarantee of equal protection. Moreover, as Justice Stevens pointed out in dissent, the Court had said in the cases leading up to *Roe v. Wade* that married and single people had a right to privacy in the bedroom. To extend this right to heterosexuals but deny it to homosexuals might also be an unconstitutional form of discrimination.

Regardless of its logical coherence, *Bowers v. Hardwick* appeared to be consistent with public opinion at the time it was decided: In July

1986, 51 percent of the respondents in a Gallup poll approved of *Bowers*.[58] The Court's refusal to constitutionalize the gay rights debate allowed public opinion to evolve in a more liberal direction during the 1980s and 1990s without being distorted by a backlash against judicial overreaching.

In 2003, the Court revisited the constitutionality of sodomy laws in *Lawrence v. Texas*. In his opinion for the Court, Justice Anthony Kennedy cited the repeal and invalidation of twelve sodomy laws in the previous seventeen years as evidence of a shift in national attitudes toward homosexual intimacy since *Bowers* was decided. "The 25 States with laws prohibiting the relevant conduct referenced in the Bowers decision are reduced now to 13, of which 4 enforce their laws only against homosexual conduct," he wrote.[59] It was, in fact, arguable whether the liberalization of twelve sodomy laws represented a precise measurement of shifting public attitudes. Between 1986 and 2003, only four sodomy laws were repealed by state legislatures; eight, by contrast, were struck down by state courts—often under the same expansive privacy reasoning that the Supreme Court had rejected in *Bowers v. Hardwick*. But there was no doubt that Texas and the three other states that prohibited sodomy when committed only by homosexuals were outliers by the beginning of 2003.

For this reason, Justice Sandra Day O'Connor offered a modest way of striking down the Texas law that would have focused on equality rather than privacy. A state should be free to criminalize acts that it considers immoral, O'Connor suggested, but may not ban those acts only when committed by certain classes of people. The only reason to ban sodomy for homosexuals but not heterosexuals, O'Connor suggested, could be "a bare . . . desire to harm a politically unpopular group,"[60] and the Court has consistently held that this is not a legitimate state interest. The constitutional guarantee of equality arguably prohibits laws passed for the sole purpose of creating a legal caste system in the United States and, for this reason, the four state sodomy laws targeting homosexual conduct alone had to fall.

An opinion striking down the Texas law on these narrow grounds would have left the states free to ban sodomy, or other sexual practices of which they disapproved, such as bestiality or prostitution, as long as they did so in an evenhanded way that wasn't intended to degrade one group at the expense of another. It could plausibly have been based on a constitutional principle that Congress had embraced ever since the framing of the Fourteenth Amendment—namely, that laws may not be passed specifically for the purpose of signaling that one group of citizens is legally inferior. Like the Supreme Court's most successful cases, it would have brought a handful of state outliers into a national consensus that sodomy cannot be criminalized for gays and lesbians alone. And an opinion along these lines would have been consistent with public opinion: in May, 2003, 60 percent of respondents in a Gallup poll said homosexual conduct between consenting adults should be legal. By contrast, after *Lawrence* came down in July, that percentage had dropped to 48 percent, the lowest number since 1996.[61]

The decline in public approval for legalizing homosexual conduct in the wake of *Lawrence* may have reflected the unnecessarily expansive reasoning that Justice Anthony Kennedy embraced in his majority opinion, which seemed to some Americans to presage a right to gay marriage. Kennedy said the case "involves liberty of the person both in its spatial and more transcendent dimensions." He then quoted his own paean to liberty from *Planned Parenthood v. Casey*, the "sweet-mystery-of-life passage." Kennedy said that states and courts should not attempt to "define the meaning of the [intimate sexual] relationship or to set its boundaries absent injury to a person or abuse of an institution the law protects."[62] In response, Justice Antonin Scalia charged that Kennedy had constitutionalized John Stuart Mills's harm principle, which holds that the state may not regulate conduct of which it disapproves absent harm to others. "This means the end of morals legislation," Scalia charged. When Kennedy announced that "liberty presumes autonomy of self," he was rejecting the foundation of the social conservatives' worldview: namely, that that "liberty . . . supposes the necessity of obedience to some supreme and eternal law," as Pope Leo XIII put it in the encyclical *Libertas*. By constitutionalizing the moral vision of the social progressives rather than the social conservatives, Scalia objected, the Court had "taken sides in the culture war." And he predicted accurately that lower courts would soon invoke *Lawrence* to demand a right to gay marriage, as indeed they did.

Kennedy was quick to protest that *Lawrence* need not lead to gay marriage; it was not, he said, a case about "whether the government must give formal recognition to any relationship that homosexual persons seek to enter."[63] Perhaps he meant that moral disapproval might not justify the criminalization of private conduct that inflicted no third-party harms on the public—such as sodomy or masturbation—but that the state was free to express moral approval or disapproval of certain public relationships (such as polygamous or gay marriages). But this reading is complicated by the fact that Kennedy's opinion is suffused with the rhetoric of equality rather than privacy. He expressed concern that sodomy laws stigmatize or degrade gays and lesbians, even if they apply in theory to all citizens. "Petitioners are entitled to respect for their private lives," he wrote. "The State cannot demean their existence or control their destiny by making their private sexual conduct a crime."[64] The concern about stigma and dignity makes it harder to read *Lawrence* narrowly as an opinion about private rather than public relationships.

After *Lawrence*, social conservatives predicted a backlash against the Supreme Court comparable to the one that followed *Roe v. Wade*, and the polls did indeed show a reaction of sorts. After the Supreme Court decision, the Gallup poll found a precipitous drop in the number of Americans who said they would support civil unions for gays and lesbians, from 47 percent in May to 37 percent in July, and those who considered homosexuality "an acceptable alternative lifestyle" fell from 54 percent to 46 percent.[65] The polls, though, may tell a more complicated story. There is clearly an age gap when it comes to gay marriage: majorities of young people under thirty-five support gay marriage, while broader majorities of those over sixty-five oppose it.[66]

In the end, *Lawrence* did not provoke a backlash from Congress or the president because regardless of Kennedy's expansive reasoning, there had been no national constituency for enforcing sodomy laws against gays and lesbians or anyone else. Social conservatives, recognizing the limited immediate effects of the decision, chose instead to see it as a harbinger of judicial rulings on gay marriage and focused their anxieties on the battles to come. And in this respect, their fears were prescient. In *Goodridge v. Department of Public Health* (2003), the Massachusetts Supreme Court struck down a state ban on marriage by same-sex couples and declared a broad right of same-sex couples to marry. As Scalia predicted, the Massachusetts court emphasized the overlap between the constitutional guarantees of liberty and equality and cited Kennedy's opinion in *Lawrence* on behalf of the proposition that "the Constitution prohibits a State from wielding its formidable power to regulate conduct in a manner that demeans basic human dignity, even though that statutory discrimination may enjoy broad public support."[67]

This position, rejected in national opinion polls by a 2–1 margin, had not been endorsed by any state government. It was not surprising, therefore, that *Goodridge*, unlike *Lawrence*, created a dramatic backlash. In the wake of *Goodridge*, thirteen states added to their constitutions amendments that ban gay marriage, all by overwhelming margins (before *Goodridge*, only four states had adopted bans on gay marriage).[68] In Congress, a proposed constitutional amendment to ban gay marriage was introduced in June 2004, with President Bush's endorsement, but failed to win the required two-thirds support in the Senate. Nevertheless the amendment, which was rejected on party lines, forced Senate Democrats to put themselves on the record as supporting gay marriage—a position that hurt them several months later in the national elections. (Indeed, some Democratic strategists suggested that the fear of judicial decisions imposing gay marriage in closely divided states such as Ohio may have helped to determine the margin of victory for President Bush over his Democratic opponent John Kerry.) Moreover, because of the reaction to the Massachusetts Supreme Court decision and to similar state supreme court decisions attempting unsuccessfully to impose gay marriage in Alaska and Hawaii, gay rights advocates now confront a series of state constitutional obstacles that would not have been passed if the state courts had declined to enter the fray.

Perhaps the biggest threat of a constitutional train wreck over gay marriage would arise if gay marriage supporters become impatient with fighting state by state and instead asked the Supreme Court to strike down state laws banning gay marriage as a violation of the federal Constitution. If the Supreme Court accepted the invitation too quickly, it would be an example of judicial unilateralism no less dramatic than *Roe*, at the very moment when the constitutional question is being intensely contested in Congress and the states. Everything we know about the wages of judicial unilateralism suggests that the national backlash would set back the cause of gay and lesbian equality rather than advancing it.

In the 1990s, three state courts—in Hawaii (1993), Alaska (1998), and Vermont (1999)—grappled with the question of gay marriage, provoking starkly different reactions. In Hawaii and Alaska, the courts produced overly expansive rulings recognizing gay marriage as a constitutional right. Both decisions quickly incited a popular backlash and were subsequently overturned by state constitutional amendments. In Vermont, by contrast, the state supreme court offered the legislature the option of creating civil unions for gays and lesbians, and guaranteeing them all the legal rights of marriage under a different name. Although this solution didn't satisfy all advocates of gay and lesbian equality, it was a plausible reading of the Vermont constitution. The Vermont court declared that the state could not exclude same-sex couples from benefits it extended to opposite-sex married couples, but then invited the Vermont legislature to craft a remedy for the violation by endorsing civil unions rather than gay marriage. The decision does not appear to be received as unilateralist in Vermont itself: in state polls after the ruling, 47 percent of Vermonters, a narrow plurality, supported the decision, while 45 percent opposed it.[69] And, because of its relative modesty, the Vermont opinion—unlike those in Alaska and Hawaii—has not been overturned.

In light of the fact that young people are far less opposed to gay marriage than older ones, I have little doubt that, within a generation or two, America and much of Western Europe will recognize a right to gay marriage in some form. Once national support for gay marriage materializes, *Lawrence v. Texas* may be seen, in retrospect, as the *Brown v. Board of Education* of the twenty-first century, an example of the justices accurately predicting the future.[70] And the fact that the Massachusetts gay marriage decision did not, in the end, provoke state or federal constitutional amendments suggests that lower courts may have more room than the U.S. Supreme Court to act unilaterally without provoking seismic backlashes, in ways that can influence the national debate without transforming it. Nevertheless, the Supreme Court would have been wrong, at the time of *Lawrence v. Texas*, to impose a right to gay marriage before a national consensus crystallized, because a decision along these lines would have triggered an even more dramatic political backlash against gay marriage than the one triggered by *Lawrence* itself. This suggests that if judges are inclined to engage in constitutional futurology, they should confine their interventions to gentle nudges toward the future rather than radical pushes or shoves. The backlashes provoked by judicial unilateralism remind us that courts will always have a limited ability to impose a social consensus ahead of schedule.

4

Politics

When the Supreme Court decided the presidential election of 2000 in *Bush v. Gore*, liberals and conservatives accused each other of opportunism and hypocrisy. Liberals insisted that conservatives had abandoned their purported commitment to having political questions decided by political actors (if the Court had not intervened, the electoral dispute would have been resolved by Congress) by inventing a novel judicial theory for one time only. Conservatives countered that liberals were happy to use the courts when it suited their purposes and insisted that the U.S. Supreme Court had to intervene to prevent the election from being stolen by the Supreme Court of Florida. Although the election of 2000 is now a distant memory, the constitutional drama that it precipitated reveals something stark and unsettling about American judicial politics at the moment: neither liberals nor conservatives are consistently committed to the proposition that political questions should be resolved in legislatures rather than courts.

This bipartisan embrace of the legalization of politics isn't hard to understand. After all, even those who are skeptical of judicial intervention in cases involving individual rights—such as sexual autonomy or property rights—agree that a fully democratic government should guarantee the rights and liberties that allow citizens to participate in politics on equal terms, including equal voting rights and equal opportunities to influence the government.[1] Moreover, when courts act to protect democratic rights—for example, when they overturn state and federal laws that limit the opportunities of citizens to vote, to assemble, and to participate in politics—their legitimacy as institutions of democracy is hard to question. Indeed, some of the most influential constitutional theorists of the twentieth century have argued that courts act most legitimately when they correct the failures of the political process, because in these cases they are helping to strengthen, rather than to thwart, the ability of political majorities to enact their will.[2]

It's easy to sympathize with those who feel earnestly and passionately that the courts are the last and best guardians of the political process. But at the same time, it's hard to avoid the conclusion that the courts have not always served either themselves or American democracy by intervening in the political process. On the contrary, in the nineteenth and twentieth centuries, it was politicians, not judges, who drove the steady expansion of political equality, and constitutional amendments, not judicial decisions, which eliminated some of the most antidemocratic features of the original Constitution. The Fifteenth Amendment (1870) extended the vote to African Americans, and the Nineteenth (1920) extended it to women. The Seventeenth Amendment (1913) replaced the election of U.S. senators by state legislators with direct election. The Twenty-fourth Amendment (1964) forbade the poll tax in federal elections that helped to prevent African Americans from voting in the South, and the Twenty-sixth Amendment (1971) reduced the voting age to eighteen. All of these amendments were passed in response to political movements that ultimately persuaded a strong majority of the American people.

At least initially, Congress played a more important role than the courts in enforcing these amendments and making their promises a reality. After the Civil War, Congress briefly committed itself to forcing black suffrage on the South, using federal troops in 1867 to allow African Americans to vote for constitutional conventions and passing laws in the 1870s to protect black voting. But these laws were undermined by southern legislatures and private violence, and most of them were eventually repealed by Congress in the 1890s as public support for Reconstruction faded. The most flagrant barriers to African American suffrage were finally eliminated when the civil rights movement of the 1960s culminated in the Voting Rights Act of 1965.

Moreover, on the occasions that judges intervened in cases involving political rights, they have been just as likely to thwart democratic values as to advance them. During the century after Reconstruction, courts, like Congress, tended to follow public opinion when confronted with cases involving political rights, sometimes ignoring the underlying constitutional principles that national majorities, at least in theory, had embraced. From the 1870s to the 1940s, courts rejected most challenges to black disenfranchisement, allowing political resistance to subvert the promises of the Fourteenth and Fifteenth Amendments. Beginning in the 1940s, however, the Court, in striking down all white primaries in the case of *Smith v. Allwright* (1944), helped to expand the franchise in a meaningful way. And during the civil rights era of the 1960s, as the president, Congress, and national opinion became committed to the expansion of the franchise, the courts supported their efforts. These belated judicial efforts to vindicate the constitutional promises of the Fourteenth and Fifteenth Amendments were welcome and overdue.

In the 1960s, however, the Supreme Court entered the political fray more aggressively and attempted unilaterally to define and enforce new political rights about which there was no broad social consensus. The results were much less successful. In the first phase of electoral litigation, the Court created a right to an equally weighted vote: that is, a vote undiluted by electoral malapportionment in which some districts had many more voters than others. In the second phase, the Court created a right to an equally effective vote: that is, a vote where different racial groups had an equal chance to elect representatives of their choice. In the third and final phase, the Court created an entitlement to electoral arrangements that gave the appearance of political fairness, which no one could define with any precision. This final phase, which culminated in *Bush v. Gore*, has dramatically exacerbated the legalization of politics, ensuring that all closely contested elections in America are ever more vulnerable to being mired in lawsuits filed for partisan purposes. This recent history suggests that when courts intervene to protect democracy, they are often forced to choose among competing and hotly contested conceptions of democracy, and they often guess wrong about which conception of democracy the country as a whole will embrace. The resulting confusion has vindicated the fears of Felix Frankfurter, who warned nearly sixty years ago of the dangers of judicial excursions into what he called "the political thicket." "It is hostile to a democratic system to involve the judiciary in the politics of the people," Frankfurter wrote. "And it is not less pernicious if such judicial intervention in an essentially political contest be dressed up in the abstract phrases of the law."[3]

The surprising inability of American courts to play a satisfying role in policing the political process stems from the inability of Congress and the courts to agree about what kind of political equality the Constitution requires. The Fourteenth Amendment (1868) was originally intended to extend to all citizens, black and white, the same civil rights (or privileges and immunities), such as the right to make and enforce contracts and to sue and be sued. But if there was any principle on which the framers of the Fourteenth Amendment agreed, it was that the amendment gave Congress or the courts no power over political (as opposed to civil) rights; and voting was the quintessential political right.[4]

The Fifteenth Amendment, ratified two years later, provided that "the right of citizens of the United States to vote shall not be denied or abridged by the United States or by any State on account of race, color, or previous condition of servitude." Although the amendment prohibited explicit race-based restrictions on voting rights in theory, it was easily circumvented in practice. Not only did the framers of the amendment reject more robust versions that would have prohibited voting qualifications that had a racially disproportionate impact on blacks, such as literacy and property tests, they also left untouched voting qualifications that were explicitly intended to prohibit African Americans from holding office—qualifications whose predominant purpose, in other words, was racial. Some framers of the amendment wanted to prohibit laws that didn't refer to race but were explicitly intended to disenfranchise blacks. The Fifteenth Amendment in its final form, however, was a compromise that only required that any qualifications for voting should be formally applied to all races, regardless of their disparate impact.[5]

Although one of its goals was to shore up the Republican Party by enfranchising blacks in the North, the Fifteenth Amendment had some initial success in achieving its primary goal: enfranchising African Americans in the South. In the 1870s, large numbers of African American men, well over a majority, were voting in the South.[6] But because the Fifteenth Amendment prohibited only the most egregious and explicit race-based disenfranchisements, it became a dead letter once the political support for Reconstruction evaporated. In the 1880s and '90s, Democratic legislatures in the South enacted a series of laws designed to reduce black voting, including complicated registration requirements, poll taxes, property qualifications, disenfranchisement for crimes committed disproportionately by blacks, and literacy tests with grandfather clauses that exempted citizens who had been eligible to vote before 1867 (when Southern blacks were first enfranchised) as well as their descendants.[7] By the first decade of the twentieth century, black suffrage had been effectively squelched throughout the South. Congress acquiesced in this brazen disenfranchisement, refusing to enforce Section 2 of the Fourteenth Amendment, which provided that states should suffer a proportionate reduction in the size of their House delegations if they refused to allow male citizens to vote. "If Presidents, in effect, ignored or repudiated the amendment after 1874, if Congress failed to provide enough troops, marshals and money to enforce it, if the Republican party, upon which the success of enforcement rested, did not retain control of both houses of Congress and the Presidency from 1875 to 1889. . . . And if the people lost interest in free and fair voting, then it was no wonder that the Amendment failed to safeguard Negro voting in the South," writes William Gillette.[8]

The courts also played a role in the elimination of black suffrage. The Supreme Court refused to enforce the few federal protections for black voting rights that had survived Reconstruction. In *U.S. v. Reese* (1876), it struck down sections of the 1870 Enforcement Act that prohibited discriminatory administration of voting qualifications by state officials. After the Republicans were wiped out in the 1874 congressional elections, this was not a very strong variety of judicial unilateralism: President Grant, in the months before, had refused to use military force to prevent whites in Mississippi from reclaiming state elections through wholesale murder.

Nevertheless, Republicans remained theoretically committed to black suffrage, which they saw as necessary to prevent the Republican Party from being swamped in the South by Democrats who were overwhelmingly favored by an all-white electorate. It wasn't until 1893/94 that the Democrats found themselves in control of the White House and both houses of Congress for the first time since the 1850s, and they took advantage of this control to repeal most of the voting rights legislation of the 1870s. When Republicans once again controlled Congress and the presidency between 1897 and 1910, they did not attempt to resurrect these laws, having established their ability to get elected without white Southern support.[9]

In the early twentieth century, after Congressional commitment to Reconstruction collapsed, the Court upheld various state efforts to disenfranchise African Americans that violated even some of the narrower original conceptions of the Fifteenth Amendment. In the most dramatic confession of judicial impotence in the face of local intransigence, the Court in *Giles v. Harris* (1903) refused to stop Alabama's massive and successful effort to disenfranchise qualified black voters. (White voters who registered before 1903 were considered registered for life, while black voters who applied after that date were subjected to a series of more severe tests.) In his opinion for the Court, Justice Oliver Wendell Holmes did not dispute that "this refusal to register the blacks was part of a general scheme to disfranchise them."[10] But he invoked a perverse catch-22: even assuming that "the whole registration scheme of the Alabama constitution is a fraud upon the Constitution," the Court could not attempt to correct it without becoming "a party to the unlawful scheme." (The odd implication seemed to be that the Court was powerless to correct even clearly unconstitutional attempts to subvert the law.) Moreover, Holmes noted with bracing candor, the courts had no practical ability to enforce political rights in the face of the determination by "a great mass of the white population . . . to keep the blacks from voting." If the conspiracy exists, he noted, a judicial decision would be powerless to defeat it. Instead, "relief from a great political wrong" must be given by the political process itself.

The *Giles* case offers perhaps the starkest confirmation of Holmes's judicial philosophy, which held above all that the law should conform to the wishes of the dominant majority in any political community. But Holmes was typically impatient with conventional legal materials that cast light on constitutional text and history, and his opinion was hard to reconcile with the constitutional judgment of the Congress that passed the Fifteenth Amendment, which had not been successfully repudiated by the post-Reconstruction Congress. Although Congress in the 1890s showed no enthusiasm for enforcing the Fourteenth Amendment's penalties for states that refused to enfranchise blacks, it declined to pass proposals by Southern representatives and senators to repeal the Fifteenth Amendment entirely. Although the president and Congress failed to criticize the decision, it was certainly a serious disappointment to black litigants who had been told to put their faith for voting rights in the courts rather than in legislatures.[11] Moreover, the decision had unfortunate feedback effects: when defenders of black suffrage called on Congress to refuse to seat representatives from states that disenfranchised blacks, the House Committee on elections declined the invitation, claiming that it was deferring to the judgment of the Court.[12] Ultimately, however, only military intervention or a federal takeover of the voting process could have effectively countered the threat of white violence, and neither of these was politically viable for nearly a century after the end of Reconstruction.[13]

During the Progressive Era, the Supreme Court was not completely impervious to the arguments of disenfranchised blacks. In *Guinn v. United States* (1915), the Court struck down an Oklahoma grandfather clause that offered an exemption from literacy tests for only those citizens who had been on the rolls in 1866, when no blacks were eligible. Because the state law made eligibility to vote before the passage of the Fifteenth Amendment the "controlling and dominant test of the right of suffrage," the Court agreed with federal prosecutors that it was an explicit attempt to subvert constitutional protections. In *Guinn*, the Court was acting as a partner of the federal government in one of the rare cases where the executive agreed to enforce the Fifteenth Amendment's commands. (The Wilson administration supported the litigation.) The case—like the Court's invalidation in 1939 of Oklahoma's subsequent attempt to entrench its grandfather clause in 1916—shows that judges in the first half of the twentieth century were willing to strike down racially based barriers on access to the ballot when Congress and the president were likely to support them.

Before World War II, there was only one area in which the Supreme Court had a dramatic and meaningful effect in expanding African Americans' access to the vote: the *White Primary* cases, culminating in *Smith v. Allwright* (1944). As early as 1927, in *Nixon v. Herndon*, Justice Holmes struck down a Texas law providing that blacks couldn't participate in Democratic primaries held in Texas. (Because the South was essentially a one-party region after the 1890s, being barred from the Democratic primaries was tantamount to being barred from office.) Holmes treated the case as an easy one, noting that the Court had long interpreted the Fourteenth Amendment to forbid race discrimination by the state, and here the state was using color as "the basis of a statutory classification."[14] The Texas law was the only one of its kind in the nation—in most southern states, African Americans were barred from voting in the primary by party practice rather than by law—and Herndon inspired no national resistance.

When Texas responded with a law authorizing party officials to prescribe the qualifications for party membership, and the Democratic Party state executive committee promptly adopted a resolution providing that only "white democrats" could vote in primaries, the Court once again struck down the law in *Nixon v. Condon* (1932). But when the State Democratic Convention responded to the second decision by passing a resolution providing that only "white citizens" who were qualified to vote in Texas were eligible to membership in the Democratic Party, the Court upheld the exclusion of a black voter in *Grovey v. Townsend* (1935), on the grounds that it represented a private decision rather than state action. Those challenging the Texas white primary persevered, however, and in the *Smith* case (1944), the Court changed its mind, overruled *Grovey*, and held that the Texas Democratic Party was not free to exclude blacks from its primary after all, because "the party takes its character as a state agency from the duties imposed upon it by state statutes."[15] In other words, since the state pervasively regulated primary and general elections—setting the dates and deciding who could appear on the ballot, for example—discriminatory decisions by political parties were tantamount to actions by the state itself.

The *Smith* decision avoided hard questions about the rights of political parties: if Texas Democrats couldn't exclude blacks, why could they exclude Republicans or advocate white supremacy? But the decision was not unilateralist, because it was consistent with the broad purposes of the Fifteenth Amendment and popular in Congress and the country as a whole. Nearly 70 percent of Americans in a 1940 Gallup poll supported repeal of the poll tax, and, in federal elections, northern Congressmen voted to abolish it. By the late 1940s, even southern majorities supported the abolition of the poll tax. And national and congressional opinion likely treated white primaries and poll taxes in similar terms, since both were deployed to limit southern suffrage only in seven or eight states by the mid-1940s.[16] The white primary case was an example of the Supreme Court doing what it does best: suppressing outlier states in the name of a national consensus. Perhaps because it was broadly popular, supported by Congress, and constitutionally plausible, the white primary decision had a dramatic and positive effect on black suffrage. In 1940, only 3 percent of adult southern African Americans were registered to vote; twelve years later, 20 percent were registered.[17]

A favorable political climate helped the Supreme Court to increase black suffrage in the 1940s where previous attempts by lower courts to invalidate white primaries in the 1930s had failed. Black servicemen returning from World War II were more determined to demand their rights; southern whites were less determined to resist; and federal prosecutors were more willing to threaten resisters with prosecution. As a result, southern judges could be persuaded to construe voting rights broadly rather than narrowly, in response to challenges brought by branches of the National Association for the Advancement of Colored People that proliferated in the South. "These legal and extralegal factors," writes Michael Klarman, "created an environment in which it was possible for *Smith* to launch a political revolution in the urban South."[18] Nevertheless, African Americans in the rural South did not become meaningfully enfranchised until the 1960s, when Congress abolished literacy and good character tests and authorized federal officials to supplant local officials who refused to register blacks, a decision that the president backed with federal force.[19]

With the exception of halting efforts to enforce the Fifteenth Amendment and to remove barriers to black suffrage, the courts generally refrained from attempting to police the electoral system for nearly a century after the Civil War. That judicial abstinence changed dramatically with the apportionment revolution of the 1960s. In the first phase of voting rights litigation, a series of cases culminating in *Reynolds v. Sims* (1964), the Court looked beyond the question of whether individuals were able to cast ballots and began to examine the very different question of whether groups of individuals were able to cast equally weighted votes—that is, votes that counted as much as those cast in different districts. Throughout the twentieth century, population changes, combined with the continued refusal of some states to redraw their legislative districts, resulted in large disparities between the value of urban and rural votes. In Tennessee, for example, which had refused to reapportion since 1901, less than a majority of the voters in the state elected more than a majority of the senators and representatives: the imbalance was so great that the state was not really a democracy. In 1962, in *Baker v. Carr*, the Court decided that the malapportionment of Tennessee could be challenged in court, overruling the 1946 holding that legislative apportionment was a "political question" that judges were powerless to review.[20] The following year, in *Gray v. Sanders* (1963), the Court struck down the county-based electoral system that Georgia used in state and congressional primary elections, on the grounds that it weighed "the rural vote more heavily than the urban vote,"[21] unconstitutionally depriving urban voters of equal protection. Finally, in *Reynolds v. Sims* (1964), the case that Earl Warren considered the most important of his tenure, the Court held that both houses of the state legislatures had to be elected from districts that contained nearly equal numbers of voters, in order to satisfy the constitutional standard of "one man one vote."[22]

Despite its clarity, the principle of "one man one vote" can't be found in the text or history or the Fourteenth or Fifteenth Amendments as originally understood; and Congress rejected it during most of American history. The Fourteenth Amendment, as we have seen, was not intended to regulate political rights at all, and the Fifteenth Amendment contained only a narrow prohibition against explicitly race-based restrictions on the suffrage. In 1946, Justice Frankfurter expressed the traditional view when he rejected a challenge by voters in urban Illinois congressional districts that had much larger populations than rural congressional districts. The Constitution gives Congress, Frankfurter noted, the duty to apportion representatives "among the several States . . . according to their respective Numbers," and yet does not require equal apportionment within each state: indeed, for much of American history, Congress refused to apportion according to the requirements of the decennial census. Not until 1842 did Congress provide for the election of representatives by districts—a requirement that was later dropped—and only briefly, between 1872 and 1929, did Congress require that the districts reflect substantial equality of inhabitants. "Throughout our history . . . the most glaring disparities have prevailed as to the contours and the population of districts," Frankfurter concluded. "Courts ought not to enter this political thicket."[23]

Although Congress acquiesced in malapportionment, the "one man one vote cases" cannot be judged by the ordinary standards for unilateralism: the reason that districts with vastly different voter populations were accepted in the House is that House districts are generally drawn by state legislatures, and therefore House incumbents had the same incentive to resist periodic redistricting that the state legislatures did. In cases where legislators are attempting self-interestedly to protect their seats, their views about constitutional questions should be entitled to less deference by the courts. For this reason, the reapportionment cases are generally acclaimed as a successful example of the courts' ability to promote democracy: because selfish political incumbents refused to support reapportionment plans that weighted all votes equally, only the courts could break the political logjam.

After *Reynolds* came down, the reaction was predictable: the House wanted to overturn the decision by a constitutional amendment, but the Senate was indifferent, since its members were elected in statewide elections. (When the courts intervene in the political process, the people elected under the old system hate the courts and those elected under the new system love the courts.) But the constitutional principle of "one man one vote" was too clear, intelligible, and nationally popular for even the House to resist for long, especially after an intervening election. When the Court decided *Reynolds*, there was nearly majority support for the principle of reapportionment based on equal population: a 1964 Gallup poll found that 47 percent approved of the principle, while 30 percent disapproved, and the rest had no opinion.[24] Moreover, because of its clarity, the one-man-one-vote principle was hard for the states to evade. The year *Baker* was decided, nearly fifty reapportionment suits were filed in thirty-four states. The threat of litigation led to compliance with the Court's commands in relatively short order. By 1966, a *Congressional Quarterly* survey found that forty-six states had substantially complied with the Court's demand for districts with equal population, and by 1968, malapportionment in state legislatures had all but vanished.[25]

Despite its rhetorical and political appeal, the one-man-one-vote principle that the Court invented in *Reynolds* opened up a series of unanswered questions: Did each district have to contain precisely the same number of voters, or was a rough form of majority rule the proper baseline? In an effort to provide a clear and enforceable rule, the Court became increasingly impatient with even minor deviations from precise equality of population. Instead of demanding mathematical equality, an alternative approach in *Reynolds* might have embraced a more modest ideal that had been endorsed by Congress itself: namely, that the inability of a majority of voters in any state to elect a majority of state representatives violated Article IV Section 4 of the Constitution, which says "The United States shall guarantee to every State in this Union a Republican Form of Government." Although subject to many interpretations over the years, the "guarantee clause," as it is known, was explicitly invoked by Reconstruction Republicans in Congress after the

Civil War as a limitation on malapportionment as well as racially motivated disenfranchisements. [26] Following this interpretation, state Supreme Courts between 1890 and 1936 held that the guarantee clause
required courts to enforce the political equality of one voter against
another, sometimes striking down cumulative or weighted voting systems, and sometimes invalidating reapportionment statutes.[27]

In a more collaborative mood, the Court in the 1960s might have
embraced the guarantee clause as a limitation on antidemocratic malapportionment, such as the system in Tennessee, which denied the ability of a majority of voters to elect a majority of representatives. A ruling
along these lines would have been more readily embraced even by the
House of Representatives, and it would have opened a dialogue with
state legislatures. If some legislatures persisted in tolerating minority
control over a majority of their own seats, Congress would eventually
have felt pressure to require something like rough proportionality.

Instead, by rigidly imposing the "one man one vote" in *Reynolds v.
Sims*, the Court precipitated a political revolution that had different
results than the justices expected. Although compliance with the one-
man-one-vote principle was easy to measure, the reapportionment revolution failed to achieve all the political goals that its supporters had
promised. It did not eliminate the self-interested manipulation of the
reapportionment process by incumbents nor did it invariably increase
the political power of urban areas at the expense of rural ones. (The
greatest beneficiaries may have been the suburbs.) Although there were
some partisan shifts in some legislatures in the immediate wake of the
decisions, some scholars have argued that the one-man-one-vote principle had the unintended effect of making partisan gerrymandering
easier. Once the Court rejected the use of established political subdivisions or the construction of geographically compact districts to justify
minor deviations from population equality, legislatures were "liberated
to snake lines all over the map to achieve their own purposes."[28] It is
hard to measure, in fact, whether partisan gerrymandering became worse

after *Reynolds* or merely took different forms; under malapportionment, self-interested legislators didn't have to ignore established political subdivisions because they were free to protect their seats simply by preserving districts that had become increasingly unequal over time.[29]

Although the Court might have taken a more modest road in the apportionment cases, the one-man-one-vote principle was a judicial success in the sense that it was easy for judges to apply, and it was ultimately supported by the national political branches. By contrast, in the 1970s, the Court took a more aggressively unilateralist turn. In the second stage of its interventions in the political thicket, the Court introduced a new and confusing right into the mix: the right to an equally effective vote. Although the reapportionment cases focused on majority rules and promised individuals an equally weighted vote, the Court in *Reynolds* had also invoked a broader right of "an equally effective voice" in the political process that would produce "fair and effective representation" for groups rather than individuals.[30] In *Reynolds*, the Court didn't explain what, precisely, an equally effective vote would entail. But in a series of cases in the following decade, it confronted claims by litigants that particular electoral arrangements denied minority voters the right effectively to participate in the political process by submerging their votes in districts where they had little ultimate chance of victory. In particular, African American voters complained that the reapportionment cases had inadvertently diluted their political influence by ensuring that rural counties, which in some southern states were disproportionately black, had equal influence with urban counties. And although Congress had reached no constitutional consensus on the issue, some litigants insisted that winner-take-all elections should be replaced with some form of proportionate racial representation.

The Court's initial response to these claims was ambiguous and uncertain. It vacillated between two very different theories of democracy—one based on majority rule, and the other based on the idea that identifiable minority groups should have a meaningful opportunity to influence the political process. The problem with the latter view was that neither courts nor litigants were able to define precisely what a meaningful opportunity would look like. In 1971, the Court rejected challenges to multimember districts in Illinois—in other words, districts represented by two or more legislators elected at-large by the voters of the district. Although acknowledging that multimember districts had the effect of making it harder for black voters to elect representatives of their choice than single member districts in which they constituted a majority, the Court in *Whitcomb v. Chavis* (1971) rejected the district court's suggestion "that any group with distinctive interest must be represented in legislative halls if it is numerous enough to command at least one seat and represents a majority living in an area sufficiently compact to constitute a single-member district."[31] This principle, said the Supreme Court, would make it difficult to reject the claims of Democrats or Republicans that their votes had been unconstitutionally diluted when submerged in multimember districts. But the Court refused to close the door on claims of vote dilution, suggesting vaguely that an apportionment scheme might be unconstitutional if it "operate[d] to dilute or cancel the voting strength of racial or political elements" of the voting age population.[32]

Two years later, in *White v. Regester* (1973), the Court tried to define what it meant by unconstitutional vote dilution. It invalidated a reapportionment plan for the Texas House of Representatives that endorsed multimember districts. Instead, the justices demanded that two single-member districts be drawn where African and Mexican American voters constituted a majority. Although disavowing any requirement that a racial or ethnic group win legislative seats in proportion to its voting potential—an intelligible if controversial standard—the Court said that plaintiffs had proved "that the political processes leading to nomination and election were not equally open to participation by the group in question—that its members had less opportunity than did other residents in the districts to participate in the political process and to elect legislators of their choice."[33] But it offered no clear guidance for lower courts to discern when, precisely, a racially identifiable group had fewer opportunities to participate in the political process. The Court did, however, note a history of racially tinged campaign appeals as well as economic and cultural barriers that might inhibit the participation of Mexican Americans.

After encouraging lower courts to evaluate the political effects of multimember districts, the Supreme Court then attempted to step back from the brink. In *City of Mobile v. Bolden* (1980), the Court refused to invalidate at-large city-council elections in Mobile, Alabama, that had been held since 1911. In Mobile, African Americans made up about a third of the electorate, and whites and blacks tended to vote racial lines. Because black voters would never constitute a majority, and whites and blacks were racially polarized, the at-large system—in which every voter cast a ballot for each of the three commissioners—meant that black candidates preferred by black voters were unlikely ever to win. But the Supreme Court refused to invalidate the at-large system. In order to violate the Constitution, the justices reasoned, a voting system would have to have been adopted with the *intent* of discriminating against racial minorities—it was not enough to allege that the system had a discriminatory *effect*. The Court rejected the claim that every political or racial minority had an independent constitutional right to elect candidates in proportion to its numbers in the population as a whole.

Congress, however, resisted the Court's efforts to withdraw from the political thicket. Having raised political expectations in the 1970s with its unilateral conception of vote dilution, the Court's intervention inspired Congress to endorse its approach. In response to lobbying by civil rights groups, a bipartisan majority Congress amended the Voting Rights Act in 1982 in a way that restored the expansive definition of vote dilution that the Court had created and then disavowed. The 1982 amendments to Section 2 of the Voting Rights Act essentially resurrected the more lenient test for vote dilution that the Court had adopted in 1973.

Illegal abridgment of the right to vote could be proved, Congress said, "if, based on the totality of circumstances, it is shown that the political processes leading to nomination or election in the State or political subdivision are not equally open to participation" by a protected minority group "in that its members have less opportunity than other members of the electorate to participate in the political process and to elect representatives of their choice." But Congress proved no more willing than the Court to agree about a precise test for how vote dilution might be measured. On the one hand, it said that "the extent to which members of a protected class have been elected to office in the State or political subdivision is one circumstance which may be considered." But on the other, it hedged its bets in the next sentence, cautioning that it was not establishing "a right to have members of a protected class elected in numbers equal to their proportion in the population."

The 1982 amendments to the Voting Rights Act show how the Supreme Court, by acting unilaterally before there is a constitutional consensus in Congress, can help a consensus to crystallize after the fact. But they also show how the Court's unilateralism can inhibit Congress from conducting its own debates in constitutional terms: instead of addressing first principles, Congress found it politically convenient merely to endorse or reject the Court's conclusions. In enacting the proposed amendment to Section 2 of the Voting Rights Act, for example, the Senate Judiciary Committee Report said that it was "designed to restore the legal standard that governed voting discrimination cases prior to the Supreme Court's decision in *Bolden*," by "codifying the leading pre-*Bolden* vote dilution case, *White v. Regester*."[34] Because of widespread disagreement among Democrats and Republicans, Congress was unable to agree on anything more than the idea that the law of vote dilution should be restored to the confusing state that the Court had created in 1973 before changing its mind.

The result of Congress's inability to define vote dilution more precisely than the Court was political jockeying of the most vigorous kind.

Energized by the Voting Rights Amendments, an unusual coalition in the late 1980s lobbied the Justice Department to demand the creation of the maximum number of majority black districts that it was geographically feasible to draw. This coalition included liberal civil rights and voting rights advocates, such as the American Civil Liberties Union and the National Association for the Advancement of Colored People, who might have been expected to support the maximization of black voting power. But the civil rights groups were joined by an improbable ally— some factions in the Republican Party—which predicted correctly that packing Hispanic and black voters into majority-minority districts would result in surrounding districts that were more conservative and more white and therefore more likely to vote Republican. (Other Republicans supported color blindness for reasons of principle rather than partisanship.)

After the 1990 census, the Justice Department in the first Bush administration abandoned its general opposition to racial classifications in search of immediate partisan results. At least partly as a result of the department's policy of maximizing minority districts, the membership of Congress in the early 1990s experienced a dramatic change that more or less vindicated the Republicans' wildest hopes. In 1993, sixteen African Americans were elected to the House from newly drawn black districts in southern states that had not sent black representatives to Congress since Reconstruction. The membership of the congressional Black Caucus increased from twenty-five members in the 102nd Congress to thirty-eight members in the 103rd, and there were nine new Hispanic members as well.[35] At the same time, the Justice Department's maximization demands had clear partisan effects: some scholars estimate that Democrats lost five seats in 1992 because of racial redistricting and another twelve in 1994. (This loss had a significant impact: in 1994, the Republicans took control of the House, and their majority in 1996 was only eleven seats)[36] The GOP's maximization strategy also contributed to a partisan shift in controls of the state legislatures, which generally control reapportionment. During the second half of the twentieth century, Democrats were stronger than Republicans in the state legislatures, holding almost 70 percent of the seats in the mid-1970s. But during the 1980s and '90s, because of a number of factors that included redistricting, Republicans began to challenge Democratic strength: in 2000, they surpassed Democrats in the total number of state legislative seats held for the first time since 1954.[37]

Although Congress endorsed the Court's original conception of vote dilution, neither Congress nor the Court managed to define a coherent standard of political fairness against which an undiluted vote should be measured. Was the prohibition of vote dilution an attempt to compensate minority voters for the discriminatory behavior of majorities who were indifferent to their interests? Arguably this was the case until the 1970s, when the Democratic Party was so dominant in the South that it could submerge black voters in majority white districts without suffering any electoral consequences. But by the 1990s—thanks, in part, to the unintended effects of the amended Voting Rights Act itself—the South had become a closely divided political battleground in which Democrats had to compete with Republicans in the most vigorous terms. In this new environment, indifference to black voters is no longer possible: both parties will treat black voters like any other bloc of reliable Democratic voters whose voting strength should be maximized or minimized, depending on who is doing the redistricting.[38]

Another vision of political fairness holds that minority groups should be represented by a meaningful number of representatives of their choice, even if the number falls short of proportional representation. But if substantive representation of minorities is the goal, majority black districts may no longer be a necessary or even an effective way of pursuing it. The rise of two-party competition in the South means that black voters are now increasingly powerful in Democratic primaries, and that black candidates are increasingly likely to be elected from majority white districts.[39] For this reason, after the 2000 census, it became conventional wisdom among some Democrats that black voters would be better served overall by "coalition districts," in which they represented about a third of the total voters, rather than being packed into majority-minority districts, in which they represented more than half.

Both majority-minority districts and coalition districts were plausible interpretations of the vague constitutional principle that Congress endorsed: namely, that minorities deserve a fair chance to elect representatives of their choice. And having inadvertently triggered a constitutional consensus in Congress, the Supreme Court should have deferred to whatever interpretation of Section 2 of the Voting Rights Act that Congress itself endorsed. Unfortunately, the Court took yet another unilateralist turn. In the third phase of its interventions in the political process, the Court tried to repudiate the congressional consensus that it had recently triggered by inventing a new and even more confusing constitutional principle: namely, the right of voters to be placed in aesthetically pleasing districts, rather than bizarrely shaped ones whose primary purpose was to maximize minority voting strength. The litigation that gave rise to this odd principle had nothing to do with aesthetics but instead involved a serious dispute about how aggressively Congress intended state legislatures to draw voting districts in which racial minorities made up a majority. In *Shaw v. Reno* (1993) and cases that followed it, however, the Supreme Court concluded that the redistricting plans that the Justice Department had imposed in North Carolina, Georgia, Louisiana, Texas, and New York and other states were infected by unconstitutional racial motivation and therefore had to be redrawn, often by federal courts themselves.[40]

The *Shaw* case involved the North Carolina legislature's effort to draw new districts for congressional elections after the 1990 census. Responding to the Justice Department's interpretation of what the Voting Rights Act required, the legislature created an oddly shaped district that was 53 percent black and snaked around the map in a way that inspired political jokes. Justice Sandra Day O'Connor, writing for a 5–4 majority of the Court, held that the district might violate the equal protection clause of the Constitution, and in the process she announced an entirely new constitutional injury: voting districts drawn along racial lines that appeared bizarre on a map might lead to racial "balkanization." After the redistricting of the 1990s, congressional districts in general became less compact and even more bizarrely shaped than they were in the 1980s, twisting in ways that some compared to a "Rorschach ink-blot test" and that the *Wall Street Journal* compared to "political pornography." These odd shapes reflected a confluence of factors: increasingly sophisticated software that allowed representatives to predict the partisan and racial identities of each household with laserlike precision; the requirements of the amended Voting Rights Act, which required the creation of some majority-minority districts to avoid minority vote dilution (although the precise number of districts was a matter of dispute); the requirements of one-man-one-vote; and the desire of incumbents to protect their seats.

If any one of these requirements had been relaxed, districts could have been drawn that were as compact and aesthetically pleasing as Fabergé eggs. In other words, it was possible to draw compact districts that maximized minority voting strength and had the same number of voters, but only at the cost of threatening incumbents. Or it was possible to draw districts that protected incumbents and maximized minority voting strength but didn't contain precisely the same number of voters. Or it was possible to protect incumbents in districts of the same size, but not to maximize minority voting strength. Because of their belief that the Constitution should be color-blind, five conservative justices came close to saying that only the final set of districts, the ones that sacrificed minority voting strength to aesthetics, was constitutionally permissible.

Why should bizarrely shaped districts violate the Constitution? They didn't implicate any of the constitutional injuries that the court had previously identified in its voting rights cases: namely, the right to an equally weighted vote or to an equally meaningful or effective vote. Instead, according to O'Connor, bizarrely shaped districts inflicted an aesthetic injury, because "reapportionment is one area in which appearances *do* matter. A reapportionment plan that includes in one district individuals who belong to the same race, but who are otherwise widely separated by geographic and political boundaries, and who may have little in common with one another but the color of their skin, bears an uncomfortable resemblance to political apartheid."[41]

Charitable legal scholars trying to make sense of the injury O'Connor was trying to describe called it an "expressive harm"—that is, an offense against the ideal of racial neutrality symbolized by an oddly shaped district that looked strange on a map—a characterization that O'Connor in a later case eagerly embraced.[42] But lower court judges struggled to make sense of whether particular voting districts were shaped so bizarrely as to inflict expressive harms, leading to a great deal of litigation without obvious benefit. And the "expressive harms" that the Court unilaterally invented have been criticized on many levels. Some objected that the aesthetic standard was so amorphous that every irregular district in the country was vulnerable to a legal challenge until O'Connor herself endorsed the shape. Others noted that far from promoting political apartheid, the majority-minority districts are in fact among the most integrated in the country. Still others criticized O'Connor for glibly asserting that race-conscious districting encourages racial block voting or sends a message to representatives that they need only respond to constituents of the same race without providing evidence to support this claim.[43]

On the Supreme Court, O'Connor's expressive harms represented an unsatisfying compromise between two factions, both of which were pressing for very different legal frameworks for the regulations of race-based redistricting. On the one hand, four conservative justices insisted that all racial classifications were inherently suspicious and came close to suggesting that the amendments to the Voting Rights Act were themselves unconstitutional. With O'Connor's support, these four justices held that minority districts should be strictly scrutinized whenever race is the "predominant factor" motivating their design.[44] Although intelligible as a constitutional principle, the claim that the apportionment process must be color-blind is impossible to reconcile with the original understanding of the framers of the Fourteenth Amendment, who said explicitly that the equal protection clause had no application to political rights. And disentangling the subjective weight that race (as opposed to politics) played in the design of any particular districts proved, in practice, to be a hopeless task.

On the other hand, four liberal justices suggested that the equal protection clause should be applied in the same way whenever an identifiable group claims that its voting power has been diluted—whether the group is defined racially, religiously, politically, or economically—and that voting districts should be upheld unless they were completely irrational. For nearly a decade, the two camps battled each other, with O'Connor swinging back and forth between them. But in 2001, the Court's experiment with the regulation of expressive harms culminated in an anticlimactic whimper when O'Connor switched sides and voted to uphold the North Carolina district that she had questioned in *Shaw v. Reno* eight years earlier. In *Easley v. Cromartie*, Justice Stephen Breyer, writing for a five-justice majority, upheld the new boundaries of the Twelfth Congressional district, which had been redrawn after the Supreme Court struck it down in 1992. Because the African American voters overwhelmingly voted Democratic, the Court held, it wasn't easy to distinguish between a legislative effort to create a majority black district from a legislative effort to create a safely Democratic one. Since the protection of incumbents was a legitimate objective, the Court concluded, racial gerrymanders were a permissible way of achieving political gerrymanders.[45]

It was ironic that the racial redistricting cases ended with the Court's endorsement of the protection of incumbents as a legitimate goal. Judges proved unwilling, in the end, to regulate the one failure of the political process where judicial intervention seemed, in theory, most justified— that is, the ability of self-interested incumbents to entrench themselves. In the 1980s and '90s, scholars such as Richard Pildes and Samuel Issacharoff called on the judiciary to scrutinize the use of the apportionment process to "lock up" what should be competitive seats. Criticizing laws that legislators pass to enhance the strength of their own party or to protect the two-party system from challenges by third parties, these scholars said judges should "destabilize political lockups in order to protect the competitive vitality of the electoral process"[46] They noted that because of the interaction of advancing computer technology and the court's unforgiving one-man-one-vote requirements, redistricting was becoming an exercise in legislators choosing their constituents, as software allowed them to predict not only the racial but also the political composition of their districts. A result of this complicated interplay of law and technology was increasingly uncompetitive elections, at the federal and local levels. After the 2001 redistricting, there were, by some estimates, only thirty competitive House seats in the country, if competitive is defined as an election won by a margin of less than 10 percent. And incumbents are similarly successful at entrenching themselves at the state level, where more than 40 percent of the state legislative seats in the 2000 elections involved uncontested Democratic or Republican candidates.[47]

Reasoning that only courts could provide a remedy for the self-interested lockup of the political process, same scholars and litigators called on the Supreme Court unilaterally to strike down partisan gerrymanders in order to promote political competition. But the Court refused to accept the invitation, largely because neither judges nor Congress nor the country could agree about how much political competition the Constitution required. Unlike *Reynolds v. Sims*, the apportionment case that produced the easily intelligible one-man-one-vote principle, judges were unable to identify a constitutional test for fair political competition that commanded national support. The result of all the indecision was a great deal of litigation without measurable results.

In *Reynolds v. Sims*, the Supreme Court criticized "[i]ndiscriminate districting, without any regard for political subdivision or natural or historical boundary lines" as "an open invitation to partisan gerrymandering."[48] And yet in repeated encounters with challenges to partisan gerrymanders, the court had a hard time articulating a standard for regulating them. In *Davis v. Bandemer* (1986), the Court held that claims of partisan gerrymandering might in theory be challenged in court if they were designed significantly to underrepresent the statewide strength of one party or another. But the Court was unable to provide a test for identifying illegal partisan gerrymandering that provided meaningful guidance to lower courts or litigants.

In *Bandemer*, Justice White announced confusingly that "unconstitutional discrimination occurs only when the electoral system is arranged in a manner that will consistently degrade a voter's or group of voters' influence on the political process as a whole," denying a particular group "its chance to effectively influence the political process."[49] He added that a finding of unconstitutionally might be "supported by evidence of continued frustration of the will of a majority of the voters" over several elections (without specifying how many) or by the "effective denial to a minority of voters of a fair chance to influence the political process."[50] The language about effective influence was drawn from cases involving racial vote dilution, but the Court was no more effective in defining effective influence in the partisan cases than it was in the racial ones.

The Court's vague but imprecise invitation to examine partisan gerrymanders without a congressional consensus on the subject proved to be, in the words of the leading scholars of the subject, "an invitation to litigation without much prospect of redress."[51] In all of the cases challenging partisan gerrymandering, lower courts rejected the challenges.[52] Confronted with the confusing and unsatisfying record of litigation, the Supreme Court remained unable to agree on an intelligible solution. In *Veith v. Jubelirer* (2004), the Court's second encounter with the subject, four justices said that partisan gerrymandering should be regarded as the kind of "political questions" that courts are powerless to answer. Four justices proposed alternative standards of their own for regulating political gerrymandering, although they could not converge on a single test. And one justice—Anthony Kennedy—confessed that he was unable to discern a practical test for the moment, but encouraged litigants to keep trying to devise one, holding out the possibility that he might change his mind in the future.

The four justices who unilaterally proposed their own standards for regulating political gerrymandering argued persuasively that without judicial oversight, self-interested incumbents will continue to entrench themselves. But none of the justices was able to produce a standard that provided meaningful guidance to lower courts. Justice Breyer, for example, would have allowed courts to strike down political gerrymanders as "unjustified entrenchment" when they denied the majority party in the state the ability to win a majority of seats over a period of, for example, two election cycles. But the challenge of measuring a particular party's statewide strength is daunting, especially in an age of split-ticket voting and declining party allegiance: for example, as Justice Scalia noted, in the 2000 Pennsylvania statewide elections, Democratic candidates received more votes for president and state auditor, and Republicans more votes for U.S. senator and attorney general. Because political parties compete for individual seats, rather than statewide vote totals, efforts to measure majority status are inevitably contested and would themselves be mired in litigation. Moreover, in a winner-take-all system, there is no guarantee that the majority party would win a majority of seats. In the 2000 Pennsylvania congressional elections, in which the map was drawn by a court and free from partisan gerrymandering, the Democrats received a statewide majority (50.6 percent) but a minority of seats (ten, as opposed to eleven for the Republicans) because the

Democratic voters were "packed" in some districts and "cracked" in others. As these statistics suggest, the capture of the redistricting system by selfish incumbents isn't the only barrier to political competition in America. In addition, single-member districts themselves (together with presidential elections and the direct primary) are responsible for shoring up the two-party system, resulting in opportunities by one party or the other to win a disproportionate number of seats. That means that even if the Supreme Court accepted the invitation unilaterally to strike down all legislative districting conducted by partisan officials and to impose instead a system of districting by nonpartisan commissions, there is no guarantee that uncontested or uncompetitive elections would decline.

As long as there is no social consensus about how much competition is appropriate, the courts would be ill advised unilaterally to impose a contested vision of political fairness on an undecided nation.[53] The Court's unfortunate intervention in *Bush v. Gore* shows the dangers of judicial efforts to save the nation from intractable political disputes. When judges invent novel constitutional principles to remove politics from the democratic process, half the country is likely to suspect them as a pretext for partisanship.

Still, there's no doubt that partisan gerrymandering has contributed to growing polarization, as candidates court their extreme right- or left-wing bases in primary elections and no longer have an incentive to move to the center in general elections, where their election is guaranteed. If Congressional Republicans and Democrats repeatedly put the wishes of their bases above the wishes of the public, a provoked national majority may eventually try to throw them out. And if unable to do so because of gerrymandered districts, that majority may be mobilized to elect more moderate politicians by popular initiative, as California voters essentially did in choosing Arnold Schwarzenegger as governor. Alas, Schwarzenegger was unsuccessful in trying to ensure that other moderates like himself could be elected in the future. He proposed a popular initiative that would have replaced California's partisan districting system with nonpartisan districting by retired judges. But the initiative was rejected by healthy majorities of voters, who decry polarization in the abstract but seem to be happy with their local representatives. Without an obvious judicial or political solution, partisan gerrymandering may be a serious problem that the people are unwilling, for now, to correct.

Although the political remedy for gerrymandering is elusive, the best judicial response seems relatively clear. Instead of treating political and racial gerrymanders as fair game for litigation, the Court should instead treat both as the kind of political questions that courts have no business reviewing. In the first reapportionment case, *Baker v. Carr*, the Court acknowledged that there was a certain category of cases raising political questions that the Court had traditionally abstained from deciding because the political branches were better equipped than judges to provide a meaningful remedy. In *Baker*, the Court set out several criteria for identifying political questions, ranging from "a textually demonstrable constitutional commitment of the issue to a coordinate political department" to the possibility of "embarrassment from multifarious pronouncements by various departments" on the question. [54]

In cases after *Baker*, the Court said that cases challenging malapportioned districts did not present political questions because the one-man-one-vote rule was a "judicially discoverable and manageable standard" that courts could easily apply. This prediction, at least, was vindicated. But the case of partisan gerrymandering was very different. Justice Scalia was surely correct when he pointed out that nearly ten years of effort by lower courts and litigants had produced no "judicially discoverable and manageable" standards for identifying an unconstitutional political gerrymander—that is, a case where the majority in a state legislature had drawn an electoral map not only to protect its own incumbents but unfairly to minimize the strength of its opponents. Because challenges to partisan gerrymanders have produced a great deal of litigation with unpredictable results, and because judges have been unable to agree on how to determine if a gerrymander is excessively partisan, Scalia wrote, the issues should be regarded as "political questions" to be regulated exclusively by legislatures, not courts.[55]

If Scalia and his conservative colleagues had applied the same standard during the presidential election of 2000 that they did in the partisan gerrymandering cases, they would have concluded that *Bush v. Gore*, too, was a "political question" to be resolved by Congress rather than the Supreme Court. In *Bush v. Gore*, however, five justices refused to view disputes about presidential elections as a political question. Instead, they invented yet another vague and ill-defined set of rights to political equality, rather than deferring to Congress's constitutional authority to settle electoral disputes. The case shows the hazards of judicial interventions in politics based on highly contested visions of equality that have been embraced neither by Congress nor by the public. As a result, it is the high-water mark of judicial unilateralism, the unhappy culmination of the Court's efforts since the 1960s to legalize the American political process.

Bush v. Gore resulted from the dispute in the 2000 presidential election about who had won Florida's twenty-five electoral votes. After the Florida executive branch certified the election for Bush, his Democratic opponent, Al Gore, contested the result, asserting that a recount of the "undervotes" from selected Florida counties would turn up enough uncounted votes for him to put him over the edge. (Undervotes involve punch-card ballots where no vote has been recorded; by contrast, overvotes are those where more than one vote has been recorded.) A trial court held that Gore hadn't met the legal standards for a contest; the Florida Supreme Court reversed and ordered a manual recount of the undervotes, and Bush appealed to the U.S. Supreme Court. On December 9, the Court issued an unusual decision halting the manual recount by a 5–4 vote. In a separate statement justifying the intervention, Justice Scalia suggested overconfidently that there was a "substantial probability" that Bush could succeed in proving that the recount ordered by the Florida Court would cast a pall over the legitimacy of his election. After the decision came down, Scalia and his colleagues in the majority justified it in essentially pragmatic terms, arguing in so many words that saving the country is a tough job, but sometimes only the Court can do it. "The Court's reputation," Scalia said in a speech in May 2001, should not be considered as "some shiny piece of trophy armor" to be mounted over the fireplace. "It's working armor and meant to be used and sometimes dented in the service of the public."[56]

But Scalia's prediction that Gore might have won the manual recount and this would have produced widespread chaos turned out to be wrong. A definitive recount of the ballots after the election sponsored by a consortium of the nation's leading media found the opposite. In a manual recount of the undervotes, rather than the overvotes. Bush was likely to have maintained his narrow margin of victory. The manual recount found that Gore might possibly have eked ahead based on a recount of the overvotes, rather than the undervotes. (When a voter both marks the ballot for a particular candidate and then writes in the same candidate's name, there is little ambiguity about the voter's intent.) But since Gore didn't request, and the Florida court didn't order, a recount of the overvotes, the predictions of chaos that the court invoked to justify its intervention were unlikely, rather than likely, to materialize.

The revelation that Bush would have won under almost any conceivable scenario muted the practical effects of *Bush v. Gore*. But the case remains uniquely revealing of the dangers of judicial unilateralism, because at every phase in the case, judges who intervened on the basis of contested constitutional principles and convinced themselves that they alone could save the country embarrassed themselves instead. This pattern began in the lower courts, when the Florida Supreme Court ordered a recount of the undervotes without responding to the observation of a dissenting justice that it would have been more fair to recount overvotes as well: if local election law demanded that officials do everything possible to discern the intent of the voters, a statewide manual recount of all ballots would have been the most effective remedy. Moreover, the Florida

Supreme Court was legitimately criticized for allowing the standards for recounting ballots to be changed in the middle of the dispute.

Nevertheless, the Supreme Court was wrong to believe that it alone could save the country from the activism of the Florida Supreme Court. In fact, both Congress and the Florida state legislature were ready to reverse the activism of the Florida Supreme Court if given the chance. If the Florida Supreme Court had certified a slate for Gore, the Florida legislature was poised to certify a competing slate for Bush. And ultimately, according to the federal law passed after the presidential election of 1876 that resulted in a similar dispute about electoral votes in Florida, Congress was the body legally authorized to choose between the competing slates. If the Supreme Court had stayed out of the fight and made clear that all electoral disputes in 2000 and in the future should be considered "political questions" to be decided by political bodies rather than lower courts, then it would have saved the country from the litigation mess that will now hang over all of our elections for the foreseeable future.

When the Court decided *Bush v. Gore*, the justices in the majority suggested that it was a ticket for one train only and would have no effect on future elections. But the hopes that *Bush v. Gore* would fade from memory like an embarrassing dinner guest have proved to be mistaken. The case has emboldened political candidates to file a tangle of litigation challenging election procedures in federal and state races. Moreover, in response to the legalization of politics that was exacerbated by *Bush v. Gore*, an army of Democratic and Republican legal SWAT teams have been assembled to challenge the results of any close election. These challenges will focus not merely on conventional efforts to discern the intent of the voter—the basis for legal fights in the past—but on constitutional squabbles about the meaning of political equality itself.

This confusion results from the Court's unilateralism, its decision to invent a series of new rights that it loosely located in the equal protection clause without the benefit of any congressional consensus on the

question. Seven justices held that Florida's failure to adopt uniform standards for recounting undervotes—ballots on which no vote was clearly
registered—violated a novel and previously unrecognized constitutional
right: namely, the right of each ballot to be counted in precisely the
same way. Because five justices thought there was no time to conduct a
uniform recount, they said no recount could occur. Three justices also
said that the decision by the Florida Supreme Court to change the standards for recounting ballots violated Article II of the Constitution, which
assigns control over presidential elections to the state legislatures.

Each of these ill-defined rights has proved to be an inexhaustible
source of rhetoric and novel lawsuits in closely contested elections. The
first set of possible challenges involves claims similar to those at the heart
of the Florida mess, arguing that each individual voter has the right to
have his or her vote counted in precisely the same way. When the Court
invented this right in *Bush v. Gore*, it was hard to fathom what the justices
had in mind, since the claim that each state had to have uniform voting standards was impossible to reconcile with local control of the
electoral process where there is enormous variation among voting technology, hours of poll access, and rules about the disqualification of
ballots.

But the fact that no one quite knows what *Bush v. Gore* means is a
fertile invitation to litigation. For example, the Help America Vote Act,
passed by Congress in 2002 to avoid another Florida debacle, requires
states to allow voters who claim they have been wrongly denied access
to the polls to cast "provisional ballots" whose status will be adjudi-
cated later. Citing *Bush v. Gore*, among other authorities, the Democratic National Committee in the presidential election of 2004 filed suits
in Florida and Missouri challenging state officials' decision not to count
provisional ballots unless they are cast in the correct precinct.

The right to have every individual ballot counted alike is the first
category of challenges that *Bush v. Gore* has spawned. But soon after
the decision came down, a second category of lawsuits began citing

the decision for a very different principle: namely, that variation in voting technology disadvantaged minority groups. Since *Bush v. Gore* came
down, scholars have established that optical scanners have a lower error
rate than the punch-card machines that are most prevalent in the urban areas that contain the most minorities. Lawsuits challenging the
use of punch-card technology have been filed in California, Georgia,
Florida, and Illinois, arguing not that the technology was intentionally
designed to discriminate against minority voters—a strong constitutional claim—but that they had the effect of doing so. In 2002, an Illinois District Court cited *Bush v. Gore* for the first time in questioning
the use of punch cards.[57]

Finally, there is a third category of possible *Bush v. Gore* challenges,
in cases where state election law has been interpreted in novel ways by
local courts or officials. In *Bush v. Gore*, three justices—Rehnquist, Scalia,
and Thomas—insisted that the Florida Supreme Court's decision to
change the standards for manually recounting ballots violated Article II
of the Constitution, which they said gives the state legislature complete
control over electoral arrangements in presidential elections. Making a
similar argument, Colorado Republicans fell one vote short of persuading the U.S. Supreme Court to review a decision by the Colorado Supreme Court invalidating an unusual mid-decade congressional
redistricting plan that Republicans had railroaded through the state legislature. Invoking the state constitution, the Colorado Supreme Court
said that congressional redistricting could take place only once each
decade, and Republicans argued that this violated Article I of the U.S.
Constitution, which gives the state legislature the exclusive power to
make rules about congressional elections.

What's striking about each of the three new rights invented in *Bush
v. Gore*—the right to equal treatment for ballots, the right to equal voting technologies that don't discriminate against minority groups, and
the right not to have election procedures changed by state courts—is
that they were invented unilaterally, without the benefit of congressional

consensus. In this sense, they are the logical but unhappy consequence of the Court's performance in the third phase of its electoral interventions, which began with *Shaw v. Reno*. As Pam Karlan of Stanford Law School has observed, *Bush v. Gore* is entirely consistent with *Shaw*.[58] Rather than focusing on the actual interests of individual voters, the Court is more concerned with the messages conveyed by particular electoral arrangements: in *Shaw v. Reno*, O'Connor said "appearances *do* matter" in apportionment cases because minority districts could "reinforce the perception" that members of the same racial group vote alike. Similarly, the *Bush v. Gore* majority was concerned that different counting standards for different ballots might *appear* unfair, even if they were designed to reveal the voter's true intent. But electoral messages are in the eyes of the beholder, which is why lower court judges and Supreme Court justices have been unable to agree about what vision of fairness a particular election should have to respect: Is it more fair to treat every ballot alike or every group of voters alike? On questions like this, judges, like citizens, will always disagree. And in the face of social dissensus, courts should resist the temptation to intervene in the political process, reserving their interventions for clearly defined rights of political equality that Congress has unquestionably endorsed, such as the right to speak, petition, organize, and the right not to be denied access to the ballot on the basis of race, gender, or national origin.[59]

The unfortunate result of the Court's unilateralism is that every contested election in the country is now vulnerable to being resolved by the justices of the Supreme Court. And the fact that they attempted in *Bush v. Gore* to deny the obvious implications of their intrusion into the political process only makes their intervention more reckless. Did they really believe they could create a right to political equality without defining it, in an age when society disagrees so vigorously about what equality requires? Did they imagine for a moment that Democrats and Republicans would meekly tug their forelocks rather than using electoral litigation as a partisan tool?

With each passing decade, these scruples about the legalization of politics may seem increasingly like the quaint atavisms of a distant era. As courts become more and more involved in policing minute irregularities in democratic elections, neither side will have an incentive to call for the judges to withdraw from the political thicket. In exceptional cases—those involving obvious fraud that thwarts majority rule or obvious disenfranchisement—courts will play a useful role in the future, as they have in the past, serving as neutral arbiters of the most partisan disputes. But the history of the Court's interventions in politics suggests that judges are less well equipped to enforce highly contested principles of political equality about which there is no widespread social agreement. By acting unilaterally and attempting to micromanage democratic politics, courts may find that they have accomplished little more than calling their own neutrality into question.

5

Civil Liberties

Since September 11, 2001, American and other Western democracies have debated the proper balance between liberty and security. A widespread assumption, in Europe and the United States, is that only courts can protect basic liberties—such as free speech and freedom from unlawful detention—against the encroachments of an overzealous executive. When the U.S. Supreme Court imposed slight restrictions on the president's power to designate enemy combatants and to detain them indefinitely, for example, the justices were widely hailed for performing what many commentators assumed was a traditional function of the courts: defending liberty in the face of indifference or hostility from the president and Congress. When Congress at the end of 2005 overturned a related Supreme Court decision allowing suspected enemy combatants held at Guantanamo Bay to challenge their detention, the notion that judges defend liberty while legislatures eviscerate it became a form of conventional wisdom, even though, in the same law, Congress also was moved to ban torture over the president's objections. And when the president insisted, with growing stridency, that unilateral executive authority should be essentially unchecked during wartime by the courts or Congress, civil libertarians focused their energies on persuading the courts, not Congress, to assert themselves.

But the idea that courts have historically taken the lead in protecting basic civil liberties during times of war is wrong. From the founding era through the 1920s, courts were often indifferent or hostile to claims by dissenters that their free speech had been suppressed, and, through the 1950s, they continued to defer to efforts by the president and Congress to suppress unpopular speech or to circumvent ordinary criminal procedures. Until the 1960s, it was not the judicial intervention but popular support for civil liberties—manifested in jury verdicts, political protests, and congressional opposition to unchecked executive authority— that provided the firmest protection for the free speech of dissenters during wartime. During the Civil War, for example, congressional Republicans insisted that the right to criticize slavery was a basic right of citizenship, and, after World War I, Congress modified some of President Wilson's most draconian efforts to punish sedition. In the last decades of the twentieth century, courts eventually embraced the idea that free speech and fair trial procedures are a bedrock of American democracy; but, by that time, a majority of the country seemed to have done so as well. Courts have been most effective in civil liberties cases when they have avoided unilateralism and encouraged cooperation among the three branches of government.

Long before the Iraq war, America squabbled with the French. In fact, we can look back to 1798 for the paradigmatic test of the meaning of free speech in America: the Alien and Sedition Acts, which allowed the president and Congress to silence their critics. After the French began to attack American ships in the wake of the Jay Treaty between the United States and Britain, President Adams sent a three-man delegation to France, led by the future chief justice, John Marshall, for secret peace talks with Talleyrand, the French foreign minister. Before agreeing to negotiate, Talleyrand demanded a bribe, forcing the Americans to deal with three deputies, whom they referred to in code as X, Y, and Z. When the XYZ affair became public in America, popular indignation was fierce and soon led to cries for war. The Federalist Congress used this patriotic fervor to pass the Enemy Alien and Sedition Acts of 1798. The Alien Acts, among other things, gave the president the power to deport dangerous foreign-born residents and label them alien enemies without a hearing. And the Sedition Act made it a crime to publish "any false, scandalous, and malicious writing . . . against the government of the United States, or either house of the congress of the United States, or the president of the United States, with intent to defame . . . or to bring them . . . into contempt or disrepute."[1]

The Sedition Act was a transparent effort by Federalists to insulate themselves from criticism by their opponents: the Republican vice president, Thomas Jefferson, was not protected; and the Act had a sunset provision that guaranteed its expiration on the last day of President Adams's term. During debates over the act, Republicans objected that it would undermine democracy by inhibiting open criticism of public policies; they also claimed that the federal government had no power to pass it.[2] Despite these constitutional objections, the act passed on a party-line vote. During the two and a half years before the Sedition Act expired—a period that Thomas Jefferson called "the reign of witches"—Federalists indicted fifteen Republicans, ten of whom were tried and all of whom were convicted.[3]

For judges to have struck down the Sedition Act during its brief and unhappy reign might have been considered an act of judicial unilateralism, since both houses of Congress supported its constitutionality and viewed it as a well-intentioned effort to protect the country from domestic subversion. Still, it's a shame that judges weren't more skeptical: because the act was clearly an attempt by congressional Federalists to entrench themselves. Congress's views were an unreliable reflection of the views of the people, who soon voted the Federalists out. Nevertheless, even when they are justified, judicial heroics tend to be in short supply: none of the judges who presided over the Sedition Act trials questioned the constitutionality of the indictments; on the contrary, they were unanimous in defending the act in charges to the jury. The typical Federalist defense was offered by Supreme Court Justice James Iredell, who wrote that the government could not issue prior restraints preventing the publication of allegedly seditious material in advance but could punish it after the fact.[4] Indeed, Federalist judges emphasized that the Sedition Act was more lenient than the common law, allowing truth as a defense to any "dangerous or offensive writings" that were of a "pernicious tendency."

There was, in fact, a competing view of the meaning of free speech, articulated not by Federalist judges but by citizens in the press, state legislatures, and public meetings. This view was embodied in the Virginia and Kentucky Resolutions, passed by the Virginia and Kentucky legislatures in the fall of 1798, which criticized the federal Sedition Act as a violation of states' rights. The Virginia Resolution, secretly drafted by Madison, also suggested that the Sedition Act was unconstitutional under the First Amendment because it was "levelled against that right of freely examining public characters and measures" that is the "only effectual guardian of every other right."[5] The question of whether government officials had failed to live up to their public trust could be determined only by free communication among the people.[6]

Although the Virginia and Kentucky resolutions were powerless to spare those convicted under the Sedition Act, public outrage at the convictions helped to trigger a congressional consensus that they were unconstitutional. Jefferson declared that Congress could not punish seditious speech, although he thought that states should have no hesitation about doing so.[7] (Indeed, Jefferson was no civil libertarian hero: he supported loyalty oaths, political internment camps, and sedition prosecutions for political enemies.)[8] By 1840, four decades after the Sedition Act had expired, the

House passed a bill recommending that the fine of one of the most prominent Republicans convicted under the Sedition Act should be repaid by
Congress. The House committee report concluded that the act was "null
and void" and that the unconstitutionality of the act had been "conclusively settled."[9] But it wasn't until 1937 that the Supreme Court found an
opportunity to recognize what the House had acknowledged nearly a century earlier: namely, that speech advocating political change could not be
banned simply because it might possibly incite illegal activity; instead,
there had to be a more direct connection between the speech and the
lawless action that followed.[10]

What caused the judges to abandon their old view—that free speech
only protected speakers against prior restraint by the government—and
to embrace a new view—that free speech allowed vigorous criticism of
government officials, unless there was a clear and present danger of lawless action? The gradual shift reflected a political consensus that the old
legal doctrine was inadequate to protect democratic values. The old legal doctrine held that speech could be banned if it had a "bad tendency,"
that is, if it might cause harm in the remote future. The new legal doctrine held that speech could not be banned unless the harm was imminent and the danger was probable. But although judges eventually
recognized and codified this shift, they did not cause it. Instead, the
shift was the result of political activity, organized around a series of
famous free-speech battles during the Civil War and World War I, and
played out in Congress before it was ratified in the courts. From the
eighteenth century until the New Deal, the primary defense for free
speech was a popular one—namely, the ability of juries to decide whether
the speech was true or intended to incite violations of the law.

The galvanizing free-speech battles of the Civil War era involved the
effort by Southern states to suppress the right of abolitionists to criticize slavery. In the late 1830s, the murder of Elijah Lovejoy, an abolitionist newspaper editor in Illinois, inflamed Northern opinion and helped
reframe the Southern assault on free speech as a threat to all Northerners,

not just to abolitionists. Former president John Quincy Adams called Lovejoy's death an "epocha in the annals of human liberty" that gave "a shock as of an earthquake throughout this continent."[11]

As a result of the Lovejoy incident (and of Southern demands that Congress refuse to accept antislavery petitions), preachers, newspapers, and citizens throughout the North condemned mob violence, and public opinion shifted toward the abolitionists. The Lovejoy affair also helped to turn Northern opinion against the "bad tendency" test, which increasingly seemed inadequate to protect free speech. In the 1830s, Southern states had passed a series of laws banning speech whose "tendency" was to incite slave rebellions. Like the Sedition Act, these prohibitions were not limited to publications that directly advocated crimes or insurrection; instead, any abolitionist criticism that had a tendency to incite bad behavior was banned; and those who circulated it were threatened with the death penalty. But unlike the Sedition Act, the Southern laws did not even allow the truth of the criticism as a defense against liability—a defect noted by Northern critics after Lovejoy's murder. "The Lovejoy experience shows that free speech is a much broader political tradition [than a legal one] and that crucial free speech decisions are made by citizens, by the press, by legislators, and by public officials who are not judges," writes Michael Kent Curtis.[12] He adds that it is just as well that courts failed to strike down the anti-abolitionist laws in the 1830s, for had they done so, the suppression of abolitionist speech would not have been seen as a threat to the speech of all citizens, and a national political consensus in favor of free speech might not have developed.

If judges had tried to strike down Southern laws restricting abolitionist speech in the antebellum era, their decisions would have been unilateralist, because questions about whether the states had the power to suppress speech under the "bad tendency test" were intensely contested across the nation until after the Civil War. When President Jackson, in 1836, recommended a federal law to "prohibit . . . the circulation in the Southern States, through the mail, of incendiary publications, intended to instigate the slaves to insurrection," his bill was opposed by Southern advocates of states' rights, who believed that Congress had no power to establish a federal standard for the suppression of free speech. (In this sense, the unconstitutionality of the federal Sedition Act was accepted relatively quickly.) Instead, Senator Calhoun proposed an alternative bill that would have punished federal officials who violated *state* laws prohibiting incendiary speech. But even this alternative was watered down because of constitutional scruples: the final version of the bill didn't try to ban abolitionist publications within Northern states or to punish abolitionists for mailing incendiary publications to the South; instead, it merely allowed Southern officials to refuse to deliver mail that violated states' laws.[13]

A series of other free speech scandals in the 1850s would finally convert the fading consensus that each state had the power to suppress speech as it pleased into a growing consensus that the right to criticize public officials was a fundamental right of all American citizens. In one case that helped to forge the new consensus, a North Carolina minister, Reverend Daniel Worth, was convicted of distributing a celebrated antislavery tract by Hinton Helper, *The Impending Crisis*. After Worth was convicted under a North Carolina law that prohibited the distribution of any pamphlet whose "evident tendency" was to "cause slaves to be discontented," Worth escaped to New York, where he objected that Helper's book was not "addressed to the colored people." (The North Carolina Supreme Court affirmed his conviction, nevertheless, holding that circulating the book within the states was forbidden, whether or not it was delivered to slaves or read in their presence.)[14]

Finally, during the first congressional campaign after the Civil War, Republicans complained about the Southern denial of free speech as a paradigmatic violation of the fundamental rights of American citizens, and these complaints influenced Congress's debates over the proposed Fourteenth Amendment to the Constitution, which prohibited states from violating the "privileges or immunities of citizens of the United

States." In proposing the Fourteenth Amendment, Republicans reaffirmed the position they had staked out during the congressional and presidential campaigns of 1856: namely, that free speech was one of the privileges or immunities of citizenship, and it should be protected from infringements by the states as well as Congress.[15]

Unfortunately, for fifty years after the ratification of the Fourteenth Amendment, judges refused to enforce the robust view of free speech that the Reconstruction Republicans attempted to embrace. From the Civil War until World War I, most judicial decisions continued to allow the suppression of free speech based on its purported bad tendency, often by ignoring free speech challenges.[16] It took yet another series of political controversies—focusing on the rights of dissenters during and after World War I—to persuade the Supreme Court to repudiate the bad tendency test in 1937. Even during these controversies, however, Congress and civil libertarian activists, rather than the courts, took the lead in debating the constitutional parameters of free speech. In 1917, for example, the Wilson administration tried to exploit antiwar sentiment by urging Congress and the courts to suppress political dissent based on its purported bad tendencies. In debates over the Espionage Act of 1917, Congress took its constitutional responsibilities seriously and rejected some of the most draconian provisions proposed by Wilson, including one that would have allowed the president to censor the press. (At this point, the prohibition against prior restraints was widely accepted.) Because of free-speech scruples, another provision that allowed postmasters to exclude from the mails any writing of a "treasonable or anarchistic character" was refined so that it only banned speech expressly "advocating or urging treason, insurrection or forcible resistance to any law of the United States."[17] This refinement represented an explicit congressional attempt to renounce the bad tendency test and to replace it with an express advocacy test more protective of free speech. The most important provision, which received the least attention, originally prohibited attempts "to cause disaffection in the military or naval forces of the United States"; this, too, was considered too broad and elastic, and it was replaced with a ban on attempts "to cause insubordination, disloyalty, mutiny, or refusal of duty."[18]

Despite Congress's attempts to protect free speech by refining the Espionage Act, lower court judges tended to construe the act very broadly, stretching it to prohibit speech that had a "bad tendency," rather than requiring the evidence of express advocacy of unlawful conduct that Congress had demanded. Like their predecessors before the war, lower court judges typically instructed juries to weigh the "tendency" of the speech in deciding whether or not it could be banned, fulfilling the fears of congressional critics.[19] As a result, about a thousand Espionage Act prosecutions led to guilty verdicts, and nearly all of these convictions were affirmed.

Only a few lower courts distinguished themselves by trying to construe the Espionage Act narrowly in ways that protected free speech rather than threatening it. A Montana district judge, George Bourquin, directed a verdict of acquittal for Ves Hall, who was charged with declaring that he hoped "Germany would whip the United States" and that "the United States was only fighting for Wall Street millionaires." Bourquin emphasized that Hall's remarks were not false, because they were statements of opinion, and were made in a location too remote from any soldiers or sailors to be "reasonably calculated" to obstruct the military. Congress, Bourquin insisted, had not intended to suppress general criticism of government officials, but only specific illegal acts.[20] The Wilson administration, however, criticized Bourquin's decision and used it as evidence of the weakness of the 1917 Espionage Act. At the urging of the attorney general, Congress in 1918 passed a new and even more draconian sedition act, which banned "any disloyal, profane, scurrilous, or abusive language about the form of government of the United States."[21]

Another notable lower court opinion fared no better. A month after Congress passed the Espionage Act, the New York postmaster banned a publication called *The Masses*, an iconoclastic collection of attacks on conventional wisdom, edited by Max Eastman; its contributors included John Reed, Carl Sandburg, and Sherwood Anderson. The postmaster objected to several antiwar cartoons and poems, including a tribute to Emma Goldman and Alexander Berkman, both in jail for opposing the draft. It read: "Emma Goldman and Alexander Berkman / Are in prison tonight. / But they have made themselves elemental forces / Like the water that climbs down rocks. . . . They are forging the love of the nations; . . . / Tonight they lie in prison."[22]

Repudiating the postmaster's ban as well as the "bad tendency" test, Judge Learned Hand, then a district judge in New York, said that publications should be prohibited under the Espionage Act only if they included "direct advocacy of resistance to the recruitment and enlistment service."[23] Hand concluded that the postmaster's effort to ban any publications that could "arouse discontent and disaffection among the people" was contrary to the intent of Congress, which had repudiated the "disaffection" standard, as well as clashing with the broad consensus that the Sedition Act of 1798 was unconstitutional.

Unfortunately, Hand's prescient opinion was reversed by the New York appellate court and eventually repudiated on the U.S. Supreme Court. The opinions were written by Hand's friend, Justice Oliver Wendell Holmes, who had endorsed the bad tendency test in 1907 and embraced it again in unanimous opinions upholding Espionage Act convictions in March 1919. In the *Schenck* case, Holmes upheld the conviction of Charles Schenck, who had circulated a pamphlet insisting that the draft was unconstitutional. In the *Debs* case, he upheld the conviction of Eugene V. Debs, the Socialist candidate for president in 1916, who had expressed his support of three Socialists imprisoned for violating the Espionage Act. After visiting the "three martyrs for freedom" in jail in 1918, Debs praised them "for paying the penalty, that all men have paid in all the ages of history for standing erect." Convicted for obstructing the recruiting of U.S. armed forces, Debs was sentenced to jail for ten years. In upholding the conviction, Holmes declared that the "probable effect" of Debs's praise for those who had opposed the war was to obstruct the war effort; therefore, the speech could be banned. These decisions were consistent with Holmes's strenuous devotion to judicial restraint and dark view of politics as a Darwinian struggle between the strong and the weak in which majorities should almost always prevail.

Between March and November of 1919, Holmes began to rethink his position on free speech. The postwar repression of dissenters intensified in a way that distressed many previously indifferent Americans, and the *Harvard Law Review* over the summer published an article called "Freedom of Speech in War Time" by Professor Zechariah Chafee, Jr., which Holmes and Chafee discussed. Intentionally misconstruing a phrase in Holmes's opinion in the *Schenck* case, Chafee emphasized that speech should be banned only when it posed a "clear and present danger" of provoking illegal activity. (Holmes had originally used the phrase "clear and present danger" as an endorsement of the "bad tendency test"; Chafee flattered him by suggesting that the phrase could be used to repudiate the bad tendency test.) With Chafee's encouragement, Holmes dissented in the next Espionage Act case decided by the Court later that year, *Abrams v. United States*. The majority upheld the conviction of Russian immigrants who had published English and Yiddish leaflets urging a general strike to protest President Wilson's decision to send Americans troops to Russia after the Bolshevik revolution. In his dissenting opinion, Holmes declared that "It is only the present danger of an immediate evil or an intent to bring it about that warrants Congress in setting a limit to the expression of opinion where private rights are not concerned."[24] The clear and present danger test was further refined by Justice Louis Brandeis: in a concurring opinion in *Whitney v. California* (1927), Brandeis emphasized that the danger had to be imminent, serious, and expressly advocated; in an earlier case, he stressed that the states as well as the federal government had to respect free speech, because it was a "privilege and immunity" of national citizenship.[25] In the

Gitlow decision in 1925, a majority of the Supreme Court agreed that the First Amendment bound the states; and in the *Herndon* case in 1937, the Court finally repudiated the bad tendency test, reversing the conviction of a Communist party activist who had urged the creation of an independent black nation in the South.

The judicial repudiation of the bad tendency test did not lead to an unbroken series of legal victories for free speech. On the contrary, the Court's devotion to the First Amendment waxed and waned during World War II, the Cold War, Vietnam, and the war against terror after September 11, 2001. When the president or Congress supported the rights of dissenters who were being menaced by the other branch, the Courts tended to uphold them; when both the president and Congress were committed to repressing unpopular speakers, the Courts tended to retreat. "A cynical, though nonetheless apparently accurate, interpretation of the Court's free speech jurisprudence is that political dissidents become entitled to significant constitutional protection only when they cease to pose a serious threat to the status quo—that is, Communists and Ku Kluxers in the second half of the 1960s, but not, respectively, in the 1950s or 1920s," writes Michael Klarman. "The Court protects the expression rights of pesky but nonthreatening dissidents (Jehovah's Witnesses) and of mainstream speakers (labor union picketers in 1940 but not 1920). Precious little corroboration of the Court's countermajoritarian heroics appears in the free speech context."[26]

Cynical or not, the observation is hard to deny. The Court was indeed sympathetic to the rights of Jehovah's Witnesses and labor organizers during World War II, when both groups enjoyed the backing of the White House and the public. For example, in 1940 the Supreme Court upheld mandatory flag salutes for the children of Jehovah's Witnesses; the decision was followed by mob attacks on Jehovah's Witnesses, vigorous criticism of the decision in the popular and scholarly press, and an increased concern about the power of totalitarian governments to coerce loyalty in Europe. Citing these criticisms, the Supreme Court reversed itself only three years later, declaring that local regulations requiring flag salutes in public and private schools were unconstitutional. In his opinion for the Court, Justice Robert Jackson noted explicitly the "fast failing efforts" to eliminate dissent by "our present totalitarian enemies."[27] He also showed a healthy respect for the constitutional views of the coordinate branches of government, noting that Congress in 1942 had chosen to make flag salutes voluntary, as well as "respecting the conscience of the objector in a matter so vital as raising the army."[28] And he explicitly embraced the clear and present danger test as a protection for free speech: "It is now a commonplace that censorship or suppression of expression of opinion is tolerated by our Constitution only when the expression presents a clear and present danger of action of a kind the State is empowered to prevent and punish."[29] Although Jackson concluded that "fundamental rights may not be submitted to vote; they depend on the outcome of no elections,"[30] his decision was hardly an exercise in antidemocratic heroics, given the political context of the moment, which was increasingly sensitive to religious and political minorities.

By contrast, as soon as the national political branches became once again hostile to political dissenters, the Court quickly reflected the change. The rise of cold-war tensions between 1948 and 1950—fanned by the blockade of Berlin and the fall of China and Czechoslovakia to the Communists, the detonation of the Soviet atom bomb, and North Korea's invasion of South Korea—emboldened the federal government to use its domestic security program to root out Communists. Between 1951 and 1952 the Supreme Court sustained the new anti-Communist policies, upholding the federal government's power to designate subversive organizations, to fire federal employees who belonged to organizations on the list, and to use the Smith Act, a federal sedition law passed in 1940, to convict Communist party leaders for antigovernment activities.[31] The decision upholding the Smith Act convictions, *Dennis v. United States*, diluted the protections of the clear and present danger

test by urging judges to balance the gravity of the harm against the probability of its occurrence. Although the Communist officials, convicted
after a highly publicized nine-month trial, had organized people to teach
and study Marxist-Leninist doctrine, they were charged and convicted
not of advocating the overthrow of the American government but of
the more remote charge of conspiring to advocate the overthrow of the
American government—a conspiracy that had little chance of imminent success. But by weighing the gravity of the harm against its immi-
nence in cases involving alleged attempts to overthrow the government,
the Supreme Court during the Cold War was able to dilute the immi-
nence requirement until it became irrelevant.

The dissenting opinions in *Dennis* assailed the majority for this and
insisted that the question of whether Communist speech was likely to
cause imminent danger should have been submitted to a jury. One of
the dissenters, Justice Black, predicted accurately that "in calmer times,
when present pressures, passions and fears subside, this or some later
Court will restore the First Amendment liberties to [a] high preferred
place."[32] But the most interesting opinion, at least for acolytes of judicial restraint, was offered by Justice Frankfurter. While acknowledging
the costs of suppressing the speech of dissenters, he insisted that judges
should defer to legislative judgments about the value of security weighed
against the value of speech that advocated violent overthrow of the government by a well-organized and substantial group. Distinguishing between the wisdom of a law and its constitutionality, he concluded: "Much
that should be rejected as illiberal, because repressive and envenoming,
may well be not unconstitutional."[33]

By the middle of the 1950s, as the excesses of the McCarthy hearings
became clear, public opinion about domestic security investigations had
begun to shift, as Justice Black predicted, and the Court shifted as well.
In 1956 in *Pennsylvania v. Nelson*, the Court, now led by Earl Warren,
struck down sedition laws in forty-two states on the grounds that Congress, in the Smith Act, had superseded state laws on the subject. The

Nelson decision created an alliance between southern segregationists, still smarting over *Brown v. Board of Education*, and northern pro-security conservatives in Congress, who were now moved to attack the Court for assailing states rights. But the foes of the Court were not able to rouse Congress to action until 1957, when the death of Joseph McCarthy and the confirmation of Justice William Brennan set the stage for a sustained judicial assault on legislative investigations, loyalty and security programs, and criminal prosecutions at the federal as well as the state level. During the 1956 Supreme Court term, no fewer than twelve anti-Communist cases were decided against the government. In the *Jencks* case, the Court gave suspected Communists and their lawyers the right to examine FBI files, which led a dissenting justice to call on Congress to overrule the decision. And on a single day, June 17, 1957, which became known as "Red Monday," the Court handed down four incendiary decisions. The *Yates* case limited the scope of the Smith Act by requiring that a defendant must incite others to engage in illegal activity in order to be convicted of subversive advocacy. The *Watkins* case called into question legislative investigations of suspected Communists that failed to give suspects basic due process rights and lectured Congress on the dangers of "broad-scale intrusion[s] into the lives and affairs of private citizens." The *Service* case reinstituted a China expert in the State Department who had been fired for alleged disloyalty. And the *Sweezy* case restricted state legislative investigations of suspected Communists in much the same way that *Watkins* had restricted Congress.[34]

Red Monday provoked a Congressional reaction and what was arguably a judicial retreat. Although the Court had ruled on statutory rather than constitutional grounds, Congress perceived the decisions of the 1957 term as a direct threat to its authority. The Eighty-fifth Congress considered a series of proposals to rein in the Court, including bills that would have allowed Congress to reverse the Court's constitutional decisions, to require unanimous votes to strike down state laws, and to disregard Supreme Court decisions that departed from previous precedent.[35]

Reflecting widespread popular criticism, a young former Supreme Court law clerk named William Rehnquist wrote an article in *U.S. News and World Report* at the end of 1957 criticizing his fellow clerks for showing "extreme solicitude for claims of Communists and other criminal defendants, expansion of federal power at the expense of state power."

In the end, Congress codified (and slightly refined) the procedures for access to government witnesses in federal prosecutions that the Court had endorsed in *Jencks*—a result that both defenders and critics of the Court claimed as a victory. But the House passed five of the anti-Court bills, and the Senate seriously considered revoking the Court's appellate jurisdiction in some domestic security cases.[36] The Court's retreat in the face of congressional pressure seemed, to some observers, swift: during the 1956 term, the term of Red Monday, the Court rejected civil liberties claims in only 26 percent of its cases; the following term, the percentage had risen to 41 percent and during the 1958 term, to nearly 50 percent.[37] During the 1960 term, the Court revisited several of the issues that it had decided four years earlier, and this time ruled against the suspected Communists on constitutional grounds. As a result, the *New York Times* was able to editorialize in 1960 that what Congress was "unable to achieve the Supreme Court has now virtually accomplished on its own."[38]

Later in the 1960s, when Communist dissenters were no longer seen as a serious threat to national security, the Court's views on subversive advocacy again shifted toward civil liberties in response. In three important decisions between 1964 and 1971, the Court enshrined a highly libertarian view of the First Amendment in order to allow vigorous criticism of public officials. In *New York Times v. Sullivan* (1964), a unanimous Court reversed a state libel verdict against the *New York Times* for $500,000, filed by an Alabama official who claimed that a *New York Times* advertisement in which civil rights advocates criticized his actions contained false statements. Writing for the majority, Justice William Brennan announced that "Although the Sedition Act [of 1798] was never tested in this Court, the attack upon its validity has carried the day in the court of history."[39] Brennan cited Madison's defense of the Virginia Resolutions on the Sedition Act and declared that his criticisms had been accepted by the nation. In order to vindicate the "profound national commitment to the principle that debate on public issues should be uninhibited, robust, and wide-open,"[40] Brennan said, public officials could not sue for libel unless the statement in question "was made with 'actual malice'"—that is, with knowledge that it was false or reckless disregard of whether it was false or not.[41] The decision protected supporters of the civil rights movement from ruinous suits and made it easier for newspapers to cover the protests without fear of being bankrupted. In this sense, *Sullivan* might also be viewed as a race case, one in which the Court was performing its traditional function of bringing a few southern outliers into a national consensus about the importance or protecting civil rights protesters.

After having codified Madison's criticisms of the Sedition Act, the Court five years later finally embraced Louis Brandeis's vision of subversive advocacy. In *Brandenburg v. Ohio* (1969), the Court reversed the conviction of a Ku Klux Klan leader who had been convicted under an Ohio law, left over from the Red Scare era, that made it a crime to advocate crime or terrorism. Brandenburg had delivered a racist speech at a Klan rally declaring that "if our President, our Congress, our Supreme Court, continues to suppress the white, Caucasian race, it's possible that there might have to be some revengeance taken."[42] Emphasizing that the Klan leader had not expressly advocated lawless action, the Court endorsed the test for subversive advocacy that Brandeis had set out in the *Whitney* case, without Brandeis's requirement that the speech in question cause serious harm. In order to protect First Amendment rights, the Court declared, a state may not "forbid or proscribe advocacy of the use of force or of law violation except where such advocacy is directed to inciting or producing imminent lawless action and is likely to incite or produce such action."[43]

The Vietnam War produced the Court's third and final encounter with a more libertarian attitude toward the First Amendment. When the Nixon administration tried to prevent the *New York Times* and the *Washington Post* from publishing the Pentagon papers, a secret account of American involvement in Vietnam, the Court rejected the injunction by a 6–3 vote. "Any system of prior restraints of expression comes to this Court bearing a heavy presumption against its constitutional validity," declared the majority in *New York Times v. United States.*[44] Justice Brennan would have recognized an exception to the rule in times of war when newspapers were on the verge of publishing "the sailing dates of transports or the number and location of troops"—both examples where serious harm to national security was imminent.[45] Justices Black and Douglas refused to recognize any exception to the rule against prior restraints. And with special sensitivity to the powers of coordinate branches of government, Justices Thurgood Marshall, Byron White, and Potter Stewart felt it was significant that Congress had failed to authorize the prior restraint in advance. In hindsight, historians have concluded that "all of the government's fears were overstated and that, in fact, none of them appear to have been accurate."[46] The Nixon administration asserted that publishing the names and activities of active C.I.A. agents would harm national security but offered no evidence to support the claim. The case suggests that government officials and judges are very bad at predicting the likely effects of controversial publications. Moreover, judicial bans on the press are likely to be ineffective: all the more so in the age of the Internet, when Daniel Ellsberg could have anonymously posted the papers online.

Taken together, the *Sullivan*, *Brandenburg*, and *New York Times* cases represented an enthusiastic if belated codification of the libertarian view of the First Amendment that had first been suggested by the Republican opponents of the Sedition Act of 1798, developed by abolitionists before the Civil War, and explicitly embraced by the Reconstruction Congress that proposed the Fourteenth Amendment. Once conservative as well as liberal justices on the Court finally endorsed the principle that speech cannot be banned unless it is likely to cause imminent harm, they were willing to apply it in ways that sometimes clashed with the views of national and congressional majorities. A survey of eighty-eight civil rights and civil liberties cases between 1953 and 1994 found that in most cases, the Court was roughly in sync with public opinion. When public opinion opposed a particular rights claim, so generally did the Supreme Court, supporting only 40 percent of the claims that the public opposed. When public opinion was evenly divided or favorable to the rights claim, the Supreme Court supported the claim as well in nearly 70 percent of the cases. But the Court and the public were farther apart in cases involving political and religious dissent, where the Court favored the rights claim in 100 percent of the cases and the public in only 33 percent.[47]

Some of the school prayer decisions, in particular, are hard to defend on majoritarian grounds: opinion polls suggested that wide majorities of the country opposed the school-prayer and Bible-reading decisions by the Warren Court. Nevertheless, the Court's decision forbidding readings of the Lord's Prayer was embraced by Catholic and mainstream Protestant leaders, who viewed denominational exercises as an affront. More to the point, when the Court struck down an anti-evolution statute, the national press was united in its praise.[48] Similarly, the Warren Court's decisions involving criminal procedure provoked intense opposition by taking on national rather than local majorities, as in the case of the decision requiring police to read suspects their Miranda rights, which initially angered the police, who feared that squad cars would have to be supplied with lawyers.[49] But even the Warren Court's criminal procedure decisions may have been more popular with national (as opposed to local) majorities than conventional wisdom assumes: in its major decisions involving cops and crime, the Court arguably "moved with the tide of public opinion rather than against it."[50]

By the 1980s, national support for free speech as an abstract value had become so widespread that the Court had broad leeway to reach particular results that the public and Congress may have questioned, such as striking down state and federal bans on flag burning. And unlike the Japanese internment cases, where there was congressional support for the principle of equal protection in theory but not in practice, the Court should have broader leeway to second-guess Congress's particular understandings in First Amendment cases, where politicians may be acting in self-interested ways to protect themselves from criticism.

The Court embraced First Amendment libertarianism more than a century after the far more equivocal embrace by some framers of the Fourteenth Amendment. Should the justices have been more aggressive in pressing libertarian claims throughout the late nineteenth and early twentieth century, rather than calibrating their decisions to reflect public opinion? It's hard not to be disappointed with the cavalier attitude toward constitutional history displayed by justices such as Holmes who, before his First Amendment conversion, ignored the rich and detailed political agitation against the bad tendency test that led the Reconstruction Republicans explicitly to reject it. Focusing exclusively and glibly on legal doctrine, the Court with Holmes's blessing showed far less solicitude for free speech than Congress intended. Nevertheless, had the Court attempted to apply the clear and present danger test with less sensitivity to public opinion, it would certainly have provoked political backlashes that made the Sedition Act of 1918 and the Jencks Act look tame. Since the Court did not create the national consensus about the importance of protecting the speech of dissenters, its politically cautious enforcement of the consensus may have preserved judicial authority while encouraging libertarian defenders to continue to make their case in Congress and state legislatures, where they were often successful. As Walter Murphy observes, "If a judge wishes . . . to protect constitutional rights rather than write libertarian tracts, he must try to visualize the possible reaction of other branches of government to any decision."[51]

The heavy-handed performance of some judges during the Civil War provides the clearest illustration that judicial unilateralism in wartime may lead to political backlashes that hurt judicial power and civil liberties at the same time. The most aggressively unilateralist decisions involved the attempt by judges to challenge Lincoln's suspension of the writ of habeas corpus, which allows suspects to challenge the legality of their detention. After the secretary of war, William Seward, suspended the writ at Lincoln's direction, thousands of citizens were arrested and detained without a judicial hearing.[52] The great constitutional question was whether Lincoln had usurped Congress's authority by suspending habeas corpus on his own, without seeking congressional approval.

During the period before Congress endorsed the suspension, one of the early detainees, John Merryman, challenged the constitutionality of Lincoln's actions, arguing that they violated Article I, Section 9 of the Constitution, which provides that "the Privilege of the Writ of Habeas Corpus shall not be suspended, unless when in Cases of Rebellion or Invasion the public safety may require it." Merryman charged that Lincoln exceeded his authority by suspending the writ without congressional authorization after a Baltimore mob blocked the passage of Union troops sent to defend the capital. Merryman's challenge to Lincoln's actions set the stage for a confrontation between Lincoln and Chief Justice Roger Taney. In ruling that Lincoln acted unconstitutionally by suspending the writ without congressional authorization, Taney, sitting as a circuit judge, offered several plausible constitutional arguments for questioning Lincoln's actions. He noted that the constitutional authorization for suspending habeas corpus is found in Article I, Section 9, which deals with limitations on the legislature's power, not in Article II, which deals with the executive power. Also, the king of England had been deprived of the power to suspend the writ, and authorities such as Chief Justice John Marshall had concluded that Congress alone had the power to suspend it.[53]

Lincoln responded to Taney's opinion by essentially ignoring it: he delivered an address on July 4, 1861, that made no explicit reference to Taney but asked whether the writ of habeas corpus could allow "all the laws, but one, to go unexecuted, and the government itself go to pieces, lest that one be violated." Lincoln also noted that the president needed the authority to suspend habeas corpus because Congress was not always in session. Congress eventually settled the dispute in March 1863, with a law declaring that the president did indeed have the power to suspend the writ of habeas corpus. (The statute was vague about whether Congress was giving the president the power to suspend the writ or recognizing the existence of the president's power after the fact.) Lincoln reluctantly expanded the scope of the suspension until it covered the entire nation, noting in a memo that "unless the *necessity* for these arbitrary arrests is *manife*st, and *urgent*, I prefer they should cease."[54]

Was Lincoln's action constitutional? The historian Daniel Farber says that "the president's power to make war in response to 'sudden attack' is the most plausible source of his authority to suspend habeas in the theater of the ensuing war."[55] Farber concludes that "on balance Lincoln's use of habeas in areas of insurrection or actual war should be considered constitutionally appropriate, at least in the absence of any contrary action by Congress."[56] Given the riots that occurred in Baltimore when the War broke out, the suspension of habeas in Merryman's case could have been justified as an emergency military measure.

As for Taney, his legal arguments were plausible, if contestable, but his heavy-handedness in challenging the president in the face of constitutional uncertainty was counterproductive. An able lawyer and not a bad man, Taney was arrogant and rigid, full of an inflated sense of judicial power, and he went out of his way to deny any flexibility to the president in a time of emergency. Refusing to allow the government to be heard, he mocked Lincoln and circulated his opinion as widely as possible to embarrass the administration. (An 1862 pamphlet of the decision, grandiosely titled *Decision of Chief Justice Taney in the Merryman Case upon the Writ of Habeas Corpus*, notes that it was published on Taney's authority.) "A judge with a little less self-righteousness and a little more humility might still have ruled against Lincoln, but he would not have overreached so badly," Farber concludes. "It was much the same arrogance that led him to think he could settle the slavery issue single-handedly with his *Dred Scott* opinion."[57] Taney's arrogance shows that plausible legal arguments are not enough; judges who act unilaterally in the face of active contestation from the president and Congress are likely to be ignored in the short term and seldom thanked in the long term for their lack of humility.

The Supreme Court as a whole was similarly unilateralist in the *Milligan* case, decided in 1866. (Perhaps a degree of unilateralism was justified in challenges to the government's efforts to try its political opponents with military tribunals; as I suggested in the introduction, courts since the founding era have been appropriately zealous in protecting their own prerogatives against executive assaults.) After Congress authorized his suspension of habeas corpus, Lincoln established military commissions to try civilians. A military commission in Indiana sentenced to death a Southern peace Democrat named Lambdin P. Milligan. He challenged the constitutionality of his conviction, and the Supreme Court agreed that he was unlawfully imprisoned because Lincoln had no power to order military trials for civilians in districts where the civilian courts were open.[58]

But four justices, led by Chief Justice Salmon P. Chase, took a much more measured and less unilateralist approach. They insisted that Congress could, if it chose, authorize the use of military commissions for civilians outside the theater of war. "When the nation is involved in war ... it is within the power of Congress to determine" the appropriateness of military commissions, since civilian judges might in some cases be disloyal to the national government.[59] But in this case, the four justices concluded, Congress had not authorized the broad use of military commissions that the president was trying to assert and in fact appeared to have prohibited them.[60] Chase's insistence on avoiding unilateralism was admirable; rather than challenging both branches of the national government, he stressed that the president could create extraordinary legal procedures in wartime, but only if Congress supported him.

Chase's warning that Congress, not the courts, would be the ultimate arbiter of civil liberties in wartime proved to be prescient. Although few people questioned the result (the Court had invalidated tribunals that were no longer being used in the North), public criticism focused on the Court's arrogance in boldly and unnecessarily questioning Congress's authority to balance liberty and security in wartime. As a result of the public reaction, Congress confronted the Court directly in order to block further attempts at judicial unilateralism. When a newspaper editor named McCardle was tried by a military commission in Mississippi for questioning Reconstruction policies, he challenged his detention. Based on the Court's aggressive unilateralism in *Milligan*, Congress feared that the Court would use the *McCardle* case to issue a direct assault on Reconstruction legislation. While McCardle's suit was pending, in March 1868, Congress passed a law over President Andrew Johnson's veto depriving the Supreme Court of jurisdiction to review the case. In *Ex parte McCardle*, the Supreme Court meekly acquiesced Congress's rebuke to its authority, ruling unanimously, in an opinion by Chief Justice Chase, that "[w]e are not at liberty to inquire into the motives of the legislature. We can only examine into its power under the Constitution; and the power to make exceptions to the appellate jurisdiction of this court is given by express words" of the Constitution.[61]

During World War II and the Cold War, in challenges to the detention of suspected domestic and foreign enemies, the Supreme Court followed the model set out by Chief Justice Chase rather than by Chief Justice Taney. Rather than attempting to unilaterally enforce individual rights in the face of hostility from the president and Congress, the Court instead sensibly focused on encouraging bilateral cooperation between the president and Congress. When the Court felt that sweeping exercises of executive authority during wartime were endorsed by Congress, it tended to uphold them. By contrast, when the Court felt that the executive was acting without congressional authorization, it tended to strike them down. Instead of casting themselves as heroic defenders of individual rights or abdicating their role entirely, the justices in the 1940s and '50s attempted instead to shift the responsibility for balancing liberty and security away from courts and toward the joint action of the president and Congress.[62]

The Court's effort to avoid unilateralism was most obvious in two cases from 1944 involving the president's efforts to detain 120,000 Japanese American citizens and aliens. In one of the darker moments in American history, a large segment of the population was sent to detention camps on ethnic grounds. In *Korematsu v. United States*, however, the Court upheld President Roosevelt's executive order authorizing the internment of Japanese residents and citizens in preparation for their evacuation from the West Coast. The order, issued despite doubts expressed by Roosevelt's attorney general, Francis Biddle, responded to public demand for dramatic action against suspected Japanese spies in the wake of Pearl Harbor: in the face of alarmism by newspaper columnists and the governor of California, General John DeWitt, the army commander on the West Coast, passed along rumors (which proved to be false) that twenty thousand Japanese Americans were on the verge of an uprising in San Francisco.[63] In justifying the internment, General DeWitt stressed the imminent danger and emphasized that there was no practical way of distinguishing between loyal and disloyal Japanese. This justification appears, in retrospect, to be an embarrassment, recycling false and inflammatory reports of potential sabotage and espionage plots that came largely from the red-baiting 1938 hearings of the House Un-American Activities Committee chaired by Martin Dies.[64] But in an atmosphere of public hysteria, Roosevelt and Congress felt strong pressure to respond: as a result, within a month, Congress explicitly ratified the executive order.

The *Korematsu* decision upholding the executive order is often excoriated as a craven failure of judicial nerve. In a 6–3 opinion by Justice

Hugo Black, the Court rejected arguments that the internment of citizens was beyond the wartime powers of the federal government or that singling out citizens of Japanese but not German or Italian descent was a form of unconstitutional discrimination on the basis of race. Justice Black emphasized that Congress had endorsed the detentions and quoted from the Court's decision the previous year upholding a West Coast curfew of suspected enemy aliens: "we cannot reject as unfounded the judgment of the military authorities and of Congress that there were disloyal members of [the Japanese-American] population, whose number and strength could not be precisely and quickly ascertained."[65] In a dissenting opinion, Justice Frank Murphy objected to what he called the "legalization of racism."[66]

Although criticized later for succumbing to popular fears, the Court in fact was careful to distinguish between the temporary executive detention—which had been endorsed by Congress as an emergency measure—and ongoing executive detention—which Congress never endorsed. In a case decided the same day as *Korematsu*, *Ex parte Endo*, the Court struck down the detention of Mitsuye Endo, a twenty-two-year-old clerical worker in the California Department of Motor Vehicles. (Endo was a loyal citizen who didn't read or speak Japanese.) The Court concluded that "Mitsuye Endo should be given her liberty" because the Congressional law authorizing curfews and evacuation on the West Coast "is silent on detention."[67] The Court noted that Congress's silence may have been especially significant, since the detentions weren't part of the original evacuation program and were only developed later by officials in the field as a response to popular hostility to the Japanese citizens and aliens who were being evacuated in their communities where they tried to relocate. Samuel Issacharoff and Richard Pildes argue that *Korematsu* should be viewed less harshly in light of *Endo*. "Evacuation and restrictions on mobility reflected military judgment (faulty or pernicious as they may have been) of what was necessary for security. Detention, however, reflected political and policy judgments, not military ones," they write. Even during one of the bleakest moments in American history, they conclude, the Court deferred to military judgments while resisting unilateral executive actions that rested on political grounds instead.[68] By insisting on explicit congressional authorization for extraordinary presidential actions during wartime, the Court encouraged both branches carefully to weigh the consequences of abridging liberty in the name of security without attempting to preempt that balance by judicial fiat.

The Court's interventions during the Civil War and World War II show that judges are better at forcing the president and Congress to act bilaterally in wartime than they are attempting to protect liberty unilaterally. Congress responded to the Court's challenge with varying degrees of concern about civil liberties. In 1950, at the height of the Korean War, Congress passed the McCarran Internal Security Act requiring "Communist-front" organizations to register with the attorney general, denying their members government jobs, and authorizing the president, in the event of war, to detain all people he reasonably believed might participate "in acts of espionage or sabotage."[69] Although the act gave suspects no right to seek judicial review, it did provide administrative hearings that gave detainees the right to appear before a hearing officer within forty-eight hours and the opportunity, with the help of a lawyer, to cross-examine witnesses in order to make a case for their release.

In repealing this egregious McCarthy-era detention law in 1971, Congress prohibited the president from detaining citizens without congressional authorization. Congress was afraid the McCarran Act could lead to a repetition of the Japanese internment during World War II, and the 1971 law was explicitly designed to avoid that unhappy possibility. But the McCarran Act, for all its faults, at least contained procedural protections for citizens who were detained; Congress feared that by repealing the act without passing new procedural protections, it might give the president an even freer hand to detain citizens indefinitely without defining the limits of executive authority. Accordingly, Congress made clear in the 1971 Non-Detention Act that "No citizen shall be imprisoned or otherwise detained by the United States except pursuant to an Act of Congress." By requiring explicit congressional authorization for the detention of citizens, Congress intended to preserve its own oversight authority in times of war, an authority that the Court in the past had been careful to respect.

Unfortunately, after the terrorist attacks of September 11, 2001, the Supreme Court found itself in a more unilateralist mood and was less concerned about Congress's earlier efforts to prohibit the detention of American citizens. In the wake of the terrorist attacks, the administration of George W. Bush embraced sweeping positions of executive unilateralism, declaring that the president has the constitutional authority as commander in chief of the armed forces to designate any citizen as an enemy combatant and to detain him or her indefinitely without any oversight by Congress or the Courts. In the past, U.S. law distinguished between lawful combatants, who were held as prisoners of war until the end of hostilities, and unlawful combatants, who were tried by military tribunals. But the Bush administration created a new category called "enemy combatants," who may never be tried by the military or the civilian justice system and who may be detained indefinitely—until the end of a war on terrorism that might, in practice, never end. And, while other Western democracies have imposed legislative and judicial oversight on the preventive detention of terrorism suspects, the Bush administration— arrogantly and inexplicably—refused to acknowledge any role for Congress or the courts.

If President Bush had had the humility to ask the Republican Congress for help, it would have immediately obliged by passing a comprehensive law of preventive detention. Instead, the administration chose to compound the dangers of preventive detention by making up its procedures on the fly, inventing new legal categories in order to avoid accountability to anyone outside the executive branch. Two of the citizens detained as enemy combatants—Yassir Hamdi, seized on the battlefield in Afghanistan, and Jose Padilla, seized in O'Hare airport in Chicago—challenged their detention, and the Supreme Court agreed to hear their cases.

In repudiating the Bush administration's unilateralism, unfortunately, the Supreme Court was more concerned about saving the president from his own excesses than it was about encouraging Congress to supervise the president. In the Hamdi case, four justices—Justice O'Connor, joined by Chief Justice Rehnquist, Justice Kennedy, and Justice Breyer—concluded that Congress had authorized the detention of enemy combatants seized on the battlefield, but they also concluded that citizens held in the United States as enemy combatants must be given a meaningful opportunity to contest the factual basis for that detention before a neutral decision maker. Accordingly, they suggested a series of judicial procedures that might allow the president to detain citizens with oversight by federal judges or by a military tribunal. The four justices rejected the administration's assertion that courts should play a "heavily circumscribed role" in times of war and insisted that, unless Congress suspended the writ of habeas corpus, judges should "play a necessary role in maintaining this delicate balance of governance, serving as an important judicial check on the Executive's discretion in the realm of detentions."[70]

In focusing self-referentially on the role of judges in checking the president, the Supreme Court slighted the role of Congress, which might have been more likely to make its views clear if the Court hadn't preempted the need for congressional action. In fact, as Justices Souter and Ginsburg argued in a separate opinion, it was hardly clear that Congress had authorized the detention of American citizens after 9/11. Congress's resolution authorizing the president to use "necessary and appropriate force" against Al Qaeda said nothing about authorizing him to detain alleged Al Qaeda operatives in the United States. During World War II, the Court had refused to interpret Congress's silence on the subject of executive detentions as implicit authorization for them; and in the 1971 Non Detention Act, Congress was even more explicit about requiring a clear statement of congressional authorization for detentions before any citizen could be detained. Moreover, in the U.S.A. Patriot Act, Congress specifically said aliens detained as terrorism suspects for more than seven days must be charged or deported in most circumstances. It seems unlikely Congress would authorize the indefinite detention of citizens but not of aliens.

Some defenders of bipartisan judicial restraint have argued plausibly that the Court should be freer to engage in adventurous interpretations of federal statutes than of the U.S. Constitution, because Congress is always free to reverse statutory decisions with which it disagrees, while constitutional decisions cannot be reversed, except by a constitutional amendment. And in an age when Congress is increasingly reluctant to take responsibility for policy choices, judicial restraint may be just as likely to encourage presidential unilateralism as it is to encourage a dialogue between the president and the Congress. But judicial creativity can remove any remaining incentives to congressional action: In the Hamdi case, for example, the Court detected congressional authorization where no explicit authorization existed and then made up judicial procedures in order to save the executive from its worst impulses. This had the unfortunate effect of removing any political pressure on Congress to adopt the comprehensive procedural safeguards that European countries with systems of preventive detention have adopted. It may have also emboldened the president to take the remarkable and unconvincing unilateralist view that the congressional resolution authorizing him to find the perpetrators of the 9/11 attacks could be stretched to authorize him to break U.S. surveillance laws with domestic wiretaps of U.S. citizens. The national scandal that erupted when this secret spying program was revealed is consistent with similar scandals that emerged in Europe during the 1980s and '90s: namely, political pressure calling for new laws to regulate the executive invariably arise in response to well-publicized executive excesses. Courts should not imagine they can create these legal regulations on their own in the absence of public support and debate.

For example, in Britain, after preventive detention of Irish Republican Army suspects led to wrongful convictions and mistaken identifications, Parliament passed a Terrorism Act in 2000 that forbids indefinite detention. Police can arrest suspected terrorists without a warrant but must charge or release them after forty-eight hours unless a court approves a maximum five-day extension. Detainees can respond to the allegations against them and must have access to counsel "as soon as is reasonably practicable." The British Anti-Terrorism Act of 2001 allows the indefinite detention of foreign nationals who can neither be prosecuted nor deported; but they have the right to appeal their designation to the judiciary and the House of Lords, and Parliament must renew the detention authority every year. In Israel, the Knesset has mandated that detainees have access to counsel to contest their status and must be brought before a court within forty-eight hours to ensure there are public security reasons to approve the detentions. Although the minister of defense can renew each detention order every six months, courts must continue to review the basis for the detention every three months. In other words, both Britain and Israel recognize the importance of oversight by the legislative branch as well as the courts.

This kind of comprehensive legislative oversight is less likely in America now that the Supreme Court has removed any incentive for Congress to act; by insisting on judicial oversight without political accountability, the Court encouraged the executive to draft a series of vague and unsatisfying procedures to regulate its own conduct. If, by contrast, the Court had struck down the executive's system of preventive detention as being unauthorized by Congress, then Congress likely would have stepped into the breach to provide whatever authorization the president thought necessary. Similarly, when the Court held that aliens detained at Guantanamo Bay, Cuba, had a right to file petitions of habeas corpus challenging their detention, Congress responded by essentially overturning the decision. If the Court had ruled more modestly—holding that enemy combatants tried before military commissions could challenge the legal basis for the their trials, but that other detainees captured and held outside the United States could not do so—then Congress might not have been roused to repudiate the Court's unilateralism.

Congress's refusal to assert its own prerogatives to authorize judicial oversight over the president in the war on terror contrasts strikingly with its response to earlier national emergencies. During debates over the Alien and Sedition Acts in 1798, the Habeas Corpus Act of 1863, and the Japanese Detentions in 1942, Congress insisted on a role for the courts in checking executive excesses, as well as asserting its own powers of oversight. In supporting the Enemy Aliens Act of 1798, for example, both Federalists and Republicans stressed that Congress had a constitutional duty to regulate enemy alien detention. In the end, the Alien Enemies Act codified Congress's insistence on multilateral action in the realm of detention: if the United States were invaded or if another state declared war on the United States, the president had power to detain enemy aliens. Absent these exigencies, Congress's constitutional power to declare war meant that it should decide how extensive the president's wartime powers to detain alien enemies would be. Moreover, both Federalists and Republicans recognized that the judiciary had a limited, but important, role in overseeing the detention of aliens. The Alien Enemies Act gave state and federal courts power to "discharge, enforce, and execute" the rules regarding detention of enemy aliens that the bill authorized the president to promulgate.[71]

Similarly, the Habeas Corpus Act of 1863 granted broad powers to President Lincoln to suspend the writ of habeas corpus, but the judicial provisions originating in the bill also provided safeguards to ensure that civilians would supervise military arrests. Chief Justice Chase's concurring opinion in *Ex parte Milligan* interpreted these judicial provisions as attempts by Congress to limit the president's authority to suspend the writ.[72] Even during World War II, when Congress ratified the president's detention of Japanese American citizens, neither the Roosevelt administration nor Congress assumed that the president could act unilaterally. On the contrary, Congress and the president acted in shameful unison. And the World War II statute criminalizing the violation of evacuation orders gave suspects a chance to contest their status in federal court.

Why then, has Congress been so passive after 9/11, refusing to assert its authority to supervise the president's broad claims of executive authority, and also refusing to authorize judges to do so? There are two obvious differences between the post-9/11 era and earlier congressional confrontations with the detention of citizens. First, the president has repeatedly asserted his own unilateral power to detain American citizens without congressional authorization. By contrast, previous congressional decisions to detain American citizens followed some sort of executive invitation to action. President John Adams thought that he needed Congress's approval to detain even aliens in wartime. President Lincoln believed that he and Congress shared the power to detain U.S. citizens, and encouraged Congress to approve his suspension of habeas corpus after the fact. President Roosevelt cooperated with Congress and as a result, Congress made it a crime to violate his evacuation orders on the West Coast.

The second difference between the current era and previous ones is a very different attitude toward judicial authority. Congress is increasingly aggressive in its attacks on purportedly activist judges, which makes congressional Republicans less likely to invite judicial oversight of the president. And the courts have contributed to this mutual suspicion by unilaterally asserting their own authority to oversee the president, without inviting congressional participation. All this suggests that healthy cooperation between the branches can take place only in an atmosphere of mutual trust. At a time when both Congress and the president view the judiciary with distrust, and the judiciary reciprocates with scarcely concealed contempt, multilateral cooperation is unlikely to occur.

The Supreme Court's confidence today that it alone can save the nation from the excesses of the executive, and the executive's indifference to congressional support, is a sign of how dramatically the civil liberties tradition has evolved over two hundred years. At the beginning, the public expected that civil liberties in wartime would be protected by democratic bodies; today we expect that they will be protected by the courts. Indeed, the Courts in the second half of the twentieth century got into the habit of standing up to the executive only after a few unusual confrontations during the McCarthy investigations and the Vietnam War. These confrontations were a dramatic contrast to the Court's performance earlier in the century, when it upheld the convictions of dissenters during World War I, the detention of Japanese Americans during World War II, and the convictions of Communist leaders during the Cold War. Because of its newfound experience in checking the executive, courts today seem to believe that without their intervention, civil liberties in wartime would have few defenders. This is, however, myopic and unconvincing. The great principles of free speech and fair trials that the Courts are willing vigorously to enforce today—in particular, the right to criticize government officials and the right to seek judicial review of convictions—were formulated and defended for most of American history not by the courts but by Congress. The courts came only belatedly to codify constitutional rights that had been defined and won in the political process.

Epilogue

Constitutional Futurology, or What Are Courts Good For?

I t should be obvious by now that the Supreme Court has followed the public's views about constitutional questions throughout its history, and, on the rare occasions that it has been even modestly out of line with popular majorities, it has gotten into trouble. Paradoxically, the federal courts, often considered the least democratic branch of government, have maintained their legitimacy over time when they have been deferential to the constitutional views of the country as a whole.

But will—and should—this historical pattern continue to hold in the future? For much of American history, liberals and conservatives were united around the importance of judicial deference to democratic outcomes. Over the next few decades, that may be less likely as activists on both sides of the political spectrum are insisting that only judges will have the expertise and stature to resolve the complex technological and scientific disputes that the future may bring. In fact, however, the issues that divide the country in coming years will continue to be political and moral, far more than they are technological, and can only be resolved by political debate. If the Court tries unilaterally to impose the views of either progressive or social conservative minorities in the face of public resistance, it may provoke social turmoil. In the future, in other words, both the temptations and the costs of judicial unilateralism may continue to grow.

Although constitutional futurology is hardly an exact science, let's try to imagine the kinds of disputes that might arise over the next few decades and how the courts might best serve the country in confronting them. Controversies might arise in areas such as genetic selection and enhancement; high-tech brain mapping that can identify criminal suspects with a propensity to violence; the demand for personalized drug and gene therapies; and efforts to patent novel forms of human life. As Congress and the states pass legislation to address these combustible issues, the laws will inevitably be challenged in court, raising novel questions about how to interpret our constitutional rights to privacy, autonomy, equality, and private property. Let's consider each in turn.

In the wake of terrorist attacks after September 11, 2001, the New York subway system implemented random bag searches, and the London Underground imposed the equivalent of electronic strip searches by high-tech body scanners that use millimeter waves to peer through clothing. In the coming years, if technology and the threat of terror continue to advance, Western democracies may confront ever more sophisticated and intrusive forms of surveillance, many of which will be challenged in court as a violation of rights to privacy and equality. It's easy to imagine, for example, the increasing use of data-mining computer programs to identify potentially suspicious individuals. As biometric camera systems become more accurate, they will be able to take pictures of people's faces, link the face to databases full of personal information, and generate a threat index based on how suspicious the individual appears. Marc Rotenberg of the Electronic Privacy Information Center, a civil liberties group in Washington, D.C., imagines a young man walking around the

Washington Monument for thirty minutes while waiting for a friend. Cameras might record his face and zoom in on, for example, the Koran he was carrying under his arm. The link between his face and his travel records and magazine subscriptions, maintained by a commercial database, might generate a threat index score that suggests further investigation. Based on his low trustworthiness score, and the copy of the Koran, the young man might be stopped by the police, who might open his backpack and find marijuana. Would the examination of the backpack be an unconstitutional search or seizure?

On the current Supreme Court, a challenge to terrorist threat indices generated by computer algorithms would face an uphill battle. In 2005, the Court upheld the dog sniff of a driver who had been stopped for speeding. (When the dog barked, the cops opened the trunk and found marijuana.) In preferring mass technological searches to police discretion, the conservative justices were joined by liberal justices such as Stephen Breyer, who has voted to uphold group drug tests of high school students as a way of avoiding the dangers of racial profiling. The only dissenters were David Souter and Ruth Bader Ginsburg, who worried that the Court had cleared the way for the police to turn drug-sniffing dogs on large groups of innocent citizens without cause to suspect illegal activity. But even Ginsburg and Breyer said there might be nothing wrong with the use of bomb-detection dogs if they were effective in identifying potential terrorists.[1]

If polls about the U.S.A Patriot Act are correct (only 22 percent of Americans say it goes too far in restricting civil liberties to fight terrorism, while 69 percent are happy with it or think it doesn't go far enough)[2] many citizens may not object to data-mining technology that claims to identify potential terrorists. But if the war against terror escalates, the government may deploy even more controversial forms of electronic surveillance, such as neuroimaging technologies that can detect the presence of electrochemical signals in the brain. The promoters of this "brain fingerprinting," which uses Functional Magnetic Resonance Imaging, or fMRI, say that it can detect brain waves that are consistent with particular kinds of recollection. In a murder case in Iowa, for example, a convicted murderer introduced an fMRI scan that suggested his brain did not contain information about the murder but did contain information consistent with his alibi.[3] Similar scans could be used in the future to interrogate enemy combatants, for example, whom officials suspect of having trained in Afghanistan. They could be shown pictures of the battlefield, and, if they have been there before, the device would detect a brain wave.

It is an open question, under the Supreme Court's current cases, whether the fMRI scans, used as a glorified, high-tech lie detector, would be considered a form of compulsory self-incrimination that violates the Fifth Amendment. If the justices viewed an involuntary brain scan as no more intrusive than a blood or urine sample or an ordinary fingerprint, there wouldn't be any Fifth Amendment problem. But if the Court decides that the fMRI scans are looking not merely for physical evidence but also for a suspect's memories and substantive consciousness, the justices might conclude that his mental privacy is being invaded, and he is being forced to testify against his will in a way that raises constitutional concerns.

There is also the possibility that police or counterterror experts may eventually search suspects for brain waves that suggest a propensity toward violence—a sort of cognitive profiling. These fMRI scans can show that the parts of the brain responsible for impulse control and empathy are underactive and those responsible for aggression and more animalistic, violent activities are overactive. In the future, suspects who show a propensity for violence might be detained indefinitely as enemy combatants, even though they have committed no crimes. Cognitive terrorist profiling seems more intrusive than brain fingerprinting deployed as a high-tech lie detector test and might put pressure in the future on the Court's traditional understanding of privacy, which has tended to focus on information that people go out of their way to conceal from the

world. Brain-scan technology can access personal information that is neither actively hidden from view nor meant to be exposed to the public.
Still, it's not clear under current doctrine that even cognitive profiling
violates the Fourth or Fifth Amendments, as conventionally understood.
This means that the fate of fMRI technology—and in particular the
difficult question of whether citizens or aliens can be detained based
on their propensity to commit future crimes—should be debated and
at least initially decided by elected representatives in Congress and
the states.

In addition to battles over the scope of privacy protected by the Fourth
and Fifth Amendments, there will also be battles over the scope of personal autonomy protected by the Fourteenth Amendment. In *Roe v.
Wade*, the Court said that the Fourteenth Amendment includes a right
to privacy broad enough to protect a woman's decision to terminate her
pregnancy. Regardless of whether *Roe* remains on the books in coming decades, America's political and legal disputes about reproduction may well have moved far beyond efforts to balance the interest of
a fetus against the interests of a pregnant mother. Instead, the country
will likely be debating the use of sophisticated technologies involving
genetic manipulation and reproductive cloning outside the womb—
controversial procedures that may prompt restrictions or bans by state
legislatures or Congress.

Already, scientists are able to analyze the genetic makeup of embryos
created through in vitro fertilization, using that information to help
aspiring parents implant in the woman's womb only those embryos that
display a specified range of desired characteristics—including not only
sex but also, perhaps someday, traits like intelligence, eye color, and
height. Not all the traits that parents demand will be conventionally
desirable: in a recent case in the United States, a deaf lesbian couple
attracted attention (and criticism) by deliberately choosing a deaf man
as a sperm donor in order to increase their chances of having a deaf
child. And if scientists ever learn to identify a genetic predisposition to

homosexuality with a high degree of certainty, genetic screening might be used to select for those embryos or to weed them out.

The political response to so-called designer babies might create strange bedfellows. "As we increasingly come to see our children as commodities to be chosen, like consumer products, they will be devalued in ways that we will come as a society to regret," says the feminist leader Judy Norsigian, co-author of *Our Bodies Ourselves*. "This kind of sex selection would create a sex imbalance, and it would reinforce preferential attitudes toward male children." Social conservatives would also oppose these efforts, but out of concern for the rights of the fertilized embryo: in 2005, in fact, a Republican state legislator in Maine introduced a bill to ban abortions based on the sexual orientation of the unborn child.

How would the Supreme Court view the constitutionality of a state law banning sex selection? In 1992, when it reaffirmed *Roe* in *Planned Parenthood v. Casey*, the court held that the Constitution protects a right of personal autonomy. The scope of this right will be at the heart of disputes over genetic technologies in the future. At the moment, the expansive vision of personal autonomy is most vigorously defended by John A. Robertson, a law professor who argues that the right to have offspring (or not), recognized in the Fourteenth Amendment and in *Roe v. Wade*, necessarily entails some right to select the characteristics of the offspring.[4] The liberal notion of autonomy over reproduction includes some right of selectivity that logically could extend to non-medical traits, he suggests.

But surely the Supreme Court should not attempt unilaterally to draw the line between those traits that parents can select for and those traits they cannot. Even justices who agree that the Fourteenth Amendment protects a certain right of personal autonomy might share a reluctance to decide, by judicial fiat, the mysterious point at which screening for genetic disabilities becomes screening for genetic enhancement. For example, genetic screening by prospective parents for Down's syndrome is already widely accepted, and couples in the future may naturally insist that if they are permitted to screen for genes associated with a low IQ they should also be allowed to screen for those associated with a high IQ. But judicial decrees about the scope of privacy rights will not settle this debate. Rather than presuming to define the boundary between therapy and enhancement on the basis of its understanding of privacy doctrine, the Court might serve the country better by leaving that agonizing decision—which has confounded our leading scientists and philosophers—to democratically accountable legislatures.

In addition to genetic selection, another area of potential controversy is reproductive cloning. At the moment, there is no widespread clamor for the practice, although parents in the future may want to clone a terminally ill child. It's also not hard to imagine a growing demand in the near future among same-sex couples for a way to produce children that are genetically related to both parents—something that reproductive cloning may be able to offer.

To consider the second possibility, here is how two men could have a child of their own: scientists would create a cloned embryo from one man, derive stem cells from the embryo, and then coax the stem cells (which can be used to create any tissue in the body) into a human ovum. The ovum would then be fertilized by the sperm of the other man, conceiving an embryo that would be implanted in a surrogate's womb for gestation and birth. It's certainly possible that Congress would be moved to ban this kind of noncoital reproduction, declaring that children shall only be conceived through the union of egg and sperm taken from an adult human.

A bill along these lines would clash with the broad vision of personal autonomy endorsed by John A. Robertson and by Justice Anthony Kennedy. In the future, however, supporters of laws banning reproductive cloning might be able to call on conservative judges and legal scholars to make arguments for upholding the legislation. Just as some liberals insist that the constitutional right of personal autonomy guarantees a right of genetic selection, some social conservatives are increasingly countering that the constitutional guarantee of equal protection of the laws should be interpreted to protect embryos from the moment of conception, including those that are destroyed in the process of generating stem cells. This view is squarely at odds with in vitro fertilization, as it is currently practiced.

For example, Robert George of Princeton, a prominent conservative legal philosopher, argues that science shows that the embryo is a full living member of the species *Homo sapiens.* If by the word "person" the framers of the Fourteenth Amendment meant to protect full living members of the species *Homo sapiens,* he suggests, then the creation of embryos for destruction would be a violation of their equal protection. Although this argument represents a minority view at the moment, there may be some political momentum in his direction. Illinois, for example, has defined human life as beginning from the moment of conception, and in 2005, an Illinois judge invoked this declaration to hold that a frozen embryo accidentally discarded in a fertility clinic was a human being whose parents were entitled to file a wrongful death suit.[5] If the Supreme Court were to hold that all embryos in America are full human beings entitled to equal protection under the Constitution, researchers engaged in stem cell research across the country might be similarly liable for homicide. And even an attempt by Congress to authorize carefully regulated stem cell research and therapeutic cloning would be an unconstitutional attempt to deny embryos the equal protection of the laws.

Set aside the historical and textual questions about the controversial claim that the framers of the Fourteenth Amendment intended the word "person" to include all living members of the species *Homo sapiens.* (It seems more likely that they were focused on distinguishing citizens from aliens.) The claim that embryos are, in fact, full living members of the species *Homo sapiens* is not a claim that can be established conclusively by science or history: it is ultimately a moral question about which Americans fiercely disagree. For the Court to impose the moral views of a social conservative minority to thwart the wishes of the majority of the American public would be unilateralist in the extreme—just as much as an attempt to impose the moral views of libertarians who exalt personal autonomy above all. Surely the justices would do better to allow the future of reproduction to be settled by Congress and the state legislatures, as even advocates on both sides of the debate acknowledge. The Court can best serve the country in cases involving reproductive autonomy by respecting the authority of other branches of government to deliberate about these vexing constitutional questions.

If Congress regulated privately funded stem cell research (for example, by mandating that it must follow the protocols of the National Institutes of Health), the law that emerged might also trigger a legal battle over the scope of Congress's power to regulate the economy, rooted in concerns about federalism. Conservatives who take a narrow view of Congress's powers might have questions about federal regulation of basic research that is not federally funded and does not take place at institutions that are federally funded. But an attempt by a conservative Supreme Court to strike down a congressional regulation of stem cell research on federalism grounds would be just as unilateralist as an attempt to strike it down as a violation of the equal protection of embryos.

If birth rates continue to fall and life expectancy continues to rise, a population made up increasingly of older people may bring a host of constitutional issues of its own—issues ranging from government financing of gene therapies to the regulation of painkilling drugs. Francis S. Collins, director of the National Human Genome Research Institute, has written that, within five years, "it is likely that predictive genetic tests will be available for as many as a dozen common conditions, enabling individuals to take preventive steps to reduce their risks of developing such disorders."[6] The medical profession may respond by customizing drugs and other treatments to suit an individual's distinctive genetic profile, possibly tailoring them not only to prevent disease but also to enhance a patient's cognitive and physical capacities.

Who will pay for these gene therapies? States or the federal government might prohibit health care organizations that receive public financing from providing access to therapies that border on enhancement. Prohibitions like this might provoke court battles over whether states are interfering with the federal government's plenary power to regulate interstate commerce, or whether the states and the federal government have an obligation to finance genetic therapies that can cure identifiable diseases. In the past, the Supreme Court has been reluctant to require the states to finance medical care for the poor. In 1977, for example, the Court upheld a Connecticut law that prohibited the use of public money for abortions, except those that were "medically necessary."[7] But identifying which genetic therapies are medically necessary to cure disease and which are merely elective enhancements may prove just as agonizing in cases involving public financing for the old as in cases involving reproduction for the young. For this reason, the Court might do best to avoid second-guessing state or federal restrictions on public financing for genetic enhancement and leave the details to the legislatures.

The Supreme Court may also face increasing pressure from an aging population to remove federal barriers on controversial drugs. In 2005, by a 6–3 vote, the Supreme Court upheld Congress's power to use federal drug policies to block a California voter initiative that authorized the use of medical marijuana.[8] William Stuntz of Harvard Law School suggests that a case like that might come out differently in a few decades, as political demands may lead states to enact more lax laws authorizing the use of various forms of morphine, which are federally prohibited but useful in treating a variety of pain. The laws might come not from California, but from Florida and Arizona, where there are many retirees. Old people are traditionally statist when it comes to drug policy, Stuntz suggests, but aging baby boomers might become more libertarian as they clamor to design everything from personalized medical treatments to the way they die. In truth, if a broad consensus developed in a majority of the country that federal drug policy exceeded Congress's power to regulate interstate commerce by targeting purely local drugs that were manufactured and consumed within state lines, it might be appropriate for the Court to follow suit. But unless that consensus is manifest in a majority of state initiatives or referenda attempting to legalize forms of painkilling drugs, the Court should be reluctant to discern a consensus before one exists.

Finally, there may be a series of important debates in the twenty-first century about the scope of rights involving private property—in particular, the ability of corporations and entrepreneurs, through the use of copyright and patent law, to control a broad spectrum of intellectual property, from digital entertainment to genetic sequences. As books, music, and movies are increasingly distributed by large corporations in digital form, entertainment and publishing corporations are clamping down on the ability to access copyrighted material—sometimes by persuading the courts to extend copyright protections, sometimes by devising ingenious technological ways to block users from making copies of the product. Many digital activists fear that free expression won't be able to thrive if people are deprived of the right to sample, remix, and tinker in a world where every copyright infringement can be recorded, punished, or technologically impeded.

The guru of digital activism is the Stanford law professor and cyberspace visionary Lawrence Lessig. In 2003, as the lawyer for an Internet publisher of works in the public domain, Lessig failed to convince the Supreme Court that the purpose of copyright law—to promote creativity—was undermined by the automatic copyrighting of all creative works for the life of the author plus seventy years (as it is after the Sony Bono Copyright Term Extension law added twenty years to existing copyright protections). Lessig argued unsuccessfully that the First Amendment is threatened in a world where artists, for example, must solicit permission from lawyers at major movie studios before using ten-second clips in their video art—virtually a requirement in the current scheme.[9] In the future, Lessig told me, the problem for digital activists will be copyright restrictions that are enforced not by lawyers but by computer code and digital rights management technology. These technologies can ensure that everyone who buys an electronic book or tune can download it as many as five times, for example, but no more.

At the moment, copyright law contains an exception for "fair use": an artist or biographer, for instance, can quote briefly from copyrighted books or songs. But as movies, books, songs, games, and the computers that transmit them are increasingly controlled by digital rights management technology, they might be made impervious to copying or sampling, even for the brief quotations that fair use now protects. Bloggers, for example, might find themselves technologically unable to cut and paste from digital books. Lessig has insisted that, in a world where most of the books, movies, and music we read and hear are experienced in digital form and every use produces a copy and is subject to copyright law, free expression won't thrive unless the Supreme Court recognizes an affirmative right to access. But he acknowledged that the Court is unlikely to create this right unilaterally on its own. Instead, the most effective way of convincing the Court to intervene is to create a constitutional and political consensus in the country in favor of the view that free expression and creativity are inconsistent with further extensions on the scope of copyright. Without a consensus along these lines, the hopes for judicial salvation seem appropriately remote.

A right to circumvent the obstacles posed by digital rights management technology might be rooted in the First Amendment. It might protect not only fair use but what Edward Felten, a professor of computer science at Princeton University, has called a constitutional right to tinker. Felten had firsthand knowledge of how the threat of lawsuits can inhibit creativity: A few years ago, he and his colleagues were about to publish an academic paper about a set of anticopying technologies being considered by the record industry. When a consortium of companies that had developed the technology threatened to sue the scholars for violating federal copyright law, Felton and his co-authors had to withdraw the paper (although they eventually won the right to publish it).

Chastened by the experience, Felton tried to articulate what, exactly, is threatened when researchers aren't permitted to experiment without first consulting their lawyers. He hit upon the concept of tinkering. Whether the Supreme Court ever recognizes tinkering as a constitutional right, the ability to tinker may be threatened not only in computer science but also in the life sciences as well. Genetic material is increasingly being patented, and many biologists worry that the tools they need in the lab to carry out research on genetic diseases, such as individual gene sequences in genetically engineered animals, may become entangled in patents.

Efforts to patent the building blocks of life may not only raise hard issues about scientific freedom. They may also ultimately force American society, and perhaps the Supreme Court, to debate the moral and constitutional issues raised by efforts to patent human life itself. These issues were explored in the 1990s by James Boyle in a prescient book, *Shamans, Software, and Spleens*.[10] Boyle notes that we already allow patents on genetically modified organisms—mice who have a predisposition to various forms of cancer suffered by humans, for example. What about a patent on a chimp with genetically enhanced intelligence? Or what he calls a "meat puppet"—not sapient but looking like a human being and intended for use as a sex toy.

Even if the market for humanoid sex puppets were to take off unexpectedly, the United States Patent and Trademark office has announced that it won't issue patents on human beings because that would violate the constitutional prohibition on slavery and involuntary servitude. But identifying what counts as a human being may be an increasingly challenging task. Confronted with patents on sapient life forms that resemble human beings, legislatures will face tremendous pressure to intervene. The task of defining human life might be so politically explosive and embarrassing that Congress might ultimately prefer to punt the controversy over to the Supreme Court. It is possible to imagine a future constitutional case being brought on behalf of what Boyle calls "a high

IQ genetically engineered dolphin" or, perhaps more plausibly, a computer program for artificial intelligence that seems to perform human functions. Either the dolphin or the machine might assert a right not just to be free of patent rights, but to be free of any ownership rights at all. There is precious little in the existing categories of constitutional discourse that would prepare the justices to identify the point at which an organism with a genetic sequence or artificial brain similar to a human deserves constitutional rights. Rather than presuming to define human life on their own, the justices would do better to defer to the definitions of elected legislatures or state initiatives, no matter how reluctant the political branches may be to address the question.

In a decade or two, many of these efforts to speculate about the constitutional future may look shortsighted and naïve; but precisely because the future is hard to predict, judges should be reluctant to second-guess the decisions of elected legislators. The world would not end if the Court upheld the restrictions on genetic manipulation that Congress might plausibly pass in the future, but the justices could do a great deal of harm if they tried to impose a hotly contested constitutional principle over the wishes of a majority of the American people—ranging from the progressive view that the Constitution prohibits any restrictions on reproductive autonomy to the conservative view that the Constitution requires equal protection for fertilized embryos from the moment of conception. Both of these views, if imposed by the Court against the wishes of the majority, could provoke political backlashes that would make the response to *Roe v. Wade* look tame.

In avoiding judicial unilateralism, it goes without saying, the Court should defer to the national majority's constitutional views, not its political views. Confident that free expression is a nationally accepted constitutional value, for example, the justices are free to interpret it in ways that may clash with the policy preferences of current national majorities. If majorities are indifferent about the technological restrictions of digital rights management, similarly the justices should be free to interpret the free expression guarantees of the copyright clause or the First Amendment in a way that recognizes some right to tinker. Such a right will not take root in America's constitutional culture, however, if it is actively contested by majorities. This is why political and constitutional transformation tend to go hand in hand.

Throughout this book, I have argued that Courts in the past have maintained their legitimacy—in both a political and principled sense—by avoiding judicial unilateralism. And these futuristic scenarios suggest that avoiding unilateralism will remain the best way for Courts to maintain their legitimacy in the future. But although maintaining legitimacy may be good for the judiciary, an obvious question arises: legitimacy for what? How can the Courts serve democracy in a positive sense, not only handing down decisions that national majorities will accept as principled but also defending constitutional values in the face of political assaults?

Some of the most distinguished defenders of judicial restraint have argued that Courts have a unique ability to predict the constitutional future, anticipating constitutional transformations before they have occurred. Alexander Bickel, for example, insisted that the Supreme Court was the only institution of government equipped to be the "pronouncer and guardian" of our "enduring values." Comparing the justices to teachers in a national seminar, Bickel wrote that "[t]heir insulation and the marvelous mystery of time give courts the capacity to appeal to men's better natures, to call forth their aspirations, which may have been forgotten in the moment's hue and cry."[11] Bickel noted with approval a story told by the legal scholar Charles Black about a French intellectual who arrived in New York harbor and exclaimed: "It is wonderful to breathe the sweet air of legitimacy!" What really intoxicated the Frenchman, Black suggested, with uncharacteristic grandiosity, was the "sweet odor of the Supreme Court of the United States."[12] Such a precious suggestion would be inconceivable today, because the idea of a fragrant Supreme Court intoxicating deferential observers is no longer plausible.

American Courts have interjected themselves too deeply into politics to have their verdicts accepted with good grace by political losers.

Those who accept the purely political vision of the Supreme Court's legitimacy—that is, those who agree that the Court's decisions are most likely to be accepted by the country when the justices accurately predict the future—may agree with Bickel that justices should try to anticipate a constitutional consensus before it occurs, as long as they guess right. But judges are often inept at constitutional futurology, and the backlashes that wrong guesses tend to provoke may delay the constitutional transformation the judges are attempting to predict. For this reason, if judges are inclined to anticipate the future, they should confine themselves to gentle nudges rather than dramatic shoves.[13]

Rather than trying to anticipate a constitutional consensus that has not yet occurred, judges often serve a more constructive role when they try to preserve a constitutional consensus that has become contested but has not yet been repudiated by a majority of the country. At important moments in history, Courts may also have an opportunity to enforce a constitutional principle that neither the president nor Congress are willing enthusiastically to embrace as long as there is no danger of active resistance. The failure to declare railroad segregation unconstitutional in *Plessy v. Ferguson* (1896) may be such a missed opportunity: only nine southern states had formally embraced railroad segregation at the time, and the Court might have claimed that it was merely bringing state outliers into a national consensus about the unconstitutionality of segregation with respect to fundamental civil rights such as the right to travel, embodied in the Fourteenth Amendment itself. Although there would have been little enthusiasm on the part of the president or Congress for vigorous enforcement of a decision banning railroad segregation, the Court might have issued a symbolic challenge to Jim Crow that, in small ways, might have slowed its expansion or perhaps even hastened its demise. In the face of congressional ambivalence, the Court has opportunities to influence constitutional debates at the margins.

Rather than trying to anticipate the future on its own, the Court can also play a constructive role by encouraging the president and Congress to reach a bilateral consensus on constitutional issues, rather than trying to monopolize the field of constitutional interpretation.[14] Throughout this book, I've pointed to cases where the Court encouraged bilateral dialogue and cooperation by refusing to endorse executive decrees whose constitutional foundations lack congressional support (such as the *Endo* decision striking down ongoing executive detention of Japanese citizens and aliens). Other productive examples of judicial attempts to encourage constitutional deliberation by Congress and the president include electronic surveillance: the Court offered a general framework for the regulation of wiretapping in 1968, and Congress responded by filling in the details, resulting in one of the most successful privacy laws ever.[15]

In addition to encouraging a constitutional dialogue between the president and Congress, courts are good at identifying constitutional principles that have emerged from that dialogue and enforcing them in a principled fashion as fundamental law. The First Amendment is the most obvious example: although representatives in Congress since the nineteenth century insisted that principles of free expression prohibited the government from banning speech unless it was likely to cause imminent harm, the claim remained politically contested until the postwar period. After the Courts in the 1960s acknowledged the constitutional status of the principle, citizens could take its judicial enforcement for granted. Once the Court embraced the principle, justices of all political persuasions were willing to enforce it, even in the face of congressional attacks. The Supreme Court and lower federal courts are good, in other words, at forcing Congress to abide by principles that Congress itself has helped to define and whose constitutional status has been accepted by the country as beyond dispute.

The claim that courts can best serve American democracy by promoting constitutional deliberation by the other branches of government will not satisfy readers who are confident that there is a single correct methodology that will produce the right answer to all constitutional questions. Lacking that confidence, I will not rehearse the various arguments for and against the major schools of constitutional interpretation. But methodologies that glorify their indifference to the views of the other branches about constitutional issues have often failed in the past to achieve their stated goals of constraining judges and promoting democracy.

Unfortunately, unilateralism is on the rise, and the commitment to bipartisan judicial restraint that united mainstream liberals and conservatives from the New Deal until the 1970s is now under siege. On the Supreme Court and in the legal academy today, the leading schools of constitutional interpretation on the left and the right tend to embrace a heroic vision of judicial power, which insists that judges can demonstrate their devotion to principle by acting unilaterally—that is, ignoring, as much as possible, the constitutional views of the president, Congress, the state legislatures, and the American people. In response to *Roe v. Wade*, conservatives embraced a series of formalist approaches to the Constitution in an effort to constrain judicial discretion, while liberals embraced an aggressively libertarian vision of personal autonomy, purportedly rooted in a growing international consensus, that was equally indifferent to the American public's common understandings of constitutional law. As a result, none of the leading schools of constitutional interpretation today—originalism and natural law libertarianism on the right and pragmatism and internationalism on the left—is consistently devoted to the tradition of bipartisan judicial restraint embodied during the twentieth century by Holmes, Frankfurter, and, most recently, Byron White.

Consider the liberal turn toward international law. If anything could reignite the culture wars, it would be a decision by the U.S. Supreme Court to thwart deeply felt currents in American public opinion in the name of a purported international consensus that does not, in fact, exist. There are, after all, dramatic legal and cultural differences between

European and American views about free expression, privacy, and due process. This means that if judges become too willing to look to Europe, they may impose values on U.S. legislatures that the American public will be moved to resist. Moreover, the U.S. constitutional tradition tends to be much more libertarian and protective of rights than the European one in cases involving hate speech, defamation, abortion, and criminal procedure. If the German Constitutional Court's far more conservative vision of abortion or free speech were imposed on the United States, for example, liberals would take to the streets in protest. To the degree that foreign authorities do agree about moral values in other cases involving basic rights, they tend to be far less consistently progressive than liberals assume.

Some liberals are indeed urging the courts to invoke international law in areas where there is intense social disagreement, such as affirmative action, gay rights, and the death penalty, and, in some cases, the Court has tentatively accepted the invitation. Consider *Roper v. Simmons* (2005), which struck down the juvenile death penalty in the name of a purported international consensus. The Supreme Court in the past has performed a legitimate role in bringing a handful of outlier states in line with genuine national consensus, as it did in 1977 when it held that the Eighth Amendment prohibited the death penalty for rape in a case where only one jurisdiction in the nation authorized the punishment. By contrast, when the Court, with aggressive unilateralism, called into question the administration of the death penalty throughout the nation in 1972, there was a dramatic backlash: 50 percent of the respondents in a Gallup poll supported the death penalty for murder in 1972; four years later, the number had risen to 65 percent.[16] Bowing to the extreme negative reaction, the Court in 1976 reversed course and allowed the death penalty to proceed.[17]

The juvenile death-penalty case falls somewhere between the extremes of unilateralism and deference: to prevent a majority of death-penalty states from retaining a long-standing practice because a narrow majority of all states have repudiated it is hard to reconcile with federalism. But the Court's suggestion that it's possible to generalize meaningfully about a purported international consensus about the death penalty was wrong as well as gratuitous. As the European response to September 11 shows, the United Kingdom, France, and Germany disagree dramatically about the appropriate line between privacy and security.[18] It was only after most national governments in Europe had abolished the death penalty on their own initiative that the Council of Europe states came to condemn it as a violation of human rights.[19] And the reason that majorities in some European countries came to oppose the death penalty in recent years reflects a growing commitment to secularism that is absent in the United States.

Comparative constitutionalism is always illuminating, and the Court has productively consulted institutional similarities and differences between Europe and America in an effort to understand the practical consequences of its decisions. Justice Breyer, for example, has usefully noted that federal systems in Switzerland, Germany, and the European Union have found that local control is enhanced, not thwarted, when constituent states, rather than federal bureaucracies, implement laws and regulation enacted by the central government[20] The juvenile death-penalty case may not have been aggressively unilateralist, because the Court struck down a practice that is supported by significant minorities (rather than majorities) in local polls. (By contrast, narrow national majorities support the practice when there is a specific murderer attached to the question.) But if the Court in the future were to invoke international decisions to strike down a practice that a majority of Americans support—such as restrictions on gay marriage—it would provoke a firestorm. By and large, liberals are winning the culture wars in the court of public opinion, and they may come to regret the effort to internationalize judicial unilateralism, which is unnecessary as well as potentially dangerous to the causes they care most about.

The mirror image of the liberal attempt to impose international values in the twenty-first century is the conservative attempt to resurrect the jurisprudence of Gilded Age. The call for the resurrection of "Constitution in Exile" comes from an article published by Judge Douglas Ginsburg in 1995, in which he urged the Supreme Court to resurrect limitations on state and federal power that have been dormant since 1937.[21] In other speeches, Ginsburg, who was nominated unsuccessfully to the Supreme Court by Ronald Reagan, has charged that the Supreme Court abandoned its commitment to the written Constitution in the 1930s, when it broadly construed Congress's power to "regulate commerce . . . among the several states." Ginsburg criticized the Supreme Court of the 1930s for upholding the National Labor Relations Act, which protects the right to organize labor unions, and for upholding parts of the Clean Air Act, which he charged gave the Environmental Protection Agency too much discretion.[22] According to Cass Sunstein of the University of Chicago, if the Supreme Court heeded Ginsburg's call to resurrect the Constitution in Exile, "key provisions of the Clean Air Act, the Federal Communications Act, and the Occupational Safety and Health Act" might be declared unconstitutional, and "important provisions of environmental laws, including the Endangered Species Act and the Clear Water Act" would also be threatened.[23]

A movement toward judicial activism, adherents of the Constitution in Exile movement acknowledge, would require the Court to impose on the country a constitutional vision that national majorities have not yet embraced. Michael Greve, one of the chief publicists of the movement, acknowledges that "[t]he lesson of 1937 is that the Court cannot enforce constitutional norms against the will of the country and against Congress." But citing Alexander Bickel, he suggests that the Court can fulfill a useful role in trying to "*anticipate* a social consensus" before it occurs. Anticipatory decisions, he suggests, "tend to legitimatize political constituencies, which in turn support the Supreme Court as an institution and protect it from political attacks."[24]

The historical reaction to judicial unilateralism suggests otherwise. America, at the moment, is engaged in an important debate about the relative merits and dangers of the market economy, and the advocates of the Constitution in Exile are aware that they cannot achieve ultimate success without persuading a majority of the American people to embrace their vision. A political transformation in their favor remains, for the moment, remote, and they appear content, even eager, to turn to the courts to win the victories that are eluding them in the political arena. Advocates of the movement are entirely sincere in their belief that the regulatory state is unconstitutional as well as immoral and that a principled reading of the Constitution requires vigorous enforcement of fundamental limits on state power. Nevertheless, it is a troubling paradox that conservatives, who continue to denounce liberals for using courts to thwart the will of the people in cases involving abortion and gay marriage, are succumbing to precisely the same temptation.

In response to liberal criticisms of the libertarian effort to resurrect the Constitution in Exile, conservatives have countered that the movement is not especially organized or influential and has few adherents on the Supreme Court today, with the exception of Justice Clarence Thomas. The movement to internationalize the culture wars, similarly, has no serious support on the current Court: the recent citations to international decisions have largely been rhetorical flourishes. But whether or not they are successful in the long run, the efforts to impose on America the Constitution of the Gilded Age or the European Court of Human Rights are harbingers of a turn toward unilateralism on the libertarian right and the progressive left.

In the political mainstream, two of the leading schools of constitutional interpretation today—originalism and pragmatism—often lead to unilateralism in practice, although neither is necessarily unilateralist in theory. (Originalists, who believe that constitutional provisions should be interpreted in light of the original understanding of their framers and ratifiers, agree on the importance of looking to the views of the

Congress that proposed the Fourteenth Amendment after the Civil War. At the same time, pragmatists, who believe the Court should approach cases with a practical awareness of the consequences of its decisions, agree on the importance of interbranch cooperation that is at the center of democratic constitutionalism.) Both originalism and pragmatism tend to be justified by their leading defenders as ways of promoting democracy and judicial restraint, but neither methodology has consistently fulfilled this promise.

Consider originalism. Invoking Alexander Hamilton's defense of judicial review, originalists insist that judges can only justify the invalidation of laws passed by democratically elected legislatures by rigorously adhering to the text of the Constitution as it was originally understood, since this original understanding helps judges to identify values that the people themselves have recognized as fundamental and enshrined in the original Constitution and in subsequent amendments. Although it has many merits in theory, originalism is not always applied consistently in practice. The scholarship of one of the most respected conservative legal historians, Judge Michael McConnell, suggests that the conservative judicial attacks on affirmative action[25] and Congress's efforts to enforce the Bill of Rights more broadly than the courts,[26] as well as the effort to resurrect prayer in schools,[27] cannot easily be justified by reference to the text or original understanding of the Constitution. Justices Thomas and Scalia, the most self-conscious originalists, have not attempted to justify their decisions in these cases in convincingly historical or textual terms. As conservative justices applied originalism inconsistently—ignoring constitutional history in the affirmative action, federalism, and religion cases—liberals concluded that the methodology was being used opportunistically and had failed to deliver on its promise of constraining judges from imposing their policy preferences.

In addition to its apparent failure to constrain judicial discretion, originalism has not led consistently to judicial deference. Judged by their willingness to strike down federal and state laws, the most activist judges on the Supreme Court between 1994 and 2000 were the libertarian Anthony Kennedy and the pragmatist Sandra Day O'Connor, followed by the two originalists, Scalia and Thomas. By contrast, the most restrained judge on the Court was Ruth Bader Ginsburg, followed by two pragmatists of very different stripes, Stephen Breyer and William Rehnquist.[28]

But pragmatism, like originalism, is also not a reliable recipe for judicial restraint: if the category includes one of the most activist judges, O'Connor, and one of the most restrained, Breyer, it must be a very large tent. In an extended defense of constitutional pragmatism, Breyer has argued that instead of focusing only on what the framers of the Constitution originally intended, judges should think about the practical effects of their decisions on the democratic process. He cites the eighteenth-century French philosopher Benjamin Constant's distinction between the liberty of the moderns —defined as freedom from government coercion—and the liberty of the ancients—defined as the freedom to participate in government—and says the Supreme Court should promote *both* forms of liberty. In the process, judges can serve democracy by encouraging broad political participation. By considering the practical tendency of their decisions to promote democracy, he says, judges "will yield better law—law that helps a community of individuals democratically find practical solutions to important contemporary social problems."[29] Breyer insists that the "philosophical tension" between his two goals—traditional judicial restraint and making society a better place by reaching pragmatically appealing results—is "sometimes less than some have imagined."[30]

Sometimes, perhaps, but not always. Although he is among the most deferential justices, Breyer does not invariably practice judicial restraint. For example, he dissented from the Court's decision to uphold school vouchers, because he feared their practical effects. Breyer suggested that the framers of the First Amendment sought to avoid the "social conflict, potentially created when government becomes involved in religious education,"[31] and he feared that vouchers, which allow parents to spend public money at religious schools, might promote religious strife. But although Breyer presented a series of hypothetical possibilities that vouchers might be administered in discriminatory and divisive ways, he failed to examine any actual evidence that voucher programs in the handful of places that have adopted them have, in fact, been divisive. Moreover, is it really the job of Supreme Court justices to decrease social strife? In fact, it's just as arguable that the First Amendment was passed to guarantee religious neutrality, not to promote political unity. It was surprising that Breyer, who approaches most historical and empirical questions in a spirit of modesty and humility, didn't give the proponents of vouchers the benefit of the doubt. And in a few other hotly contested cases, Breyer has voted to prevent the people from deciding highly divisive social issues, such as his vote to strike down bans on so-called partial birth abortions, even though the empirical effect of those bans was also open to dispute. Like the originalists, Breyer (and other more activist pragmatists, like O'Connor) seems ready to abandon a general counsel of deference to legislatures in the cases where deference clashes with strongly held policy preferences.

Since neither originalism nor pragmatism seem consistently to lead to judicial deference in practice, I find myself increasingly losing interest in abstract debates about which constitutional methodology best promotes democratic values. No matter what methodology they choose, judges can best promote democratic values by consistently and straightforwardly practicing judicial deference—that is, by avoiding judicial unilateralism and embracing a sensibility of bipartisan judicial restraint. Judges should be hesitant to strike down laws unless many of the traditional tools of constitutional interpretation—text, original understanding, historical traditions, previous judicial precedents, current constitutional consensus, and pragmatic considerations—seem to argue in favor of invalidation. In other words, judges should be evaluated not by what they say but by what they do: by their willingness to embody the restrained judicial virtues of modesty and humility not in theory but in practice.

It may seem surprising that Democrats and Republicans turned away from judicial deference in the 1960s and 1980s respectively—the very moment when both parties began consistently to win national elections. The turn toward judicial unilateralism at a moment of political victory is often, however, a sign of trouble to come. In the years leading up to the Civil War, for example, the South was doing quite well in national politics. But at their moment of national triumph, after winning the presidential election of 1856, Southern Democrats began to embrace extremist theories about constitutional restrictions on Congress's power to resolve the slavery question, which the Supreme Court endorsed in the *Dred Scott* decision. Southerners spoke of themselves as principled and derided their opponents as craven politicians; but this exaltation of principle over politics proved to be their undoing.

Today, on the right and the left, there are similarly combative declarations about the importance of defending constitutional principle regardless of the political consequences. By embracing judicial unilateralism as a mark of their devotion to principle, the extremists on both sides risk dooming themselves to electoral failure. If the courts embrace the invitation to unilateralism, they risk a backlash that could imperil their effectiveness and legitimacy in ways that will make the current attacks on judges look like shadowboxing. The courts can best serve the country in the future as they have served it in the past: by reflecting and enforcing the constitutional views of the American people.

Notes

INTRODUCTION

1   Jonathan Rauch, *The Right Went Wrong on Schiavo Because Law Trumps Life*, NATIONAL JOURNAL, April 29, 2005.

2   When the Supreme Court decided Lawrence v. Texas in 2003, 50 percent of the country said that homosexual relations should be legal, while 39 percent said that homosexual marriages should be recognized by law. See Karlyn Bowman, *Attitudes About Homosexuality and Gay Marriage*, A.E.I. Studies in Public Opinion (May 20, 2005), available at http://www.aei.org/publications/pubID.14882/pub_detail.asp

3   In 2003, 57 percent of those polled by the Pew Forum supported affirmative action programs that gave special preferences to qualified women and minorities in hiring and education in an effort to overcome past discrimination, while 72 percent disagreed that blacks and other minorities should get preferential treatment. See The Pew Research Center for the People and the Press, Survey Report, "Conflicted Views of Affirmative Action" (May 14, 2003), available at http://people-press.org/reports/display.php3?Report ID=184.

4   Everett Carll Ladd & Karlyn H. Bowman, *Public Opinion about Abortion Twenty-Five Years after ROE V. WADE* (Washington: A.E.I. Press, 1997), pp. 32–33.

5   Michael J. Klarman, *Rethinking the Civil Rights and Civil Liberties Revolutions*, 82 VA. L. REV. 1, 6 (1996).

6   The political scientist Gerald Rosenberg has examined nine periods in American history where judicial decision lead to meaningful congressional opposition, measured by the number of bills introduced in the House and Senate attempting to curb the Supreme Court. In three of the nine periods, congressional opposition was so intense that it led to a full judicial retreat: Congress's assault on the Marshall Court's ability to control its own agenda between 1802 to 1804; its response to the Dred Scott decision and to Presidents Lincoln and Johnson between 1858 and 1869; and its assault on the conservative Court's effort to strike down the New Deal between 1935 and 1937. In another three periods, congressional opposition was less intense and led the Court to moderate its views rather than abandoning them entirely: Congress's resistance to the Marshall Court's nationalizing decisions between 1823 and 1831; its assault on the Warren Court's efforts to defend free speech against the anticommunist investigations between 1955 and 1959; and its response to *Roe v. Wade* between 1977 and 1982. In the final three periods, the Court maintained its independence because congressional opposition was diffuse and weak: Congress's response to the Court's pro-business decisions between 1893 and 1897; its response to the judicial invalidation of minimum wage and maximum hour laws between 1922 and 1924; and its response to the Warren Court's school prayer decisions between 1963 and 1965. Gerald N. Rosenberg, *Judicial Independence and the Reality of Political Power*, 54 REV. OF POL. 369, 396 (1992).

7   Keith Whittington, "The Political Foundations of Judicial Supremacy" in *Constitutional Politics: Essays on Constitution Making, Maintenance, and Change* S. A. Barber & R. P. George, eds., (Princeton: Princeton University Press, 2001).

8   Alexander M. Bickel, *The Least Dangerous Branch: The Supreme Court at the Bar of Politics* (New Haven: Yale University Press, 1986), pp. 16, 18, 17.

9   THE FEDERALIST No. 78 (Hamilton), pp. 524–25.

10   Walter F. Murphy, *Congress and the Court: A Case Study in the American Political Process* (Chicago: University of Chicago Press, 1965), p. 264.; *see also* 2 George H. Gallup, *The Gallup Poll: Public Opinion 1935–71*, pp. 1250, 1332–33 (1972) (54 percent public approval of *Brown* in June 1954).

11   *See, e.g.*, Barry Friedman, *Dialogue and Judicial Review*, 91 MICH.L. REV. 577 (1993); *see also* Barry Friedman, *Mediated Popular Constitutionalism*, 101 MICH. L. REV. 2596 (2003).

12   Robert A. Dahl, *Decision-Making in a Democracy: The Supreme Court as a National Policy Maker*, 6 J. PUB. L. 279 (1957), *reprinted in* 50 EMORY L.J. 563, 570 (2001).

13   Mark Graber, *The Non-Majoritarian Difficulty: Legislative Deference to the Judiciary*, 7 STUD. IN AM. POL. DEV. 35, 37 (1993).

14 Robert G. McCloskey, *The American Supreme Court* (Chicago: University of Chicago Press, 2005), p. 14.
15 Michael J. Klarman, *Brown and Lawrence (and Goodridge)*, 104 MICH. L. REV. 431, 487, 489 (2005).
16 David P. Currie, "Prolegomena for a Sampler: Extrajudicial Interpretation of the Constitution, 1789–1861," pp. 21–22 in *Congress and the Constitution*, Neal Devins and Keith Whittington, eds. (Durham: Duke University Press, 2005).
17 Ibid., pp. 28–31.
18 James Bradley Thayer, *John Marshall* (Boston: Houghton, Mifflin, 1901), p. 107.
19 Kelo v. City of New London, 125 S. Ct. 2655 (2005).
20 http://www.castlecoalition.org/announcements/kelo-polls-6-28-05.asp
21 http://www.castlecoalition.org/legislation/states/index.asp, http://www.castlecoalition.org/legislation/federal/index.asp
22 Thayer, *John Marshall*, p. 109.
23 *See, e.g.* Stanford v. Kentucky, 109 S. Ct. 269, 2971 (1989).
24 Jeff Rosen, *Was the Flag Burning Amendment Unconstitutional?* 100 YALE LJ 1073 (1991).
25 The vision of democratic constitutionalism I endorse should be distinguished from a recent movement called "popular constitutionalism." The popular constitutionalists argue that the framers of the Bill of Rights and the Civil War Amendments expected that the meaning of the Constitution would be debated and enforced not primarily by judges but by the people themselves—through petitions, juries, voting, and civil disobedience. See Larry Kramer, *The People Themselves: Popular Constitutionalism and Judicial Review* (New York: Oxford University Press, 2005). I am less convinced that populist resistance to judicial decisions has always been the most effective way of enforcing constitutional principles; regional minorities have thwarted the constitutional views of national majorities in cases such as the "massive resistance" by southern states to the Supreme Court's decisions striking down school segregation and school prayer. See Lucas A. Powe, Jr., *Are "The People" Missing in Action (And Should Anyone Care)?*, 83 TEX. L. REV. 855 (2005).
26 *See generally* William Michael Treanor, *Judicial Review Before* Marbury, 58 STAN. L. REV. 455 (2005).
27 Cooper v. Aaron, 358 U.S. 1, 17 (1958).

CHAPTER 1

1 Michael Klarman, *How Great Were Those 'Great' Marshall Court Decisions?*, 87 VA. L. REV. 1111, 1120 and n. 42 (2001).
2 Michael W. McConnell, "The Story of Marbury v. Madison: Making Defeat Look Like Victory," in *Constitutional Law Stories* (New York: Foundation Press, 2004), pp. 14–16.

3   Ibid., pp. 19–22.
4   James M. O'Fallon, *Marbury*, 44 STAN L. REV. 219, 258 (1992).
5   McCloskey, *The American Supreme Court*, p. 26.
6   Marbury v. Madison, 5 U.S. (1 Cranch) 137, 176 (1803).
7   Ibid., p. 177.
8   McCloskey, *The American Supreme Court*, p. 25.
9   Marbury, 3 U.S. (1 Cranch) at 166.
10 Ibid., p. 171.
11 McCulloch v. Maryland, 17 U.S. (4 Wheat) 316, 435–36 (1817).
12 Daniel A. Farber, "The Story of McCulloch: Banking on National Power," in *Constitutional Law Stories*, pp. 36–37.
13 Ibid., pp. 37–43.
14 Jean Edward Smith, *John Marshall: Definer of a Nation* (New York: Henry Holt, 1996), p. 441.
15 Farber, "The Story of McCulloch," pp. 47, 49.
16 Ibid., p. 48.
17 McCulloch, 17 U.S. (4 Wheat) at 405.
18 Ibid., p. 415.
19 Ibid., p. 413.
20 Ibid., p. 421.
21 McCloskey, *The American Supreme Court*, p. 45.
22 Smith, *John Marshall*, pp. 393, 394.
23 Ibid., p. 480.
24 *See, e.g.*, Mark A. Graber, *The Passive Aggressive Virtues:* Cohens v. Virginia *and the Problematic Establishment of Judicial Power*, 12 CONST. COMMENTARY 67 (1995).
25 Don E. Fehrenbacher, *The Dred Scott Case: Its Significance in American Law and Politics* (New York: Oxford University Press, 1978), pp. 109–10.
26 Ibid., pp. 160–61.
27 Michael Kent Curtis, *Free Speech, "The People's 'Darling Privilege'": Struggles for Freedom of Expression in American History* (Durham: Duke University Press, 2000), p. 265.
28 Fehrenbacher, *The Dred Scott Case*, p. 141.
29 Ibid., p. 194.
30 Ibid., pp. 201–2.
31 Ibid., pp. 292–93.
32 Ibid., p. 312.
33 Mark A. Graber, *Dred Scott and the Problem of Constitutional Evil*, p 59 (unpublished manuscript on file with the author).
34 Ibid., pp. 80–81.
35 *See generally* Howard Gillman, *The Constitution Besieged: The Rise and Demise of* Lochner *Era Police Powers Jurisprudence* (Durham: Duke University Press, 1993).

36 Lochner v. New York 198 U.S. 45, 75 (1905) (Holmes, J., dissenting).
37 Donald G. Stephenson, *Campaigns and the Court: The U.S. Supreme Court in Presidential Elections* (New York: Columbia University Press, 1999), p. 124.
38 Gerald Rosenberg, *Judicial Independence and the Reality of Political Power*, 54 Rev. of Pol. 369, 384–85 (1992).
39 Stephenson, *Campaigns and the Court*, p. 135.
40 West Coast Hotel Co. v. Parrish, 300 U.S. 379, 399 (1937).
41 Cooper v. Aaron, 358 U.S. 1, 17 (1958).
42 United States v. Nixon, 418 U.S. 683, 704 (1974).
43 Ibid., p. 705.

Chapter 2

1 Cong. Globe, 39th Cong., 1st Sess., 129 (1866) (codified as amended at 42 U.S.C. § 1981 (1996).
2 Herbert Hovenkamp, *Enterprise and American Law 1839–1937* (Cambridge, MA: Harvard University Press, 1991), pp. 118–19.
3 Cong. Globe, 39th Cong., 1st Sess. 2766 (1866).
4 Hovenkamp, *Enterprise and American Law*, p. 117.
5 The Slaughter-House Cases, 83 U.S. (16 Wall.) 36, 78 (1973).
6 Akhil Reed Amar, *The Bill of Rights and the Fourteenth Amendment*, 101 Yale L.J. 1193, 1219 (1992).
7 The Slaughter-House Cases, 83 U.S. (16 Wall.) 36, 96 (1973) (Field, J. dissenting.).
8 Michael Klarman, *From Jim Crow to Civil Rights: The Supreme Court and the Struggle for Racial Equality* (New York: Oxford University Press, 2004), p. 5.
9 C. Vann Woodward, *The Strange Career of Jim Crow* (New York: Oxford University Press, 1974), p. 6.
10 United States v. Stanley, 109 U.S. 3, 28 (1883) (Harlan, J., dissenting).
11 Klarman, *From Jim Crow to Civil Rights*, p. 18.
12 Louisiana ex rel. Abbott v. Hicks, 44 La. Ann. 770 (1892).
13 Chiles v. Chesapeake & Ohio Railway, 218 U.S. 71 (1910).
14 Ex parte Plessy, 45 La. Ann. 85 (1893).
15 Plessy v. Ferguson, 163 U.S. 537, 550 (1895).
16 Ibid., p. 551 (Harlan, J., dissenting).
17 Klarman, *From Jim Crow to Civil Rights*, p. 23.
18 Plessy, 163 U.S. at 559 (Harlan, J., dissenting) (emphasis added).
19 T. Alexander Aleinikoff, *Re-Reading Justice Harlan's Dissent in* Plessy v. Ferguson: *Freedom, Antiracism, and Citizenship*, U. Ill. L. Rev. 961, 970 (1992).
20 Klarman, *From Jim Crow to Civil Rights*, p. 19.
21 Ibid., p. 38.
22 Mark A. Graber, *Judicial Recantation*, 45 Syracuse L. Rev. 807, 809 (1994), citing H.B. Brown, *The Dissenting Opinions of Mr. Justice Harlan*, 46 Am. L. Rev. 321 (1912).

23   Klarman, *From Jim Crow to Civil Rights*, p. 49.
24   Ibid., p. 50.
25   McCabe v. Atchison, Topeka & Sante Fe Railway Co., 235 U.S. 151, 163–64 (1914).
26   Buchanan v. Warley, 245 U.S. 60, 82 (1917).
27   Mary L Dudziak, *Cold War Civil Rights: Race and the Image of American Democracy* (Princeton: Princeton University Press, 2000), pp 79–80.
28   Sweatt v. Painter, 339 U.S. 629, 634 (1950).
29   Klarman, *From Jim Crow to Civil Rights*, p. 254.
30   Walter F. Murphy, *Congress and the Court: A Case Study in the American Political Process* (Chicago: University of Chicago Press, 1965), p. 264.
31   Klarman, *From Jim Crow to Civil Rights*, pp. 308–9.
32   Kevin J. McMahon, *Reconsidering Roosevelt on Race: How the Presidency Paved the Road to Brown* (Chicago: University of Chicago Press, 2004), p. 17.
33   Ibid., p. 200.
34   Klarman, *From Jim Crow to Civil Rights*, p. 306.
35   Michael W. McConnell, *Originalism and the Desegregation Decisions*, 81 Va. L. Rev. 947 (1995).
36   Lucas A. Powe, *The Warren Court and American Politics* (Cambridge, MA: Harvard University Press, 2000), p. 47.
37   McMahon, *Reconsidering Roosevelt on Race*, pp. 194–95.
38   Klarman, *From Jim Crow to Civil Rights*, pp. 325–26.
39   Cooper v. Aaron, 358 U.S. 1, 18 (1958).
40   James R. Dunn, *Title VI, the Guidelines, and School Desegregation in the South*, 53 Va. L. Rev 42, 44 (1967).
41   J. Harvie Wilkinson III, *From Brown to Bakke: The Supreme Court and School Integration: 1954–1978* (New York: Oxford University Press, 1979), pp. 108, 121.
42   Klarman, *From Jim Crow to Civil Rights*, p. 364.
43   Briggs v. Elliot, 132 F.Supp. 776, 777 (E.D.S.C. 1955) (per curiam).
44   Powe, *The Warren Court and American Politics*, p. 294.
45   Wilkinson, *From Brown to Bakke*, pp. 113–14.
46   Green v. County School Board of New Kent County, 391 U.S. 430, 442 (1968).
47   Wilkinson, *From Brown to Bakke*, p. 217.
48   Ibid., p. 202.
49   James E. Ryan and Michael Heise, *The Political Economy of School Choice*, 111 Yale L.J. 2043 (2002).
50   Missouri v. Jenkins, 515 U.S. 70, 114 (1995) (Thomas, J., concurring).
51   Malcolm X, *By Any Means Necessary: Speeches, Interviews, and a Letter* (George Breitman, ed., 1970), pp. 16–17.
52   Alex M. Johnson, *Bid Whist, Tonk, and United States v. Fordice: Why Integrationism Fails African-Americans Again*, 81 Calif. L. Rev. 1401, 1425 (1993).
53   Jeffrey Rosen, *Translating the Privileges or Immunities Clause*, 66 Geo. Wash. L. Rev. 1241, 1254 (1998).

54 Herman Belz, A *New Birth of Freedom: The Republican Party and Freedmen's Rights, 1861 to 1866* (Greenwood-Heinemann, 1976), pp. 101–2 (1976).

55 Adarand v. Pena, 515 U.S. 200, 227 (1995).

56 Ibid., p. 237.

57 Adarand v. Slater, 228 F.3d 1147, 1168 (2000).

58 Charles Alan Wright, Douglas Laycock, & Samuel Issacharoff, Amici Curiae Brief filed in Board of Educ. v. Taxman, No. 96-679 (1997) pp. 14, 3 (available at 1997 WL 626055).

59 Grutter v. Bollinger, 539 U.S. 306, 350, 360, 368 (2003) (Thomas, J., concurring in part and dissenting in part).

60 Douglas G. Smith, *Originalism and the Affirmative Action Decisions*, 55 CASE WESTERN L. REV. 1 (2004).

CHAPTER 3

1 Planned Parenthood v. Casey, 505 U.S. 833, 851 (1992) (plurality opinion).

2 Lawrence v. Texas, 539 U.S. 558, 588 (2003) (Scalia, J., dissenting).

3 Christine Rosen, *Preaching Eugenics: Religious Leaders and the American Eugenics Movement* (New York: Oxford University Press, 2004).

4 Philip R. Reilly, *The Surgical Solution: A History of Involuntary Sterilization in the United States* (Baltimore: Johns Hopkins University Press, 1991), pp. 46–47.

5 Ibid., p. 51.

6 Ibid., p. 52.

7 Ibid., pp. 84–85.

8 Buck v. Bell, 274 U.S. 200, 205 (1927).

9 Albert W. Alschuler, *Law Without Values: The Life, Work, and Legacy of Justice Holmes* (Chicago: University of Chicago Press, 2000), p. 65.

10 Buck, 274 U.S. at 208.

11 Ibid., p. 207.

12 Daniel J. Kevles, *In the Name of Eugenics: Genetics and the Uses of Human Heredity* (Berkeley: University of California Press, 1985), p. 97.

13 Reilly, *The Surgical Solution*, pp. 87, 97.

14 Ibid., p. 136.

15 Ibid., p. 148.

16 John D'Emilio & Estelle B. Freedman, *Intimate Matters: A History of Sexuality in America* (New York: Harper & Row, 1988), p. 245.

17 Ellen Chesler, *Woman of Valor: Margaret Sanger and the Birth Control Movement in America* (New York: Doubleday, 1992), p. 216.

18 Deborah R. McFarlane & Kenneth J. Meier, *The Politics of Fertility Control* (New York: Chatham House, 2001), p. 30.

19 Ibid., p. 32.

20   David J. Garrow, *Liberty and Sexuality: The Right to Privacy and the Making of* Roe v. Wade (New York: Macmillan, 1994), pp. 42–43.

21   United States v. One Package, 86 F.2d 737, 739 (2d Cir. 1936) (Hand, J., concurring).

22   D'Emilio & Freedman, *Intimate Matters*, pp. 247–48.

23   Ibid., pp. 249–50.

24   McFarlane & Meier, *The Politics of Fertility Control*, p. 41.

25   Ibid., pp. 41–42.

26   Ladd & Bowman, *Public Opinion about Abortion Twenty-Five Years after* Roe v. Wade, (Washington: A.E.I. Press, 1997), p. 43.

27   Ibid., p. 32; *See also,* Thornburgh v. American College of Obstetricians & Gynecologists, 476 U.S. 747 (1986).

28   Ibid., p. 33.

29   Paul Benjamin Linton, Planned Parenthood v. Casey: *The Flight from Reason in the Supreme Court*, 13 St. Louis U. Pub. L. Rev. 15 (1993).

30   McFarlane & Meier, *The Politics of Fertility Control*, p. 36.

31   Kristin Luker, *Abortion and the Politics of Motherhood* (Berkeley: The University of California Press, 1984), p. 65.

32   Rosemary Nossiff, *Before* Roe: *Abortion Policy in the States* (Philadelphia: Temple University Press, 2001), p. 41.

33   Ladd & Bowman, *Public Opinion about Abortion Twenty-Five Years after* Roe v. Wade, pp. 25–30.

34   Ibid., p. 37.

35   Gerald N. Rosenberg, *The Hollow Hope: Can Courts Bring About Social Change?* (Chicago: The University of Chicago Press, 1991), p. 181.

36   *See* People v. Belous, 71 Cal. 2d 954 (1969).

37   *See* Roe v. Wade, 314 F. Supp. 1217 (1973).

38   United States v. Vuitch, 402 U.S. 62 (1971).

39   *See* Eisenstadt v. Baird, 405 U.S. 438, 453 (1972).

40   David J. Garrow, Roe v. Wade *Revisited*, 9 Green Bag 2D 71, 80 (2005).

41   *See* Ruth Bader Ginsburg, *Speaking in a Judicial Voice*, 67 N.Y.U. L. Rev. 1185 (1992).

42   Laurence H. Tribe, *Abortion: The Clash of Absolutes* (New York: W.W. Norton, 1990), p. 50.

43   Ladd & Bowman, *Public Opinion About Abortion*, p. 42.

44   Rosenberg, *The Hollow Hope*, p. 187.

45   Ibid., p. 186 & n. 16.

46   Ibid., p. 187.

47   Ladd & Bowman, *Public Opinion About Abortion*, pp. 32–33.

48   Planned Parenthood v. Casey, 505 U.S., p. 836.

49   Ibid., p. 963 (Rehnquist, C.J., concurring in part and dissenting in part).

50   Ibid., p. 999 (Scalia, J., concurring in part and dissenting in part).

51 *See, e.g.*, Richmond Med. Ctr. for Women v. Gilmore, 219 F.3d 376 (4th Cir. 2000).

52 Compassion in Dying v. Washington, 79 F.3d 790, 813 (9th Cir. 1996) (*en banc*) (overruled by Washington v. Glucksberg, 521 U.S. 702 [1997]).

53 Washington v. Glucksberg, 521 U.S. 702, 703 (1997).

54 Ibid., pp. 703–4.

55 Ibid., pp. 790–91.

56 Bowers v. Hardwick, 478 U.S. 186, 192 (1986).

57 Ibid., p. 194.

58 *See* George Gallup, Jr., *The Gallup Poll: Public Opinion 1986* (1987), p. 214, cited in Barry Friedman, *Dialogue and Judicial Review*, 91 MICH. L. REV. 577, 608 & n. 153 (1993).

59 Lawrence v. Texas, 539 U.S. 558, 573 (2003).

60 Ibid., p. 580 (O'Connor, J., concurring).

61 Karlyn Bowman, "Attitudes about Homosexuality and Gay Marriage," *A.E.I. Studies in Public Opinion* (2005), p. 4, available at http://www.aei.org/docLib/20050520_HOMOSEXUALITY0520.pdf

62 Lawrence v. Texas, 539 U.S. at 567.

63 Ibid., p. 578.

64 Ibid.

65 Richard Morin & Alan Cooperman, "Majority Against Blessing Gay Unions," *Washington Post*, Aug. 14, 2003, p. A01.

66 Linda Lyons, "U.S. Next Down the Aisle Toward Gay Marriage?" Gallup Poll Tuesday Briefing, July 22, 2003.

67 Goodridge v. Department of Public Health, 798 N.E.2d 941, 959 n.17 (Mass. 2003).

68 *See, e.g.*, Linda Feldmann, "How Lines of the Culture War Have Been Redrawn," *Christian Science Monitor*, Nov. 15, 2004, p.1.

69 Gwen Florio, "Fight Rages as Civil Vows Take Effect in Vermont," *Philadelphia Inquirer*, July 1, 2000, p. A8.

70 Michael J. Klarman, Brown *and* Lawrence (*and* Goodridge). 104 MICH. L. REV. 431, 489 (2005).

CHAPTER 4

1 Robert A. Dahl, *How Democratic Is the American Constitution?* (New Haven: Yale University Press, 2001), p. 136.

2 John Hart Ely, *Democracy and Distrust: A Theory of Judicial Review* (Cambridge, MA: Harvard University Press, 1980), p. 117.

3 Colgrove v. Green, 328 U.S. 549, 553–54 (1946).

4 Akhil Reed Amar, *The Bill of Rights and the Fourteenth Amendment*, 101 YALE L.J. 1193, 1261 & n. 295 (1992).

5   William Gillette, *The Right to Vote: Politics and Passage of the Fifteenth Amendment* (Baltimore: Johns Hopkins University Press, 1965), pp. 71–72.
6   Michael Klarman, *From Jim Crow to Civil Rights: The Supreme Court and the Struggle for Racial Equality* (New York: Oxford University Press, 1974), p. 30.
7   Ibid., pp. 30–31.
8   Gillette, *The Right to Vote*, pp. 163–64.
9   Klarman, *From Jim Crow to Civil Rights*, p. 38.
10 Giles v. Harris, 189 U.S. 475, 482 (1903).
11 Richard Pildes, *Keeping Legal History Meaningful*, 19 Const. Commentary 645, 661 (2002).
12 Samuel Issacharoff, Pamela S. Karlan, & Richard H. Pildes, *The Law of Democracy: Legal Structures of the Political Process* (New York: Foundation Press, 1998), pp. 74–75.
13 Klarman, *From Jim Crow to Civil Rights*, p. 55.
14 Nixon v. Herndon, 273 U.S. 536, 541 (1927).
15 Smith v. Allwright, 321 U.S. 649, 663 (1944).
16 Klarman, *From Jim Crow to Civil Rights*, p. 200.
17 Ibid., p. 236.
18 Ibid., p. 237.
19 Ibid., p. 253.
20 Baker v. Carr, 369 U.S. 186, 210–11 (1962).
21 Gray v. Sanders, 372 U.S. 368, 379 (1963).
22 Reynolds v. Sims, 377 U.S. 533, 560 (1964).
23 Colegrove v. Green, 328 U.S. 549, 555–56 (1946).
24 Gerald N. Rosenberg, *The Hollow Hope: Can Courts Bring About Social Change?* (Chicago: University of Chicago Press, 1991), p. 299.
25 Ibid., p. 295.
26 William M. Wiecek, *The Guarantee Clause of the U.S. Constitution* (Ithaca: Cornell University Press, 1972), pp. 200–201.
27 Ibid., p. 271.
28 Michael W. McConnell, *The Redistricting Cases: Original Mistakes and Current Consequences*, 24 Harv. J.L. & Pub. Policy 103, 112 (2000).
29 Richard L. Hasen, *The Supreme Court and Election Law: Judging Equality from Baker v. Carr to Bush v. Gore* (New York: New York University Press, 2003), p. 55.
30 Reynolds, 377 U.S. at 565.
31 Whitcomb v. Chavis, 403 U.S. 124, 156 (1971).
32 Ibid., p. 144.
33 White v. Regester, 412 U.S. 755, 766 (1973).
34 Issacharoff, Karlan, & Pildes, *The Law of Democracy*, p. 425.
35 Maurice T. Cunningham, *Maximization Whatever the Cost: Race, Redistricting, and the Department of Justice* (Westport: Praeger, 2001), p. 1.

36 Ibid., pp. 107–8.

37 Table of Partisan Control of State Legislatures, 1938–2004, National Conference of State Legislatures, available at <http://www.ncsl.org/programs/legman/elect/hstptyct.htm>

38 Samuel Issacharoff & Richard H. Pildes, *Politics As Markets: Partisan Lockups of the Democratic Process*, 50 STAN. L. REV. 643, 703–4 (1998).

39 Richard H. Pildes, *Is Voting-Rights Law Now at War with Itself? Social Science and Voting Rights in the 2000s*, 80 N.C.L. REV. 1517, 1534 (2002).

40 Cunningham, *Maximization Whatever the Cost*, p. 1.

41 Shaw v. Reno, 509 U.S. 630, 647 (1993).

42 Bush v. Vera, 517 U.S. 952, 960, 984, citing Pildes & Niemi, *Expressive Harms, "Bizarre Districts," and Voting Rights: Evaluating Election-District Appearances After Shaw v. Reno*, 92 Mich. L. Rev. 483 (1993).

43 Hasen, *The Supreme Court and Election Law*, p. 141.

44 Miller v. Johnson, 512 U.S. 900, 916 (1995).

45 Easley v. Cromartie, 532 U.S. 234, 245 (2001).

46 Issacharoff & Pildes, *Politics As Markets: Partisan Lockups of the Democratic Process*, 50 STAN. L. REV. at 649.

47 Samuel Issacharoff, *Gerrymandering and Political Cartels*, 116 HARV L. REV. 593, 623 (2002).

48 Reynolds, 377 U.S. at 579.

49 Davis v. Bandemer, 478 U.S. 109, 110, 133 (1986).

50 Ibid., p. 133.

51 Issacharoff, Karlan, & Pildes, *The Law of Democracy*, p. 563.

52 Preliminary relief was granted in only one case—a challenge to North Carolina's statewide system for electing superior court judges, which had resulted in the election of only one Republican since 1900. After a trial judge concluded that a statewide election scheme had prevented Republicans from winning in the past and was likely to continue to do so in the future, an election held only five days later resulted in the victory of every Republican candidate. Veith v. Jubelirer, 541 U.S. 267, 287, FN 8, (2004) citing Republican Party of North Carolina v. Hunt, 1996 U.S. App. LEXIS 2029, No. 94-2410, 1996 WL 60439 (CA4, Feb. 12, 1996) (per curium) (unpublished), judgt. order reported at 77 F. 3d 470.

53 Hasen, *The Supreme Court and Election Law*, p. 163.

54 Baker, 369 U.S. at 217.

55 Veith v. Jubelirer, 541 U.S. 267, 281 (2004).

56 Greg Pierce, "Inside Politics," *Washington Times*, May 25, 2001, p. A6.

57 *See* Black v. McGuffage, 209 F. Supp. 2d 889, 899 (N.D. Ill. 2002).

58 Pamela S. Karlan, *Nothing Personal: The Evolution of the Newest Equal Protection from Shaw v. Reno to Bush v. Gore*, 79 N.C.L. REV. 1345 (2001).

59 Hasen, *The Supreme Court and Election Law*, p. 82.

CHAPTER 5

1   Michael Kent Curtis, *Free Speech, "The People's Darling Privilege:" Struggles for Freedom of Expression in American History* (Durham: Duke University Press, 2000), p. 63.
2   Ibid., pp. 66–69.
3   Geoffrey R. Stone, *Perilous Times: Free Speech in Wartime from the Sedition Act of 1798 to the War on Terrorism* (New York: W. W. Norton, 2004), pp. 46, 63.
4   Ibid., p. 68.
5   Ibid., pp. 44–45.
6   Curtis, *Free Speech*, pp. 96–97.
7   Ibid., p. 101.
8   Leonard W. Levy, *Jefferson and Civil Liberties: The Darker Side* (Chicago: Ivan R. Dee, 1963), p. 18.
9   Curtis, *Free Speech*, p. 84.
10   Herndon v. Lowry, 301 U.S. 242 (1937).
11   Curtis, *Free Speech*, p. 228.
12   Ibid., p. 257.
13   Ibid., pp. 159, 174–75.
14   Ibid., pp. 293–95.
15   Ibid., pp. 360–64.
16   David M. Rabban, *Free Speech in Its Forgotten Years* (Cambridge: Cambridge University Press, 1997), p. 131.
17   Stone, *Perilous Times*, p. 150.
18   Ibid., p. 151.
19   Rabban, *Free Speech in Its Forgotten Years*, p. 257.
20   Stone, *Perilous Times*, pp. 161–62.
21   Ibid., p. 186.
22   Ibid., pp. 165–65.
23   *Masses*, 244 F. 535, 542 (S.D.N.Y.), rev'd 246 F. 24 (2d Cir. 1917).
24   Abrams v. United States, 250 U.S. 616, 627-28 (1919).
25   Gilbert v. Minnesota, 254 U.S. 325, 336 (1920).
26   Michael Klarman, *Rethinking the Civil Rights and Civil Liberties Revolution*, 82 VA L. REV. at 14–15.
27   West Virginia State Board of Education v. Barnette, 319 U.S. 624, 641 (1943).
28   Ibid., p. 638.
29   Ibid., p. 633.
30   Ibid., pp. 638–39.
31   Lucas A. Powe, *The Warren Court and American Politics* (Cambridge, MA: Harvard University Press, 2000), pp. 15–16.
32   Dennis v. United States, 341 U.S. 494, 581 (1951).
33   Ibid., p. 556.
34   Powe, *The Warren Court and American Politics*, pp. 93–98.

35 Walter F. Murphy, *Congress and the Courts: A Case Study in the American Political Process* (Chicago: University of Chicago Press, 1965), p. 116.

36 Ibid., p. 183.

37 Ibid., p. 246.

38 Ibid., p. 245.

39 New York Times v. Sullivan, 376 U.S. 254, 276 (1964).

40 Ibid., p. 270.

41 Ibid., pp. 280–81.

42 Brandenburg v. Ohio, 395 U.S. 444, 446 (1969).

43 Ibid., p. 447.

44 New York Times Co. v. United States, 403 U.S. 713, 714 (1971).

45 Ibid., p. 726 (Brennan, J., concurring).

46 Floyd Abrams, *Speaking Freely: Trials of the First Amendment* (New York: Viking, 2005), pp. 50–51.

47 Thomas R. Marshall & Joseph Ignagni, *Supreme Court and Public Support for Rights Claims*, 78 JUDICATURE, pp. 148–49 (1994).

48 Powe, *The Warren Court and American Politics*, pp. 358–78.

49 Ibid., p. 399.

50 Corinna Barrett Lain, *Countermajoritarian Hero or Zero? Rethinking the Warren Court's role in the Criminal Procedure Revolution*, 152 U. PENN. L. REV. 1361, 1451 (2004).

51 Murphy, *Congress and the Courts*, p. 263.

52 Daniel Farber, *Lincoln's Constitution* (Chicago: The University of Chicago Press, 2003), p. 157.

53 Ex parte Merryman, 17 F.Cas. 144, 147 (C.C. Md. 1861) (Taney, C.J., presiding).

54 Farber, *Lincoln's Constitution*, pp. 158–59.

55 Ibid., p. 162.

56 Ibid., p. 163.

57 Ibid., pp. 199–200.

58 Ex parte Milligan, 71 U.S. 2, 121 (1866).

59 Ibid., p. 140.

60 Ibid., p. 141.

61 Ex parte McCardle, 74 U.S. 506, 514 (1869).

62 Samuel Issacharoff & Richard H. Pildes, *Between Civil Libertarianism and Executive Unilateralism: An Institutional Process Approach to Rights during Wartime*, 5 THEORETICAL INQ. L. 1, 5 (2004).

63 Stone, *Perilous Times*, p. 290.

64 Ibid., p. 295.

65 Korematsu v. United States, 323 U.S. 214, 218 (1944).

66 Ibid., p. 242.

67 Ibid., pp. 283, 301.

68   Issacharoff & Pildes, *Between Civil Libertarianism and Executive Unilateralism*, 5 THEORETICAL INQ. L. at 21.

69   Stone, *Perilous Times*, p. 335.

70   Hamdi v. Rumsfeld, 124 S. Ct. 2633, 2650 (2004).

71   8 Annals of Cong. 1786v.

72   Ex parte Milligan, 71 U.S. (4 Wall.) 2, 133; Cong. Globe, 37th Cong. 3rd Sess. 1207 (1863).

EPILOGUE

1   Illinois v. Caballes, 125 S. Ct. 834 (2005).

2   http://www.lifeandliberty.gov/subs/s_people.htm

3   Harrington v. State, 659 N.W.2d 509, 516 (2003).

4   John A. Robertson, *Children of Choice: Freedom and the New Reproductive Technologies* (Princeton: Princeton University Press, 1994), pp. 151–52.

5   Steve Patterson & Abdon M. Pallasch, "Destroyed Embryo Deemed Human," *Chicago Sun Times*, Feb. 5, 2005, p. 3.

6   Francis S. Collins, "Personalized Medicine: A New Approach to Staying Well," *Boston Globe*, July 17, 2005, p. E12.

7   Maher v. Roe, 432 U.S. 464 (1977).

8   Gonzales v. Raich, 125 S. Ct. 2195 (2005).

9   Eldred v. Ashcroft, 537 U.S. 186 (2003).

10   James Boyle, *Shamans, Software, and Spleens: Law and the Construction of the Information Society* (Cambridge, MA: Harvard University Press, 1997).

11   Alexander M. Bickel, *The Least Dangerous Branch: The Supreme Court at the Bar of Politics* (New Haven: Yale University Press, 1986), pp. 24, 26, 30–31.

12   Ibid., p. 29.

13   *See, e.g.*, Dan M. Kahan, *Gentle Nudges vs. Hard Shoves: Solving the Sticky Norms Problem*, 67. U. CHI. L. REV 607 (2000).

14   *See, e.g.*, Barry Friedman, *Dialogue and Judicial Review*, 91 MICH.L. REV. 577 (1993).

15   Orin S. Kerr, *The Fourth Amendment and New Technologies: Constitutional Myths and the Case for Caution*, 102 MICH. L. REV. 801 (2004).

16   John C. Jeffries, Jr., *Justice Lewis F. Powell, Jr.: A Biography* (New York: Scribner's, 1994), p. 414.

17   Compare Furman v. Georgia, 408 U.S. 238 (1972) with Gregg v. Georgia, 428 U.S. 153 (1976).

18   Kim Lane Scheppele, *Other People's Patriot Acts: Europe's Response to September 11*, 50 LOY. L. REV. 89 (2004).

19   Frank E. Zimring, *The Contradictions of American Capital Punishment* (New York: Oxford University Press, 2003), p. 23.

20   Printz v. United States, 521 U.S. 898, 970 (1997) (Breyer, J., dissenting.)

21 http://www.cato.org/pubs/regulation/reg18n1f.html

22 Cass R. Sunstein, *Radicals in Robes: Why Extreme Right-Wing Courts Are Wrong for America* (New York: Basic Books, 2005), pp. xx–xxi.

23 Ibid., pp. xvii–xviii.

24 Michael S. Greve, *Real Federalism: Why It Matters, How It Could Happen* (Washington: A.E.I. Press, 1999), pp. 21–22.

25 Jeffrey Rosen, *Translating the Privileges or Immunities Clause*, 66 Geo. Wash. L. Rev. 1241 (1998); *see also* Michael W. McConnell, *Originalism and the Desegregation Decisions*, 81. Va. L. Rev. 947 (1995).

26 Michael W. McConnell, *The Supreme Court, 1996 Term: Comment: Institutions and Interpretations: A Critique of* City of Boerne v. Flores, 111 Harv. L. Rev. 153 (1997).

27 Michael W. McConnell, *Religious Participation in Public Programs: Religious Freedom at a Crossroads*, 59. U. Chi. L. Rev. 115 (1992); *see also* Michael W. McConnell, *State Action and the Supreme Court's Emerging Consensus on the Line Between Establishment and Private Religious Expression*, 28 Pepp. L. Rev. 681 (2001).

28 Thomas A. Keck, *The Most Activist Supreme Court in History* (Chicago: University of Chicago Press, 2004), p. 251.

29 Stephen Breyer, *Active Liberty: Interpreting Our Democratic Constitution* (New York: Knopf, 2005), p. 6.

30 Ibid., p. 20.

31 Ibid., p. 120.

Index